Trans Kids

Trans Kids

*Being Gendered in the
Twenty-First Century*

TEY MEADOW

UNIVERSITY OF CALIFORNIA PRESS

University of California Press, one of the most
distinguished university presses in the United States,
enriches lives around the world by advancing scholarship
in the humanities, social sciences, and natural sciences. Its
activities are supported by the UC Press Foundation and
by philanthropic contributions from individuals and
institutions. For more information, visit www.ucpress.edu.

University of California Press
Oakland, California

Library of Congress Cataloging-in-Publication Data

Names: Meadow, Tey, 1976– author.
Title: Trans kids : being gendered in the twenty-first
  century / Tey Meadow.
Description: Oakland, California : University of
  California Press, [2018] | Includes bibliographical
  references and index. |
Identifiers: LCCN 2018006254 (print) | LCCN 2018012748
  (ebook) | ISBN 9780520964167 (epub and ePDF) |
  ISBN 9780520275034 (cloth : alk. paper) |
  ISBN 9780520275041 (pbk. : alk. paper)
Subjects: LCSH: Transgender children—United States.
Classification: LCC HQ1075 (ebook) | LCC HQ1075 .M425 2018
  (print) | DDC 306.76/8083—dc23
LC record available at https://lccn.loc.gov/2018006254

26   25   24   23   22   21   20   19   18
10   9   8   7   6   5   4   3   2   1

To the kids who are different
and the adults who ease their way

Contents

Tables and Figures

TABLES

FIGURES

Acknowledgments

A book is a yardstick of time and relationships. Any creative process, no matter how solitary, is underwritten by the care and labor of others. This book took me a long time to write, and I've had the tremendous fortune to be surrounded by kind and brilliant colleagues and friends in graduate school, during my postdoc, and as a junior faculty member. Those listed here are among many who touched this project—and me—along the way.

My first and deepest thanks go to the children and families who so generously shared their time and their stories with me, along with their community and parent activists, physicians, and mental health professionals. Joel Baum, Stephanie Brill, Kim Pearson, and Kenneth J. Zucker were key interlocutors, and each provided extraordinary assistance in locating and recruiting participants. "Claudia" and "Rachel" did me the tremendous honor of providing me with the stunning cover photograph.

The research and writing of this book was supported by a series of generous grants from the New York University Department of Sociology, the Institute for Public Knowledge at NYU, the Princeton Society of Fellows, the President and Fellows of Harvard University, and the Provost of Columbia University.

Faculty and students who attended talks I gave vetted, questioned, challenged, and enriched the arguments in the text. My thanks go out to audiences at Columbia, Georgetown, Harvard, Harvard Medical School, Northwestern, NYU, Pace, Princeton, Rutgers, UC Berkeley, UC Riverside, University of Chicago, University of Denver, University of Illinois at Chicago, University of Oregon, University of Pittsburgh, University of Virginia, and Yale for their critical engagements.

Material in this book appeared previously as "Deep Down Where the Music Plays: How Parents Account for Childhood Gender Variance," *Sexualities* 14, no. 6 (2011): 725–747; "Studying Each Other: On Agency, Constraint, and Positionality in the Field," *Journal of Contemporary Ethnography* 42, no. 4 (2013): 466–481; and "Child," *Transgender Studies Quarterly* 1, nos. 1–2 (2014): 57–59.

My editor at UC Press, Naomi Schneider, believed in this project in its infancy and saw it through to the end with steadfast support and saintly patience. She has been invaluable in ways both psychic and material. Editorial assistant Benjy Mailings, project editor Kate Hoffman, and copyeditor Anne Canright shepherded me through the steps to publication with great care and attention to detail.

Judith Stacey taught me that feminist mentorship is much like good parenting; she provided a solid base of support, allowed me to chase my own questions on my own terms, and was always there when I scraped my knees. Craig Calhoun, master of sociality, created an intellectual community that became the container for my graduate studies; he was and is always on hand and in good humor. Richard Sennett taught me volumes about what it means, on a technical level, to treat people as "competent interpreters of their own lives." Ann Morning, Paisley Currah, and Betsy Armstrong all read and commented on the final draft of my dissertation, preparing me for the work of forming it into this book.

Colleagues at Harvard—Jason Beckfield, Robin Bernstein, Genevieve Clutario, Deb DeLaurell, Elizabeth Hinton, Sasha Kilewald, Michele Lamont, George Paul Meiu, Afsaneh Najmabadi, Mario Small, and Jocelyn Viterna—and at Columbia—Maria Abascal, Peter Bearman, Shamus

Khan, Jennifer Lee, and Mignon Moore—read drafts, supported me, asked important questions, and provided invaluable thought partnership along the way. D'Lane Compton, Kimberly Hoang, C.J. Pascoe, Carla Pfeffer, Kristen Schilt, and Judith Stacey read the first book draft and offered wonderful editorial advice and intellectual community. Estela Diaz, Joss Greene, and EunSil Oh provided extraordinary research assistance at various stages of the project. Important interlocutors in queer and trans studies, Kate Bornstein, Alexander Davis, Jack Halberstam, Eric Plemons, Avgi Saketopoulou, Gayle Salamon, and Jane Ward, conversed with me, read drafts, or otherwise inspired my thinking.

My beloved friend Gayle Salamon wrote with me, talked with me, read drafts, traveled with me, and cooked me beautiful food, gifts unquantifiable. Chase Joynt was the best and most fun housemate and life collaborator. Jody Davies, my sighted guide, walked beside me for the last stretch of this important journey. The completion of this book feels like a gift from the three of them.

Such deep gratitude goes to my wonderful friends and chosen kin, the ones who show up in hours dark and light, Lia Brooks, Zahid Chaudhury, Jody Davies, Jen Handler, Arielle Herman, Chase Joynt, Alice Mangan, Elizabeth Mikesell, Gayle Salamon, Sonja Shield, Judith Stacey, and Rachel Winard: many of you have been with me since the beginning, and your presence in my life makes many things more possible.

To my family: my parents, Mark and Jamie Meadow, who believed in me long before they had any idea just what it was I would do with my life—and continued to, even once they found out; my grandparents, Marge and Stanley Lewin and Frances and Isidore Meadow, who gave me lifetimes of love and support; and Matt and Cara Meadow, Gavin, Miles, Grant, and Varick, who always keep it silly.

Finally, with love and pride, to Alice Mangan, my queerest of queer kin, for her steadfast faith and support. To Noa Eleanor Mangan-Meadow, the light at the center of my life. And to all her young friends, with the hope that the coming years usher in a gentler and more expansive world.

CHAPTER ONE

Studying Each Other

I heard Rafe before I saw him. His lilting voice cut through the din of animated chatter in the crowded sitting area of a large hotel suite. Around him, a group of thirty-five teenagers lounged trading magazines and junk food. Even among the dizzying movement of denim-clad legs, brightly colored sneakers, and sweatshirts, I picked him out immediately. He was positioned in front of a cluster of seated kids around his age, gyrating his hips with his hands crossed over his chest. He spun around several times and abruptly stopped, planting his feet with improbable force. I later learned he was demonstrating a move from a recent Britney Spears video. I remember I was struck at the time by the intense hot pink of his skinny-legged jeans, how they set off tiny flecks of bright neon colors in his otherwise muted black T-shirt. Rafe was very stylish.

He wore slouchy boots and an artfully arranged scarf. His deliberately coiffed brown hair was streaked with highlights, cut in a jagged, punky, feminine style. It fell in front of his eyes, which he accentuated with smoky shadow. He shook it from his face with a toss of his head. His comportment suggested dance training. Much about his presentation of self, his dramatic vocal inflections, artful makeup, fluid graceful body movements, reminded me of the gay men of musical theater I met

I

when I first moved to New York City as a teenager. Yet Rafe confounded easy interpretation. I caught myself looking at him intently. While some may have read his posture and campy humor as classically "gay," it was also evident that what was on display was far more than a performance of sexuality; some core part of the being that was Rafe was deeply and essentially feminine. He drew me in from the start, and I found myself gravitating over to his group, where I attempted to perch myself on the edge of a sofa to watch him command the attention of his peers. He immediately paused, jutted a hip in my direction, pointed his finger, and loudly challenged, "And *who* are *YOU?*"

In that moment, Rafe was asking me the very question that was so often, and by so many adults, directed at him.

Rafe was sixteen years old and lived with his parents, Claudia and Rick, in a middle-class mid-Atlantic suburb. We met at a weekend conference for transgender and gender nonconforming teenagers, children and their families. Claudia explained that she and Rick were engaged in a process of supporting Rafe in his ongoing efforts to understand his own identity. The onset of puberty had been an excruciating time emotionally for Rafe. He was devastated by the idea that his body would masculinize, that his voice would deepen, and that he would begin to sprout facial hair. He said it felt like a betrayal. With the support of his parents, he elected to go on a newly available hormone regimen that suspended his male puberty. Two years later, Rafe was still actively considering whether he wished to make a social transition, to live in the world and be recognized as female. His parents told me they discussed these issues often.

They are not alone.

Doctors, psychiatrists, politicians, parents, and journalists are all talking about transgender children. From medical journals to neuroanatomy labs, from mainstream magazines to personal parenting websites, from churches to college classrooms, people are puzzling out what makes some small minority of very young boys and girls depart, sometimes radically, from the type of gender behavior other children appear to enact naturally and automatically. Is it something intrinsic to their physiological makeup? Is it something in the wiring of their brains? Is it the product of poor, deficient, or absent parenting? Or is it simply benign human variation? Should boys be allowed to wear dresses? To use girls' restrooms? Or should we, instead, be encouraging these children to acclimate to their socially assigned genders? Why do we see so many transgender children today when in previous generations they were all but absent from public sight?

We have reached what some cultural commentators are calling a "transgender tipping point."[1] From Caitlyn Jenner to Chaz Bono, images of adults who elect to change their social gender categories are now a mainstay of media discourse. Concomitant with the increasing visibility of transgender adults, a new vocabulary for understanding childhood gender nonconformity as incipient transgenderism has changed the way parents think about gender.

This transformation in cultural understandings of gender has led parents and some medical professionals to argue for significant changes to institutional practices around gender categorization. And they have been remarkably successful. Gender is no longer simply sutured to biology; many people now understand it to be a constitutive feature of the psyche that is fundamental, immutable, and not tied to the materiality of the body. While psychologists have been thinking this way since the late 1950s,[2] it is only in the last decade or so that this sex/gender split has affected the administrative and institutional categorization of children.

That change has been sweeping. On June 13, 2010, the U.S. Department of State issued a new passport policy, in effect allowing parents to change the legal gender of their minor children.[3] Because passports are "breeder documents,"[4] they can be used to change state identification, school records, health records and more. Parent activism is similarly changing the medical management of transgender youth; endocrinologists now widely recommend the use of puberty-inhibiting hormone therapies for transgender adolescents.[5] Medicare lifted its ban on coverage for transgender health care, making such treatments more widely available to families.[6] In 2013, the 5th edition of the *Diagnostic and Statistical Manual* debuted a new version of its clinical diagnostic criteria for "gender dysphoria," which limited the diagnosis to individuals experiencing "clinically significant distress" about their gender (rather than applying the diagnosis to all transpeople) and separated gender into a category wholly apart from sexuality. Finally, in late 2017, the Endocrine Society updated their initial guidelines, urging research into the biological underpinnings of gender identity and installing a multidisciplinary, team approach to gender management in children, consisting of psychological and endocrinological care, administered in concert.[7]

Some local administrative practices around the country are changing dramatically as well. By 2017, thirteen states had enacted laws prohibiting discrimination based on gender identity or expression in schools that are enforced by the state or human rights agencies, and hundreds of school districts around the country have instituted similar policies on a local level.[8] High school students have successfully lobbied for genderless bathrooms and locker rooms in schools across the country. Some worry that the election of President Donald Trump will erode some of the laws protecting trans youth, and indeed, since 2016, North Carolina and Texas both introduced so-called bathroom bills, laws that specifically require transpeople to use public restrooms associated with the gender they were assigned at birth.[9] The federal government rescinded a directive mandating the provision of transgender students with gender-appropriate bathrooms in schools.[10] Bathrooms are a locus for cultural disagreements about trans inclusion;[11] and trans youth in other states continue to lobby successfully for gender-neutral facilities or use of those consistent with their identities.[12]

Transgender children are popular subjects of reality television shows, the news media, documentary films, and children's books. National Geographic released a documentary called *The Gender Revolution* in 2017, along with a print edition of the magazine that depicted the first transgender person ever featured on its cover; that person was a nine-year-old child.[13]

This followed on the heels of similar documentaries by independent filmmakers,[14] as well as large-scale investigations by the BBC, PBS, and others.[15] There are children's books about children who identify as members of the other gender[16] or who enjoy dressing or playing in gender-diverse ways.[17] There are guides for parents on raising a gender nonconforming child[18] and a rapidly expanding literature for the clinicians who serve them.[19] There are dozens of personal stories by parents and young people themselves.[20] There are self-help books for teens and parents.[21] In short, "trans" is not just an identity; it's an industry.

It appears we are "surrounded by evolving notions of what it means to be a woman or a man."[22] Facebook now offers some fifty custom gender options to its users who eschew male and female labels. The dating app Tinder lists thirty-seven.[23] Oregon offers a third gender category on driver's licenses, and there is political momentum for such a policy in California.[24] Some expect that other state agencies may soon follow suit. Is this, as some commentators have opined, "the beginning of the end of the gender binary?"[25] Or are we heading into a new era where proliferating gender categories supplement existing notions of male/female complementarity?

Some conservatives worry that we are eroding gender distinctions altogether. Erin Brown, writing for the Culture and Media Institute, lamented that "propaganda pushing the celebration of gender-confused boys wanting to dress and act like girls is a growing trend, seeping into mainstream culture."[26] Fox News psychologist Dr. Keith Ablow declared that "this is a dramatic example of the way our culture is being encouraged to abandon all trappings of gender identity—homogenizing males and females, when the outcome of such 'psychological sterilization' ... is not known."[27] He warned other would-be gender-lenient parents that supporting deviant behavior in children poses serious danger, not merely for them, but for the larger culture that relies on adherence to ideas of sexual difference.

On the other side of the debate, facilitative clinicians dismiss the connections between social supports for gender nonconforming behavior and the active encouragement of adult LGBT identities. What's notable is not that they do this, but *how* they do this. Gay psychiatrist Jack Drescher notes, "I can say with 100% certainty that a mother painting her son's toenails pink does not cause transgenderism or homosexuality or anything else that people who are social conservatives would worry about." Indeed, he continued, feminist notions that gender is culturally determined are themselves erroneous. "Most studies show that if boys were given Barbie dolls, they would pick them up and use them as if they were guns."[28] In Drescher's estimation, most children are gender typical, and socialization is unlikely to turn them into trans kids; by the same token, some kids are trans, and no amount of social engineering will change their innate identities.

PERFECT GENDER

Transgender children "throw into sharp relief"[29] the social process of gendering to which all children are subject, as well as the important ways in which that process has shifted in recent decades. There is a long and studied tradition within ethnomethodology of using gender transitions to illuminate the underlying, often obscured, social processes that consolidate social gender relations. Rather than "inverting" gender, transpeople "elaborate the particular configurations of sexuality, gender and sex that undergird and give meaning to [the concepts] man and woman."[30] Anthropologist Don Kulick, in his study of Brazilian *travesti*, suggested that transpeople "perfect" gender expectations, that their mobilization of ideas, representations, and practices associated with maleness and femaleness "clarify and distill them, draw them to a logical conclusion, purify them to an extent that it becomes possible to see in them central elements of [culture]."[31]

Like Kulick, I draw on ethnomethodology in an attempt to situate the families I study within the context of contemporary American culture. "Doing gender," being a man or a woman in a social sense, is not an ontological position. Instead, as sociologists Candace West and Don

Zimmerman tell us, it is something we "do" because our very "competence as members of society is hostage to its production." Gender is a "routine, methodical and recurring accomplishment."[32] Individuals organize interactions and engage in social activities to reflect or express our gender, and we interpret the behavior of others as expressions of the same. This is not unlike Judith Butler's theory of gender performativity, typically understood[33] as a poststructuralist and psychoanalytically informed correlate of symbolic interactionism. Gender is culturally "citational," always in a state of being iterated or reproduced. As Butler says, "We act and walk and speak and talk in ways that consolidate an impression of being a man or being a woman."[34] The ways individuals signal gender, and the ways those signals are received, interpreted and integrated are the material of this book.

Postmodern gender theory and symbolic interactionism share an approach to understanding the social reproduction of gender. Our individual selves are forged through interaction.[35] We assume social roles, with an eye to how they are received by the audiences with whom we interact.[36] In "Doing Gender," West and Zimmerman separate out sex, sex category, and gender. While "sex" is determined by normative biological standards, our "sex category" is a social assignation based on sex but established and sustained by the "socially required identificatory displays" that accompany maleness and femaleness. "Gender," in contrast, is the "activity of managing situated conduct in light of normative expectations of masculinity and femininity."[37]

The interactional work of "being" a man or a woman in society requires that there be a relationship among these three elements. We are assigned a sex category based on our biology, which we must then maintain with our quotidian behavior. Gender performances are structured to appear as if they are naturally occurring;[38] thus it is the reiterative power of the social that produces the very forms of gender it then constrains and regulates. Gender is an achievement, rather than an attribute, one that is aimed at significant others assumed to be oriented to its production.[39] We do gender with others to establish ourselves as fluent actualizers of our bodies, and always "at the risk of assessment" by others.[40] Negative assessments of gender performance can result in stigmatization and loss of social and material capital.[41]

This is a paradigmatic example of interpellation, though sociologists don't typically think of gender in this way.[42] In "Ideology and Ideological State Apparatuses," Louis Althusser described the ways that the State—by which he meant the duality of the actual regulatory, repressive state apparatus and the invisible ideological schemas through which it executes control—calls upon each individual to become a subject, to participate in the community as a particular type of person and to accept the overall ideological structure.[43] This process happens entirely outside our awareness, one might even say prior to it, relying on our psychological need for recognition in order to develop a psychic life.[44] There are both ideological and material manifestations of this process, the sense of "being" and of "doing" through which we experience and execute gender. So when a baby is born and the pronouncement is made, "It's a boy!" the baby is both hailed into gendered subjectivity, and simultaneously becomes accountable to maintain that subjectivity. Both the child and the adult experience this hailing as a benign statement of fact; indeed, most people would resist the notion that this is a moment of ideology. To paraphrase Althusser, one of the practical effects of ideology is the denigration of the ideological character of ideology.[45]

This concept of assessment yokes it to normative gender. We are beholden to reproduce normative masculinity or femininity, and failure to do so results in failed social integration. But what if assessment is no longer merely the process through which hegemonic gender reproduces itself through threat of sanction? What if it is now a moment where the hegemony might, in some cases, also re-sort individuals into new gender categories that may or may not adhere to their bodies? Our symbolic understandings of gender are multiple and emergent, and have concretized into a social classification system that encompasses new forms of gender.

Transgender children, hailed into an originary gender category, actually seek to incite that very accountability process, using it to make claims on otherwise prohibited forms of action and identity. Through a sociological examination of their interactions with parents and social institutions, we can see that accountability is constitutive of gender, even in its nonnormative forms. Accountability processes function not only to restrict, but also to elaborate rapidly proliferating forms of gender. Gender is a process of interpellation. We are hailed into maleness or femaleness by others. Once hailed, we are accountable to maintain the boundaries of that category with our quotidian gender behavior. Small infractions, of course, trigger precisely the kinds of sanction West and Zimmerman outlined. But there is a certain threshold beyond which transgression can change the very category into which one is interpellated. Parents, doctors, psychologists, teachers, can move an individual child from one category to another, and the entire apparatus, all the social processes previously employed to shore up an individual child as male, then shift to consolidate the very same person as female. In this way, gender is fundamentally relational, though paradoxically, many of us also believe it to be immutable. And while gender assessments are routine parts of social interaction, assessments of nonnormativity incite a range of social processes, from sanction to celebration. As gendered subjectivity is relieved from a rigid and dependent relationship to the body, our lexicon for communicating the subtleties of gender in all its varied configurations is expanding exponentially. And individuals, for their part, are examining one another with ever greater attention to detail.

BEING GENDERED

It is rare to have an opportunity to watch an emergent social category in formation. Transgender children provide us with precisely this opportunity. Yet the contemporary struggles to understand and define the category itself inflect ethnographic encounters with a sense of urgency for the research subjects themselves. The desire for epistemological clarity led parents, physicians, and children to investigate the

gender of those around them with incredible nuance. Gender assessments bled from their original objects (in this case, kids) to those who
surrounded them. I found this gaze impossible to escape. As I scrutinized people whose precise predicament was that they were being
scrutinized, they turned their gaze back on me. It was a perfect reciprocity, a projection of precisely the social process at play, and my first
lesson about the implications of these new social gender processes.

Early on in my fieldwork, I spent several hours in the empty mezza-
nine lobby of a conference hotel interviewing Dr. Kenneth J. Zucker, a
world-renowned but increasingly controversial psychologist who ran
an outpatient gender identity clinic housed in a major teaching hospital
in Toronto. I was initially surprised by his willingness to speak with
me. During the months prior to beginning my fieldwork, I read dozens
of his articles, as well as an equal number of fierce critiques of his methods by transgender activists and some other clinicians. I expected him
to be defensive, or at the very least self-protective. He wasn't. He agreed
immediately to be interviewed, and even suggested I visit his clinic to
form my own impressions of his work. Of all the medical professionals I
met during my fieldwork, he was the only one to extend such an offer
unsolicited. I went to the interview with great anticipation.

During the three hours we spent together, the first of many such
conversations, we discussed his views on the difficult process of differ-
entiating gender nonconforming behavior that signals emergent transgender identity from that which signposts emergent homosexuality. We
also discussed his concern with misdiagnosis and the pervasive, and in
his opinion erroneous, conflation of his treatment methods with "reparative therapy." Midway through our conversation, he presented a dig-
ital camera with an image of a young adult formerly in his care for
severe gender dysphoria. A soft and somber face gazed into the camera,
and as Ken proceeded to describe his gender trajectory, I struggled to
discern the work this image was supposed to do. Was I supposed to see
femininity in the gentle contours of his face? Was I to focus on the male
insignia he wore? Was there something about the solemnity of the

image that should communicate the gravity of the choices he faced at the threshold of adulthood? What was Ken expecting me to see? To him, the image, the person in the image, was an object with its own communicative value. The gender inhered in the person, in the materiality of his body, the fabric of his psyche, in how he inhabited both of those things. To comment on what I saw would be to collude with him in evacuating gender into the image. What I was coming to understand in my own work, however, was that this person's gender, this person's gender category, resided more in us than it did in him. It wasn't that I didn't see gender in the image; it was that I was discovering that the gender I did see was alloyed, more a projection of my own subjectivity and cultural frames than something innate to that individual person. Were I to collude with Dr. Zucker in making a gender attribution, I would, in effect, be arguing that gender is a static property, about which evidence can be procured. Gender is, instead, an iterative, interactive process, constantly in negotiation among individuals. The anxiety I saw in this stranger's face was as much my own anxiety as Ken's. We met his image with our own unanswered questions.

As we concluded the formal part of our conversation and I switched off my recording device, Ken presented the camera again and showed me several more photographs. He then asked me if he could take my picture. I asked him why he wished to do that, and he responded, "I just like taking pictures," and proceeded to pull up several others, one of his own child smiling into the screen. I felt immediately uncomfortable, found out, at issue. I imagined myself among the faces arranged in his album of gender variants. I took a mental inventory of my own gender transgressions that day. I had gotten a haircut earlier that week, and it was quite short. I wore no makeup. My button-down shirt was boxy, but open at the throat. I felt acutely aware of the contours of my body, of the way I was holding myself. I had to remind myself that my gender presentation was cultivated with great care. That I was comfortable with it and felt entitled to it. That I was an adult, a professional. I would not be conscripted into the role of gender deviant. I wondered if the young person in the initial photo felt similarly exposed when faced with his camera. I wondered if he, like me, found it easier to relent than to manage the discomfort of noncompliance. Ken seemed oblivious to my discomfort, which somehow made it worse. Although I acquiesced, I wondered what I would become an example of for his next interlocutor. Only at that moment did I register that of all my subjects, only he asked if he too could record our discussion, and his tape recorder sat on the table beside mine. It was then that I realized I was not just studying him; *we were studying each other.*

In the frame of Ken Zucker's camera lens, I felt as if I had moved from the space of colleague, interlocutor, or even just researcher and into the realm of study object, of case example: a gender variant in my own right. My image, the contours of my face, my clothing and hairstyle, were worth adding to the anthology he drew from to make intellectual arguments about the line between typical and atypical gender. I fell on the atypical side, I was noteworthy, a specimen worth collecting. In some ways, this taste of objectification offered me the closest approximation of what I imagine the children parented by my research subjects experience: objectification in the service of affirmation. My decision to relent to the lens offered me continued access to this clinician, and it was a deliberate methodological choice. But it was one that left an emotional residue of shame.

This interaction provided me with a deep, affective, and embodied comprehension of the experience of being observed. I allowed Ken Zucker to take my picture that day. I focused on squelching the sting of abjection, smothering the unease I felt under a false bravado. I thought to myself, and then repeated silently, "I am comfortable enough with myself to do this." What I really meant was, "You are an expert and I want something from you. I will put myself, my body, on the line to get those things that I want." This places me akin to so many transgender people who, like Ken's young patient, submit to scientific objectification in an instrumental way, to get something we need. For me, it was data; for them, it was perhaps life-saving medical care. It is precisely that clinical gaze, that has for decades positioned gender-nonnormative people as psychiatric subjects, which is resisted in the new gender stories we are telling about children in the twenty-first century. In its place is a proliferating lexicon for experiencing, communicating, and interpreting the gender signals that float all around us.

EMBODIED ETHNOGRAPHY

This is a book about the social process of gendering. It is about the way we have come to scrutinize the gender displays of others, to make meaning of those displays, to interpret, identify, classify, catalogue, and critique the behaviors, statements, and affiliations of others. It is also about the ways the genders of others come to influence our own sense of self, and the possibilities we believe exist for the children in our lives. It outlines the new sets of choices emerging in the early twenty-first century, and the kinds of excitements, fears, and frustrations they elicit. In the contemporary moment, one cannot study gender without being a subject of study. One cannot be an analyst without also being data for someone else's identity project. In this research, I was both.

Gender hovered ambiently around each interaction I had in the process of researching this book. My gender could render me suspect, it could make me into an ally or even data, depending on who was on the other side of my table. Sometimes this reading of me was made explicit; often it took the form of veiled questions about the origins of the project, my interest, or aspects of my appearance. Indeed, it became clear to me that, much like the child subjects of my research, I too lacked control over the meanings made by others of my body and my identity. It seemed to matter greatly to my research subjects just who and what I was. They labored to decipher my identity, my relationship to communities with which they identified, and my political perspective. In short, they returned my gaze, and the ways they did so were themselves valuable data on how individuals make sense of gender in others, and how that sense-making affects interactions and relationships.

My own gender presentation structured my experience of my research subjects in important and occasionally conflicting ways.[46] My life and my gender were frequent topics of commentary and speculation, from the parents who alternately endeavored to expose or remove their children from my presence, to the children themselves who often asked questions or made comments about my body or my clothing. The subjects of my research—parents, doctors, and psychologists—were actively seeking to understand the very same phenomenon I was, yet with vastly different epistemological orientations and for different sets of reasons. We were participants in what Judith Stacey called a "collaborative, reciprocal quest for understanding."[47] We were co-creating the very questions we sought to resolve. And what we each saw in the "material" of gender was ordered by who we ourselves were.

Parents struggled with whether to identify or reject the meanings of transgender created by previous generations. For many of those parents, gender nonconforming adults, myself included, were deeply symbolic in a variety of conflicting ways. We functioned as floating signifiers for the hopes and fears they attached to their children's uncertain futures. For some parents, the deep pain and pervasive discrimination experienced by transgender adults was too much to bear emotionally; for others, it was the notion that their child might cultivate an oppositional identity, one that radically departs from social norms, that was of primary concern. These parents attempted to disassociate their child from dominant cultural images of transgender adults. For still others, constructing taxonomies of different forms of adult gender allowed them to exert more careful control over precisely what *sort* of influence connections to the adult transgender community might have on their child's evolving self-understandings. It was around these issues of identification and disidentification that I felt my own gender presentation become most salient for my interview respondents. Navigating those moments proved treacherous, both methodologically and emotionally.

Colten's mom, Deirdre, told me her biggest fear was that Colten would spend a lifetime hiding the truth of his body from potential intimate partners. Deirdre hoped that exposing Colten to genderqueer adults who live in intermediate gender spaces without making full medical and social transitions[48] might provide him with a sufficient model for how to articulate his own gender, thus alleviating his desire to make a full transition himself. I felt her eyes travel the planes of my body as we spoke. She commented on my earrings. She told me Colten had a jacket like mine. As we concluded our interview, she asked me if I would join them for lunch that afternoon. She told me she'd really like me to spend some time with Colten. When I asked her why, she replied,

> My feeling is, the more varied kinds of people that Colten talks to, the better. I want him to see more and more of those people in the gray area. I want him to meet more people that are like him. I want him to meet more people that are female but not all the way at *that* end of female. In that way, it's kind of like when I discover somebody who speaks Italian, because my husband is Italian, it's like, *Oh, speak Italian to him, please. Speak French to him. He can do it.*

Deirdre read me as "like Colten," fluent in a language of self-understanding that might offer him an alternative to gender transition. She paused, made direct eye contact, and said, slowly and thick with emotion, "*Please*... Speak gender stuff to him in a way that I can't."

This was a peculiar kind of carnal sociology,[49] a learning of the other through the acquisition of a bodily disposition. My body became a screen for the projected gendered fantasies of others, and as a result, my attunement to the way my body was received heightened. Parents imagined my gender to be a finished product, one they could mobilize to assist them in uncovering a hidden truth about their own child. Deirdre imagined that Colten and I shared a fluency in a foreign language, a kind of bodily and psychic knowing that inhered in the particularity of our genders. An urgency attended that imagined connection, a need for a feeling of commonality, of being able to place Colten among like objects. Deirdre felt inarticulate in a language of gender she presumed both Colten and I spoke. She needed a translator, and she hoped Colten and I might be able to work out his grammar together.

The management of this and others' reactions to my gender, their assumptions, discomforts, and interests became an embodied ethnographic project. It was in those self-conscious moments that I believe I came closest to knowing the gender nonconforming child, by which I mean living the experience of having one's body and identity be the object of a particular type of searching gaze, one tinged with worry, fear, expectation, sometimes hope. This mirrors in some sense the kind of scrutiny politically inflected ethnographic research fixes on the lives of those we seek to understand, and it is a mistake to think that our subjects don't feel that gaze.

Because the gender categories and identities I studied were in a process of active iteration, they were exceedingly porous to the ethnographic encounter itself. This presented me with certain methodological challenges in the field that warrant examination. Would I participate in organizing activities for the children, knowing that it was in the context of their shared community that many of them labored to form coherent identities? Would my presence and participation ultimately overdetermine what I would find? Would an investigator with a different gender configuration draw forth different gendered messages in others? These very questions from my fieldwork with families and clinicians underscored how individuals engage in the process of making the new social categories into which they may then be hailed, and the many ways gender structures relationships in the ethnographic field. Perhaps, most importantly, they underscore the ways in which our genders are profoundly, inescapably both a deep subjective reality and a mode of relationality, always in the hands of others.

UNDOING GENDER?

Feminists did not invent the concept of gender, nor were we the first to separate cultural ideas of male-female difference from their biological or bodily origins. We inherited our contemporary concept of gender from scientists who worked on, and often pathologized, intersexuality and transsexuality.[50] At the turn of the twentieth century, most presumed that masculine and feminine mapped neatly onto male and female and came yoked to a sexuality aimed at those in the other category (heterosexuality). To psychologists of that era, being a man who desired other men sexually was like being a woman, and vice versa. There was little conceptual separation between male, masculine, and gynophilic.[51] What Margaret Mead labeled "sex roles," the "culturally constructed behaviors expected of women and men," were not indistinct from the biological functions of reproduction.[52] In fact, they were co-determinate. Yet, as Mead and others also began to chronicle the different ways in which sex roles manifested across cultures, they introduced into the anthropological imagination the concept of a socially learned, psychological component to sex. This set the stage for later notions of gender that emerged in the 1950s.[53]

In surveys of the introduction of the gender concept, historian Joanne Meyerowitz and Australian gender scholar Jennifer Germon traced its etiology to a series of articles written by Johns Hopkins psychologist John Money in the mid to late 1950s.[54] An expert on intersexuality in children, Money argued that it was not the anatomy or physiology of the body that determined a child's internal sense of being a boy or a girl, but instead the sex assigned at birth and the way the child was subsequently raised.[55] In 1955, he employed the term *gender* for the first time to refer to "all those things a person says or does to disclose himself or herself as having the status of boy or man, girl or woman."[56] He compared gender to a "native language" learned in childhood, and reasoned that while some piece of the capacity to learn language is biological, specific languages (and genders) are learned through a process of social engagement.[57]

Robert Stoller, a psychiatrist working with transsexuals at UCLA, refined Money's concept in 1964, introducing the term *gender identity*, which subsequently came to dominate the literature on transsexuality. He used it "much as others had used psychological sex, to refer to 'one's sense of being a member of a particular sex.'"[58] Stoller was the first psychoanalyst to separate the concept of gender identity from sexual orientation; this separation allowed the critical disaggregation of the subjective or felt sense of self from the behaviors we associate with maleness and femaleness, masculinity and femininity.[59]

Since the 1960s, gender has come to mean two different sets of things. In one set of meanings, feminists describe a "sex/gender system," by which we mean "the set of arrangements by which a society transforms biological sexuality into products of human activity."[60] The social correlates of biological sexual difference operate as "a complex of socially-guided, perpetual, interactional and micropolitical activities that cast particular pursuits as expressions of masculine and feminine 'natures.'"[61] Gender isn't a form of personal property, but rather "an emergent feature of social situations," "both an outcome and a justification for outcomes," and at its center, a vehicle with which to "legitimate a fundamental social division" between men and women.[62] This concept of social gender persists as a useful analytic in much current feminist theory,[63] even as feminists trouble the sex/gender divide itself, pointing to the ways even our scientific understandings of biology are strained through the mesh of gender ideology.[64]

Alongside and occasionally in dialogue with feminist notions of gender, psychoanalytically-informed gender theories evolved dramatically in the ensuing half century as well. Some clinicians still espouse a "developmental, biopsychosocial" theory of gender acquisition,[65] a trinity of biological and genetic makeup, culture/environment/family composition, and child/caregiver interaction patterns.[66] Others, however, eschew traditional normative, developmental models in favor of viewing gender as a phenomenon idiosyncratically sutured together,[67] a complex assembly[68] of intrapsychic, relational, and cultural influences, always in a process of iteration.[69] Far from viewing trans and other forms of atypical gender as per se psychopathological, some have gone so far as to suggest that the repetitive misattribution of gender, or persistent failure of significant others to recognize the identities of transpeople, is "gender trauma," which can itself cause significant psychic debility, even mental illness.[70] Despite the plurality of etiological and clinical orientations, there is an emerging consensus that facilitating transition in trans-identified people is preferable to older models aimed at cure.

How might we understand the implications of the disaggregation of gender from biology, and the increasing conceptualization of psychological gender development as an assemblage of often divergent forces? To the extent that these evolutions in thinking create the condition for the emergence of the transgender child, one plausible conclusion we might draw is that these families are dismantling the sex/gender system as we know it. Perhaps we are headed into the "post-gender world" imagined by some feminist sociologists, one in which cultural ideas of gender are undone, disrupted and disestablished on both cultural and institutional levels. Perhaps, as Francine Deutsch argued, we should consider dispensing with the concept altogether.[71] Perhaps it's time for the utopian context imagined by Judith Lorber, Barbara Risman, and Jessica Sherwood, where gender becomes increasingly irrelevant, where men and women will not be held accountable to gender norms, and where gender will cease to be a master status. Perhaps it is time, as they argue, to "undo gender."[72] If gender was in a process of erosion, we would expect to see a relaxation of identity discourse, greater fluidity and flexibility in labeling behaviors, and greater demedicalization of care.

Or instead, as I will argue in this book, maybe gender is both proliferating and becoming ever more important. Parents are becoming ever more likely to fight for a child's chosen identity, to contest the labeling practices of others, to engage in more directed interpersonal work to assist children in further articulating a discrete identity, to purchase clothing and toys that reinforce that identity, and to enlist social institutions in identity creation and maintenance. The notion that "gender identity," or the felt sense of gender subjectivity, is fundamental, immutable, and not tied to the materiality of the body makes it possible for parents to begin to understand some children to be transgender and to alter their social environments to accommodate that subjectivity.

Atypical gender was once considered a form of psychopathology; it was a failure of gender. Now, for the first time, atypical gender is understood not as a failure of gender, but as *a form* of gender. Gender transgression marks the insufficiency of reified gender categories (male/female), and not of the individual who inhabits them. Gender nonconformity now constitutes social identity, rather than eroding it.

And we will see that the material of gender is being used in a multitude of ways, that gender identities are replicating, not dissolving, and that they are deeply held and increasingly institutionally embedded. Gender, in its institutionalized forms, accumulates various feeling states, relationships, medical and scientific apparatuses, and cultural forms. All of these constitute social gender. As transpeople and their parents assert their identities in increasing numbers to medical professionals, they become installed as legitimate categories of being, analysis, and study. As they assert these identities to schools, churches, and communities, they change the architectures of those institutions, becoming embedded in the very ways they function. These families may be doing gender at the risk of assessment, but they are also demonstrating the ways gender requires assessment, even in its most nonnormative forms.

OUTLINE OF THE BOOK

Chapter 2, "Gender Troubles," introduces the families in the study and the diverse ways they came to understand that their child had a gender issue that penetrated to the level of core identity. While many children engage in atypical forms of play, certain types of gendered statements and behaviors led these parents to decide that their child had a problem significant enough to seek support from an outside expert or advocate. Some also came, in time, to understand that their child had a gender identity that conflicted with their social assignment. The processes through which parents generated these understandings differed significantly for male and female children, reflecting how we valorize normative masculinity while simultaneously treating the category "male" as exquisitely fragile. Parents then shift their behavior, "giving gender" differently to their children, revealing the ways our identities come into being in interaction with significant others.

In previous generations, families with significantly gender-transgressive children with sufficient financial means would almost uniformly bring their child for corrective psychiatric treatment. Today, they are doing something different. Chapter 3, "The Gender Clinic," follows families through the arduous process of medical decision-making for transgender-identified adolescents. The anxiety generated by the gravity of social and medical decisions underwrites a rapidly expanding research agenda by clinicians seeking stable predictors for adult transgenderism. Chief among its architects was Dr. Ken Zucker, who once ran the world's most respected clinic treating transgender youth. We enter his clinic and meet some of the families who utilized its services, and then accompany Dr. Zucker as he faces his dismissal and the subsequent closure of his clinic. The complexity of these medical decisions, and the rapid decline of Zucker's clinic from the very vanguard of childhood gender to a relic of an outmoded and largely abandoned clinical practice, tell the story of larger cultural shifts in the science of gender.

Chapter 4, "Building a Parent Movement," introduces the two organizations responsible for the bulk of family advocacy work done during my research period. Begun by parents of transgender children, these organizations employed vastly different rhetorics in their education efforts and cultivated distinct presentations of self. Despite these often conflicting efforts at impression management, they aligned in certain key ways to create a movement distinct from earlier attempts by adult transgender people to secure social acceptance. Today's parent movement is fundamentally a movement by cisgender people for transgender people, and it suggests that today's trans children will look vastly different than those who came before them.

Chapter 5, "Anxiety and Gender Regulation," returns to the concept of gender assessments, this time examining how they work after a parent has determined their child is transgender. While many parents perceived themselves to be acutely vulnerable to state regulation, families with sexual-minority parents or racial-minority children were much more likely to have interventions into their lives by the state. When the state actually did intervene, however, it was with great consequence, and those interventions intensified the inequalities those families already suffered. Families with the greatest emotional and material resources, however, could marshal the state to assist them in problem-solving, demonstrating the double life of the state as enforcer and as resource provider, and the ways in which it functions as its own, important locus of recognition.

Chapter 6, "Telling Gender Stories," outlines a new set of narratives parents consolidate to make sense of their child's gender. While we typically think of medical and psychiatric discourses as inherently normative, these families appear to repurpose them, along with biomedical discourses, to fashion a more mutable construct of gender than they once held. Families used rhetorics from biomedicine, psychiatry, and even religion to imagine worlds in which their child's self-understandings were inevitable, intrinsic, and immutable, the sorts of justifications demanded by the institutions from which they sought social support.

Finally, in the conclusion, we return to Rafe, now a young adult, on the other side of puberty and living in the world. Returning to the questions that animated the initial study, I draw conclusions from Rafe's story about the significance of childhood transgenderism for understanding the ways we all gender one another in the contemporary moment. Gender is, at once, a deeply personal, subjective identity and a way of anchoring social relationships. We are interpellated into gender categories, and in the moments we contest them, rather than evacuating them of their meaning, we draw them more fully into our subjectivities and intimate, relational lives.

· · ·

Perhaps while reading this chapter, you turned the book over in your hands, searching for an author photo. Perhaps you wondered if, in fact, I am transgender, what I look like, what, were we to sit across from one another, you might discern in the contours of my face. If so, *you are like many of us,* on a distinctly contemporary quest to understand the complexities of gender, to position others in the cultural folds of masculinity and femininity, to grapple with the increasing presence among us of people who deliberately violate gender's mandates. The people in this book share your questions.

CHAPTER TWO

Gender Troubles

Josephine and Ari had a few things in common. For both children, by the time they could walk, ordinary household objects held within them the power to transform reality. Bath towels, scarves, and sarongs became flowing locks of their imagined hair. T-shirts and sweaters cinched tightly around the waist were the billowing skirts of flamenco dancers. Drinking straws danced together like ballerinas under their fingertips. For their parents, what began as the typical creative play of very young children became increasingly worrisome as they grew older and entered the public world. In preschool, the "dress-up corner" was their domain of choice. Both children would gravitate there immediately to put on frilly tutus and hats and gloves. Their parents waited and watched with concern for the reactions of teachers and peers. Some were appreciative, others angry and reproachful. Josephine and Ari were born little boys and, in the eyes of adults, were engaging in socially inappropriate behavior. Both children, however, delighted in their play, in the small space in their lives in which enacting their femininities was permitted and facilitated.

Josephine, at eight years old, attended school as a girl. She used a female name and female pronouns, dressed in feminine clothing. She used the girls' bathroom and participated with the girls in gender-segregated activities. Some children and parents at Josephine's school knew about her boy history; others didn't. Her parents were educating themselves, in anticipation of her impending puberty, and they planned to place her on "blockers," a controversial hormone therapy that would prevent her from ever going through male puberty. Ari, age twelve, attended school as a boy, though his manner of dress and style of behavior remained markedly feminine. He vacillated between using male and female names and pronouns, though he was most frequently found in the company of female classmates, doing theater and making art. He favored mostly androgynous clothing: flowing pants in bright colors, patterned shirts, and scarves. His hair grew long and was carefully arranged. His mother spoke nervously about his recent struggles with depression at the onset of puberty and the daunting choices she faced helping him to cope with the changes in his body. She wasn't sure whether Ari would be a gay man or a transgender woman, and felt a tremendous amount of discomfort with that uncertainty.

Both Josephine and Ari had parents who not merely supported, but who actively facilitated their gender nonconformity. I met both families through their involvement with Gender Spectrum, a small nonprofit organization that provided support and advocacy for parents of gender nonconforming youth. Both children, like all the others profiled in this book, deviated enough from the behavior expected of typical boys and girls that their families needed support to understand precisely why their children acted the way they did. Often, it began with something small—a request for a Barbie doll at Christmas, the rejection of a holiday dress in favor of pants, some inexplicable sense of upset over seemingly mundane interpersonal interactions. Over time, parents began collecting evidence of a deeper problem: the requests persisted, the emotional distress intensified, they began receiving concerned comments from teachers, neighbors, other family members. At a crucial tipping point, these parents shifted their fundamental understandings of their children. Whereas initially they thought their child unusual, perhaps acutely sensitive, maybe even troubled, they began to wonder if, in fact, their child had a different form of subjectivity, if they no longer belonged in the gender category initially assigned to them. Their children became not atypical, but gender nonconforming; not boys or girls, but transboys or transgirls. Their gender categories revealed their porosity: children's behavior spilled over the edges, or it fell out of its container completely.

A given child might reject the clothing a parent provided, might express distress over their appearance, or might make requests for activities or toys that were unexpected. Individually, these experiences were difficult for parents to comprehend or easy for them to dismiss. Over time, these disparate behavioral fragments accrued a kind of density. Parents began identifying them as *gender fragments,* and they began to seem like barriers to their child's social integration. At a critical point, parents concluded that their child's gender caused enough worry, conflict, or social disapproval that they required expert support. I call these "gender problems," by which I mean something specific. *Problem* is not an ontological category; I do not consider these forms of gender aberrant. Nor is it a philosophy, an instance of gender subversion that aspires for political reasons to antinormativity. Instead, what I mean to signal is that the act of reaching out beyond the family, to someone with expertise in gender, transformed these gendered processes from the private realm of the family to the social, from interpersonal negotiations to a larger question of where individual children fit in the social order. In those moments, that child's gender became the definition of a problem, an "intricate, unanswered question [requiring] consideration or solution."[1]

Judith Butler has argued that there is no ontological unity that constitutes gender, that, rather, it is produced through a series of acts that consolidate into culturally recognizable forms.[2] We tend to consider moments when these disparate indicia of gender conflict, when the presumed harmony of bodily sex and social gender misalign, moments of "gender trouble."[3] We think that these ruptures indicate the instability of gender; something about gender is failing or fracturing. An individual is revealed to be an incompetent inhabitor of their body, their social position. For the families in this book, however, these were moments of recognition and coherence, a starting point from which a different gender trajectory might be defined. They were the moments when parents began to think of their child as a new type of gendered person. The way this happened differed for boys and girls, reflecting the paradoxical way we value masculinity while also treating the category "male" as peculiarly fragile.

UNCOVERING AN UNDERLYING IDENTITY

The families profiled here are "facilitative"; each contains at least one adult who chooses to support their child's gender nonconforming expression. Most of these parents and caregivers shared a sense that gender identity is a static property that individuals possess, rather than a set of interactional accomplishments. Their children *were* boys, or girls, or something else. The notion of gender as a property of the psyche, immutable, present long before it is discovered by others, was a symbolic resource that allowed parents to understand gender nonconformity as evidence of an underlying identity, rather than psychopathology. Parents employed it routinely in their descriptions of their children's early development. Many, though certainly not all, parents of gender nonconforming children said that in retrospect, their child's atypical gender was readily apparent from an early age, but they had few tools at their disposal for deciphering the cues provided by pre- or minimally verbal children that their gender infractions actually signaled something deeper or more pervasive about their identity. Parents of children on the feminine spectrum recounted stories of their toddlers simulating long hair by draping T-shirts, towels, and scarves on their heads. Parents of masculine-spectrum children recalled emphatic rejection of "dressy" clothing in favor of jeans and sweatshirts. Parents of both groups described their children's disappointment over birthday and Christmas gifts, distress over preparations for the school day, and other interpersonal conflicts that seemed incomprehensible at the time, yet wove a fabric of consistent, small upsets and transgressions. Many parents described attempts to read their children's emotions as if they were tea leaves, a scattered series of protests and outbursts, puzzling joys and disappointments, that washed together to produce a picture of gender distress.

The ways this happened differed for assigned male and female children. Masculine girls typically needed to have significant, repeated emotional outbursts or to make ardent claims to a different gender for parents to notice. Parents of feminine boys, however, faced high levels of social disapproval from adults outside the family, sometimes for very minor infractions. They were often confronted by extended family members, teachers, clergy, or doctors and cautioned that they should step in and address their child's femininity.

David was one of those parents. He said that, in retrospect, any of a thousand cues should have alerted him and his wife, Lyn, that their child Jade wasn't like other little boys. By the age of three and a half, Jade was wearing towels on her head to simulate long hair, fashioning adult T-shirts and belts into dresses and engaging in cross-gender play.

> I think what was probably the most powerful is a lot of her fantasy play was in the guise of female characters. So, you know, we had some buddies, two boys in particular that were her closest friends, and we'd do play dates together, and they would just be running around like crazy people, running from the bad guys, and one of the kids would be all "I'm the Hulk!" and the other one would be like "I'm Batman" and Jade's like "I'm a butterfly princess!" All running from the same bad guy, all, you know, kooky and nutty, but that's how Jade was doing it. That's *who Jade was,* doing it.

Jade's inner life was projected onto her stuffed animals and artwork as well, which David came, over time, to interpret as a sign that she conceptualized herself in the feminine from the start. Her stuffed animals all had girls' names; she identified with female characters in movies and storybooks. Like many other parents, David and Lyn simply assumed their child was exhibiting early signs of being gay; yet, David said, they grew concerned when they began also to see signs of increasing anguish.

She would sometimes go to preschool like that, like wearing Lyn's shirt or my shirt or whatever as a dress. And pretty soon—I would say, like, you know, in a matter of a few weeks, it seems like now—she started getting, like, more and more perturbed ... that is, quote-unquote, "It's not right. It doesn't look right." And so she clearly had what "right" was in her mind and she became increasingly distressed at getting ready to go to school in the morning. I mean, not like out of control, but she'd be crying and sad and just ... [David shook his head and sighed.]

As David spoke, his body told the story of Jade's torment. He scrunched up his face, pulling at his T-shirt and moving his body tensely beneath it, laying and re-laying the clothing on his hunched shoulders. He was a picture of distress, discomfort, and anxiety, and I felt his overwhelm as he depicted his child's suffering. Many parents, like David, told their child's story this way, through a combination of language and affect. Their bodies held poses of hiding or shifting to find comfort. They mimed their children's grief and frustration. The emotionality in the stories became contagious. The room stilled.

Lyn said that one particular afternoon, during one of Jade's emotional outbursts, she finally realized that Jade was trying to say that she really wanted a dress. "So I just decided I'd ask her. I said, 'Honey, do you want to go to the store and get a dress?'" She remembered being taken aback by the reaction: Jade could barely contain her excitement enough to get her body into the car and into the store. Her delight was so exuberant, so thorough, so unlike her responses to smaller joys, that both Lyn and David recognized that something significant had happened. That moment prompted them to begin discussing Jade's gender in earnest between themselves and with others. It was a sobering realization, one that opened into a universe of unfamiliar questions and ideas. David and Lyn, perceiving independently that Jade wanted to cross-dress, began a series of conversations about whether Jade was transgender. They lived in a fairly liberal metropolitan area, so they'd encountered the idea of transgender before, but they remained, for a time, unsure if and how it applied to Jade.

For other parents, however, it wasn't until they encountered observations or criticisms from other adults that they fully understood the extent of their child's deviance. Lucia explained with obvious pride that she was surprised by her husband José's ready acceptance of their child Isabelle's interest in feminine things. Lucia worried when, at age two or three, Isabelle began wrapping towels around her waist to make skirts and resisted taking off girls' dress-up clothes at the end of the preschool day. José didn't seem to share her concern. When Isabelle had just turned four, they spent the Christmas holiday with Lucia's extended family in the Colombian countryside. Issy swam and lounged by the pool playing with sarongs and Lucia's sister's dresses. Lucia said she didn't pay much attention, until her mother pulled her aside.

> She said that she was very concerned about this. That is ... that we were being very, very permissive and that that probably could lead Issy to confusion about her gender roles. That then triggered my concerns, you know, because if my mom was concerned, then ... then I should be concerned. So when I came back, basically something changed, with that trip, you know ... in me. I came back, yeah, very much concerned, trying to ... you know, before that we were being very permissive and we ... all these play roles and dress-up and, you know, all these things. And then, something in me changed and I started to reverse.

For Lucia, seeing Issy's gender through her mother's eyes brought everything into clearer focus. When they returned to their West Coast suburb, she found herself thinking more deeply and consistently about Issy's desire for dresses and feminine toys. She researched children and gender online and found a pamphlet, available in both English and Spanish, from a Washington, DC, children's hospital gender clinic for parents wishing to support gender nonconforming children. The notion that such a program existed brought Lucia some comfort, because, as she said, "Now I had a name for it. I knew that this happened to other people too." She and José began attending a nearby support group for parents of gender nonconforming children and experimenting, slowly and incrementally, with allowing Isabelle to wear girls' clothing. She recalled a particularly poignant conversation, a few months later, in which Isabelle told her she was angry at God. "Why?" Lucia asked. "Because She made me a boy," Isabelle replied. Lucia now paused, her eyes filling with tears, and said, "So, in that moment, I knew, I started to understand." What it was, precisely, that Lucia began to understand would become better articulated with time. Isabelle, she said, was telling her she felt like a different kind of person, not a boy but a girl.

The emergent understanding that a child was different didn't necessarily lead smoothly to action. Parents often moved back and forth between attempts to prevent and facilitate the gender nonconforming expression of their children. Many families tolerated (and even ignored) a fairly substantial amount of transgressive behavior,[4] before confronting the question of whether and how to respond. However, this latitude only extended so far. As long as parents considered each transgressive action to be an isolated incident, they gave their children some room for fluidity and experimentation. Once they began to consider the possibility that there might be some deeper or more systemic meaning to these behaviors, most did engage in some efforts to correct or to minimize the extent of their child's difference. They described this form of gender management as a reaction to fear, confusion, and distress. In some families, the responses of parents aligned; in many, however, parents approached a child's gender trajectory from very different ideological or emotional positions.

The Lopez family had a typical story. Charlotte Lopez was a forty-nine-year-old mother living in a small Midwestern town she described as "very conservative." Her youngest child, Ashley, was a nine-year-old transgirl. Charlotte worked from the family's home, providing day care for neighborhood children. She had been married to her husband, Damian, for twenty years, and she and her family were active participants in their community's church. They had six children, all of whom were assigned male at birth. Charlotte's description of her very male-dominated household seemed to suggest it would be an ideal breeding ground for hegemonic masculinity. And indeed, she told me she never gave much thought to gender at all, until at the age of two and a half, Ashley began asking for girls' toys. At first, Charlotte said, she didn't pay much attention. One day at Wal-Mart, Ashley was begging Charlotte for her very first Barbie doll. Her initial impulse was to buy the doll; but Charlotte didn't quite feel she could make that decision alone. These sorts of gender choices felt heavy, worthy of reflection and discussion.

> I thought I had better call my husband and ask him first because my husband is a Latino. He is extremely manly, and we have five very manly boys. They are all very athletic, very daredevil, very rough and tumble, VERY manly.

Damian told her he thought buying a Barbie doll was okay. At that point, she said, neither parent considered occasional gender-deviant behavior to be any big deal. They had five other male children, all of whom seemed securely situated in their gender identities. She never imagined a single Barbie doll might become so symbolic. Several of her sons had tried on high heels as young boys. The children in her day care often played with a wide range of toys. But she and Damian quickly understood that their youngest child would have a different developmental course from their other children.

> The minute the Barbie hit her hand I think I realized that there was something there. She stroked the hair incessantly. The Barbie never left her hand. If she went to sleep, the Barbie went with her. If she went to the bathroom, the Barbie went with her. If she watched TV, the Barbie was with her. Barbie actually had painted-on panties, and the panties wore off from her hand being around the waist. That was how frequently she held on to that Barbie.

Over the next year or so, Ashley began engaging in other forms of cross-gender play. Since Damian cut all of the boys' hair into military-style fades, Ashley took to wrapping towels around her head, walking around in Charlotte's shoes, and periodically asserting to her parents and siblings that she was a girl. While her oldest son occasionally commented on this behavior, and while Charlotte recalled exchanging concerned glances with Damian from time to time, she still assumed this was a developmental phase that Ashley would outgrow.

Like Lucia and José, an intervention by outside adults provoked Charlotte and Damian to consolidate their respective responses to Ashley's gender transgressions. At four and a half, Ashley began attending a local Christian preschool affiliated with the family's church. Charlotte, Damian, and their other children were all devoted participants in weekly services, as well as in children's programming and summer camps; Charlotte volunteered in the nursery, and Charlotte and Damian belonged to a local group that met weekly to discuss Christian books, parenting, and family issues. It was a natural choice to enroll Ashley in this school, which she attended with her cousin and several neighbors who had been her primary playmates since birth.

At midyear, Charlotte and Damian went into school to discuss Ashley's progress with her teacher. The meeting did not go quite as they expected. After preliminary comments about how intelligent and affable Ashley was, Charlotte remembered the teacher saying, "Oh, and by the way, we had a meeting... the pastor, the director, and I even brought some of the other teachers in because I wasn't sure what to do. And we decided to tell your child that he will not be allowed to play in the dress-up area any longer because boys don't wear skirts."

Charlotte was livid. She exclaimed, "Nobody called me. Nobody consulted me. They just told my child, 'You are not allowed to play in the dress up area any longer because boys don't wear skirts.'" That the school would discuss this with Ashley without notifying her was mortifying. She said it took tremendous effort for her to remain calm. She remembered Damian rolling his eyes and asking if Ashley ever played with boys' toys. The teachers replied that she did join the boys in building with blocks but that when left to her own devices she preferred the company of female classmates. Charlotte remembered Damian's entire body tensing up. "What he projected was anger," she said, "but what he was really feeling was fear and uncertainty, and embarrassment."

> My husband was horrified. He was so embarrassed. He was not angry that they had said that to our child. He was angry that it needed to be said. He was embarrassed. His manhood was threatened. He was being told that his son was a sissy, and he did not like it.

Before their humiliating encounter with Ashley's school, both parents tolerated and even participated in facilitating Ashley's cross-gender play. After the meeting, however, Damian began displaying more of the constraining behaviors commonly associated with men in other sociological studies on gender and childrearing.[5] He engaged with Ashley more frequently and, Charlotte noticed, with a more distinctly masculine style. Instead of giving her a hug, he'd pick her up and roughhouse. He invited her to play baseball; when she refused, he became angry. Charlotte sensed that his efforts were having an entirely different outcome than what he intended.

> Obviously, she didn't want to do any of the things that he was proposing. And the more she was reluctant, or the more she refused, or the more she complained, the more he pushed. And the angrier he got. And the more determined he became to change this behavior. And what ended up happening is she hated him. She absolutely hated him. I don't mean she disliked him. I mean she hated him. Every fiber of her being displayed her hatred for him. [...] She wanted nothing to do with him.

During this time, Ashley's older brothers began to echo some of their father's disdain. They called her a sissy, told her boys don't play with Barbie dolls, gave her G.I. Joe figurines instead. Tension emerged between Charlotte and Damian over how to respond to the mounting strain in their household. Charlotte felt a gender divide emerging, with Damian and the boys on one side and Ashley and Charlotte on the other.

Charlotte and Ashley began having what she called "secret girl time." They would get together and dress up, and Ashley would tell

Charlotte to call her girls' names. Charlotte participated, but she felt deeply conflicted about doing so.

> I saw how much she enjoyed it and how happy it made her to hear those things. And how her behavior evolved. She was so confident when she was that person being told those things, which I was happy for her, but yet I was also quite honestly a little sick to my stomach because it was so odd to me to say something like that to who I thought was my son.

Ashley's distress and its effects on the family intensified as she began her kindergarten year. She would cry each morning while getting ready to go to school. When Charlotte asked her why she was so upset, Ashley replied, "Because it's too hard for me to pretend to be a boy for that long." Charlotte was devastated, and frightened. Ashley began being taunted by other children. She came home one day and asked Charlotte what the word *faggot* meant.

In the end Damian, despite his discomfort with Ashley's preoccupation with feminine things, wasn't unwavering in his commitment to hegemonic masculinity. Charlotte recalled feeling a knot in the pit of her stomach when she saw Ashley's Christmas list that year. It was all girls' toys: Barbie, My Little Pony, Strawberry Shortcake. She worried that Damian would be terribly upset. She tried intervening, telling Ashley she didn't know if Santa would bring girls' toys for a boy. Finally, she showed the list to Damian. Damian had grown up with a single mother and two siblings. They hadn't celebrated holidays because there was no money for toys. "Santa didn't visit their house," Charlotte recounted. As a result, holidays with his own family were hugely important to Damian. She said he decorated like the "Griswold house at Christmas." Damian, weighing his childhood poverty and his desire for his children to have beautiful, magical holidays against his fear and frustration, told Charlotte, "Whatever, just buy the toys."

For both Charlotte and Damian, decisions to monitor, facilitate, or attempt to prevent Ashley's gender transgressions were inconsistent, often made in interaction with competing desires of their own. Damian was not unilaterally intolerant of Ashley's femininity. In fact, until called upon to account for it to school administrators, he was almost indifferent to it. He experienced the censure as shaming, however, and after that point his orientation shifted. For Damian, despite his discomfort with Ashley's femininity and concern about the scrutiny of others, the scars of his own childhood deprivation prevented him from withholding his child's desired Christmas toys. Charlotte was willing to allow Ashley to violate gender norms, and was angry when confronted by the school's intervention. She also occupied the role of mediator, attempting to mitigate both her child's and her husband's distress. While Charlotte responded to Ashley's requests for affirmation of her female identity, she would temper some of those with warnings or reproaches, in an attempt to minimize the tension between her husband and her child.

Damian's response to Ashley's Christmas requests was a relief, but Charlotte was still left with lingering questions. Was Ashley gay or was this a deeper manifestation of her gender identity? How should she understand these desires and behaviors? Then Charlotte had what she called her "epiphany day." One morning, while Charlotte was preparing the family for the school day, Ashley approached her and asked for an advance on her allowance. "What for?" Charlotte asked. Ashley said, "Well, I want a quarter and I need it today, not Saturday. Because on the way to school we pass a house that has a wishing well, and I'm gonna ask the bus driver to stop so that I can wish to be a girl." Charlotte explained, "I felt like ... here's a five-year-old who conjured up this wish that seems so far out there, but yet so poignantly real. This was something about *who she is*." For Charlotte, it wasn't just the complexity of this thought process her five-year-old was having that was so sharply painful, it was also Ashley's essential belief that her mother could help her realize this wish she so desperately held: to be and to live as a girl.

I feel like my kids look at me as omnipotent. And as a mother you want that, and you want to be able to give them the best of everything and everything that they want. You make sacrifices for yourself in order for them to have what they want. And you go without the new shoes so that they can have the exact shoes they want rather than just the shoes they need. And her saying that to me, she put her absolute faith in telling me that and believing that the quarter that I gave her, you know, she knew I was trying to make it better for her. She knew I wanted her to feel good. [...] And her having the complete faith to ask me for that quarter and to share that with me, combined with the fact that that's a big thought process for a five-year-old. Most five-year-olds think in terms of today, right now, what can I get now, maybe what am I having for lunch, but really not beyond that. And this five-year-old is talking to me about the rest of her life. And that was huge to me. That had such an impact on me.

Charlotte remembered spending much of that day in tears. It was the first day she looked on the internet for information about children and gender, and the first day she reached out for support from other parents of gender nonconforming children. Charlotte and her family began to come to terms with Ashley's transgender identity and to move into community with other families with children like her.

Most parents, like Charlotte, described the process of grappling with their child's identity as confusing and confounding. They described a series of opaque conversations with children and partners, working with clues that seemed at the time incomprehensible. They reported moving back and forth between restricting the gender behavior of their children and allowing or even at times facilitating it, all the while searching for clues about what the underlying set of issues might be. Once experiences accrued enough density, many parents reported having a kind of "epiphany day," a moment, an interaction, where these disparate fragments cohered into something they understood as core gender, as a "part of who [their children] are." This was the phrase they used over and over. They began an interpretive process, then, to situate their child among the multitude of new gender identity categories they encountered in their research. They experienced those questions and the responsibility to ask them as weighty.

Some other parents didn't suspect their child might be transgender until they were explicitly told. Haley's parents, Roni and George, never gave any thought to Haley's gender until she told them she was a girl, on a trip home from boarding school when she was sixteen. Likewise, Devon's mother, Natalie, said that it never crossed her mind that Devon had gender identity issues. She always assumed he was a tomboy. She sensed he was deeply unhappy from a young age, and remembered him always wearing his hair short and preferring baggy clothing, provoking frequent questions and occasional harassment in women's restrooms. Still, she was shocked when he came to her at thirteen and said, "Mom, I finally know what's bothering me. I'm a boy; I've always known it, and I'm actually a boy." She explained that in the moment, she told him everything would be all right, and that she and his father would always support his choices, but part of what prompted that response, she admitted, was her belief that his feelings would resolve themselves in time, would go away. Nonetheless, she reached out to a parent organization for support.

Certain interactions between parents and children, emotional distress, requests for highly gendered objects and certain play styles, and most notably, outside censure, were the most common fragments of gender that provoked parents to understand a child's inner self differently. That child's gender inhered in their body, in the sense that these behaviors and interactions either felt consistent or inconsistent with their body. But they were not of the body. Gender—the sense parents had of their child's maleness or femaleness—became knitted to things they said and did, types of affirmations they required, how they managed the gaze of others, how at ease they felt in their own skin.

UNTANGLING GENDER AND SEXUALITY

Bess, a forty-six-year-old mother of two from a Northeastern suburb, remembered thinking long and hard about how to understand her daughter's masculinity. Always a staunch tomboy, Benjamin, then an eighteen-year-old transboy, had always played mostly with boys, and favored Pokémon cards and hockey games over other forms of recreation. But he was solitary, often preferring to hang out alone in his room. Bess remembered vividly sitting on the family's sofa one day, when Ben was twelve or thirteen.

> I was sitting on the couch and going, "What is going on with this kid? This kid is not like other kids. I don't think she's a lesbian." [...] I just didn't know what it was. I remember, as I was sitting on the couch, thinking, "If I had to peg this child, I would say it's a gay boy, but that's ridiculous because this is a girl. That doesn't make sense."

Bess described understanding that Benjamin was masculine, but not being able to comfortably situate him in any of the cultural categories she had at her disposal. He didn't seem gay. She said, even in retrospect, he didn't seem entirely male, either. So, what was he?

Many of Bess's struggles with Ben unfolded over shopping for clothing. She explained that she, too, had a tomboy history, and so she didn't worry too much when Benjamin asked for clothing from the boys' section of the local store. "I believe in picking your battles," she said, "and that was okay. I mean, you're buying a fleece jacket, so you get to have dark blue instead of pink." Several mothers, both gay and straight, recalled tomboy girlhoods that were mostly ignored by their own families. They referenced a cultural tolerance of moderate forms of girlhood masculinity that didn't exist for the feminine boys. Bess could tie Ben's smaller gender behaviors to her own history of incidental gender transgression, indicating that it would take a more significant disruption before she realized there was more at stake than color preferences.

The moment of revelation for Bess came one afternoon in the car, on the way to another fraught shopping trip. Benjamin, a gifted martial artist, was preparing to accept an award at a formal ceremony and had asked Bess if he could wear a tuxedo rather than a dress. She acquiesced, despite her anxiety that peers might think his choice strange. On the drive to pick up the tuxedo from a rental shop, Bess and Benjamin were arguing about buying clothing for school, and she asked in frustration, "Why is it so difficult for you to just go out and buy a pair of slacks?"

Benjamin retorted, "Because when I wear girls' clothes, I feel like I'm cross-dressing!" Bess was shocked. She had no idea what this declaration meant. She remembered thinking only that her heart was pounding out of her chest, but that for Ben's sake she needed to remain calm. She had some sense that this declaration was related to her own struggles to understand his identity. Her stomach, she said, was "like ice water."

Bess reached out to a friend who taught psychology at an Ivy League college and who had gay children. She found websites and reading material about transgender children. It took her a few days to confide in her husband, Ronald, about what she was learning, and she said that he struggled with the news at first. Ronald worried that Benjamin was seeking attention, or that perhaps he had been sexually abused. Even when we spoke, Bess still struggled to explain Benjamin's gender. Although by that point Benjamin fully identified as male, Bess thought of him as a "feminine boy." It made sense to her, yet other people found the distinction confusing.

The conclusion that an individual child had an underlying gender problem represented only the beginning of what many parents experienced as a long, often confusing process of trying to disentangle gender from sexuality. The first clues for incipient homosexuality and transgenderism often look the same: small, quotidian gender infractions.[6] How were parents to determine which was which? Were these autonomous phenomena, or were they, perhaps, connected? Were they even possibly manifestations of sexual abuse? How could they tell what was about sex and what was about gender, when the lines so often blur and overlap? In this crisis of uncertainty, parents often turned to mental health professionals to assist them in untangling the knots.

Rafe's parents, Claudia and Rick, had their first consultation with a psychologist when Rafe was four years old. They recalled telling the psychologist that they were perfectly comfortable with the idea that Rafe might grow up to be a gay adult, but in the short term they feared that his feminine behaviors would make him a target for bullying by other children. Over the next weeks and months, with the support of a handful of sessions with this psychologist, they engaged in what Claudia labeled "an intensive effort" to socialize the feminine behaviors out of Rafe. While they didn't punish him for playing with girls' toys while visiting friends or family members, they carefully edited his surroundings at home, his wardrobe, and his toys, and permitted him only traditionally masculine haircuts. Rick signed him up for karate classes. Claudia reflected on that time with a furrowed brow, telling me that Rick's disappointment in Rafe's resistance to these efforts was palpable. She thought Rafe sensed it, too. Karate became a site of symbolic struggle over control of Rafe's person. Rafe would cry and refuse to go, and Rick would force him. They became increasingly estranged. Over the next two years, Claudia says, Rafe's behavior began to shift markedly.

> By the age of six, he went from the happiest baby on earth to a nasty, angry, unhappy, crazy, awful child. I used to tell people, "Don't call me at home after work, I live in a battle zone." I would go home, I would battle with the child till he passed out. At the age of six, for some seemingly inconsequential reason, he stood at the sink and looked up at me and said, "Mommy, I'm gonna get a real gun and kill myself." And I thought, "Okay, I'm obviously in over my head, I have no idea what's going on or why this is happening."

Claudia next called a child psychiatrist, who diagnosed Rafe with anxiety and depression. They discussed the probability that he would grow up to be gay but didn't focus specifically on his gender behaviors. The psychiatrist recommended a local family counselor, and they began to meet with her regularly.

It appeared, for a period of time, that the psychiatrist was correct. In eighth grade, at the age of thirteen, Rafe came out to his mother as bisexual. But Claudia continued to struggle with a sense that something wasn't quite right. She remembered feeling uncertain about what exactly Rafe's identity was and what it meant to him. She felt deeply conflicted about his feminine clothing choices and mannerisms. "This didn't feel like 'bisexual' to me," she said, making scare quotes with her hands. At this moment in our conversation, Rick entered the room and the atmosphere changed. Claudia began to choose her words more slowly and carefully. Rick sat in silence as Claudia described the family's emotional conflict. She said that she and Rafe continued to argue. The strain was taking its toll on Claudia and Rick's marriage. As the three of us sat together in the interview, I felt the air thicken with tension. At one point, Claudia paused, then said, as if speaking to Rafe, "I didn't know where this was going to end, you know? I'm giving you the pinkest room on earth and this isn't enough? Good heavens to God, what is this? What do you need? And how far can I take you, and how far can I drag this loving wonderful man whom I adore, you know?" Claudia put her hand on Rick's arm as she spoke, to affirm both his efforts to parent Rafe and his discomfort with Rafe's femininity. Claudia seemed anxious as she described all these conflicting experiences— her child's pain and distress, her desires and resistances and those of her husband. I sensed that she felt it was her responsibility to maintain the emotional temperature in the room. It looked exhausting.

She wasn't always successful. On one particularly difficult day, she remembered shouting at Rafe, "You can be as gay as you want, but if you ever go trans, it's on your own time and your own money out of my house!" She said she couldn't remember what precipitated the outburst, but the moment itself was emblazoned on her memory, and as she recounted it she flushed red with shame. She told me that shortly thereafter she heard a segment on NPR about transgender adults and realized, with shock, that many of the same things these adults were saying had, at one time or another, come out of her own child's mouth. She recalled Rafe telling her he was born in the wrong body. She remembered him describing his gender as embodying "the best of both worlds." "I just reflected back on that moment, what I'd said ... and I went, *oh, shit!*" That was her epiphany moment and the moment she realized Rafe was something other than male.

Gender and sexuality evolve in intricate relationship to one another. Emergent sexuality often trades in gender behavior; it can be a way we signal availability to the objects we desire. And many gay and lesbian adults reflect back on gender nonconforming childhoods, remarking that the responses of others to their mannerisms and play styles were the first clue to their parents and even to themselves that they might by gay. Claudia and Bess initially wondered if Rafe's and Ben's clothing preferences, play styles, and friend choices signaled the beginning of adult homosexuality, but both ultimately concluded that what they saw was "about gender." Once they did, a new question emerged: how would they interact with these children they suddenly understood differently?

GIVING GENDER

On a balmy early June afternoon, I sat in the main lobby of the Philadelphia Convention Center with Nan, a thirty-eight-year-old mother from the West Coast. Nan was staffing a table in the exhibition area of a large conference, for an all-volunteer organization called Trans Youth Family Allies (TYFA). We sat together chatting about her family, and exchanging information with other parents who came by to ask questions, look at the organization's brochures, or grab a piece of chocolate from the large bowl of candy displayed on the table. Nan's child, Hunter, a transboy, was six years old at the time. Over the previous year, he decided to change his name and begin attending school as a boy. He did this with Nan's knowledge and full support.

While we were talking, Hunter came running up to us and grabbed his mother's legs. "Mom, guess what?!" he exclaimed. "Did you know that Colten and Tommy both have *vaginas?*" (Colten was another kid a year older than Hunter with whom he'd been running around that morning, and Tommy was the twenty-two-year-old volunteer in the child care area of the conference.) I watched with surprise as Nan looked at Hunter, shrugged her shoulders and said, noncommittally, "Sure honey ... lots of boys have vaginas."

With this simple descriptive statement, Nan made Hunter a boy. She architected a world for him in which his body and identity were not in conflict. She narrated for him a way to alter his "felt sense"[7] of his body, that his body could feel like a boy body, could, in fact, *be* a boy body. In referring to Colten and Tommy *as* boys, she created a similar rhetorical space in the world for Hunter to occupy; the offhand way with which she spoke was a kind of emotional labor,[8] one that made his identity unremarkable, obvious, and taken for granted.

If we take the notion of subjective gender identity in its conventional form, Hunter exists "as a boy" prior to his relation to his mother; instead, he is in the world, occupying space as a particular kind of being with a static self-understanding, whether or not that subjectivity is recognized by others. But the notion of gender identity as a subjective phenomenon sits in an uneasy tension with the ways gender actually comes into being in the world through intricate processes of social assignment, recognition, and regulation. The parents I spoke with felt that small, routine decisions about how to interact with their children acquired a new significance. The enormity of the process of negotiating gender with their children underscores the extent to which gender is woven into the fabric of many quotidian social interactions. Parents bought children clothes, painted their rooms, referred to them by name and pronoun, signed them up for activities and sports teams, took them into public restrooms, and encouraged friendships with other children. In each of these encounters, they were making decisions about what was possible in their child's world, in who they would be and to whom they would be in relation.

On the most intimate level, parents decided whether they had sons or daughters (or, on rare occasions, something else). They did this in language, in play, in the ways they touched their children, in the emotional closeness or distance they cultivated in the face of their child's behavior or distress. Sociologist Jane Ward describes this as "giving gender," the interpersonal, affective labor we undertake to assist others in shoring up their identities.[9] Because, by definition, the children had limited agency, many of the ways they enacted their genders were circumscribed by what their parents permitted. As parents began to interpret their children's identities differently, they made tentative forays into gendering their children differently. Often it was an initial toy purchase or article of clothing. Sometimes parents restricted the use of such objects to private spaces, slowly allowing their child increased room for public expressions of their gender. Eventually, many parents began making more significant aesthetic decisions—a new haircut or a seasonal piece of clothing like a winter coat or pair of shoes. They might allow their child to redecorate their room or participate in a new activity or social group. Finally, children whose parents understood them as trans were allowed to change their names and social gender categories, this representing the final step toward inhabiting a new social identity.

It is through these interpersonal processes that children become boys or girls. Although the lexicon we have for understanding identity imagines it as fixed, as existing in some stable form, and sitting in wait for discovery by others, it makes more sense to view the assumption of a gender category as an interactional, social process, happening in concert with the others from whom we seek recognition.[10] This recognition can only occur within a field of cultural constraint, which sets the linguistic parameters of communication, the conditions of possibility for personhood, and the legible modes of address and response.[11]

Sometimes parents made explicit their permission, acceptance, and acknowledgment of their child's person by materially changing their environment. Claudia did this for Rafe when he was fifteen years old. It was a difficult time for the family. She and Rick argued regularly about how to address Rafe's gender, even as she noticed Rafe growing more and more withdrawn. She felt his ambient discomfort in public spaces and even in the shared space of their home. Rafe had asked repeatedly to redecorate his bedroom, and she had resisted. "He'd always wanted pink and we'd always railroaded him into the guy stuff," she said. Eventually, she relented. She told him he could have any kind of space he wanted. She gave him the basement of their house as his own private space. She said she wasn't entirely prepared for the outcome.

> We went down to that basement and he had the pinkest ... just the absolute pinkest pink ... [she shakes her head.] I'm talking pom-poms, hanging beads, talking mirrors with fluff and frou-frou. I mean, the girls in our neighborhood wanted this bedroom so bad.

Claudia admitted, with more than a hint of irony, that she would never allow a daughter to have a room like that, but she felt a sense of relief as she watched Rafe's anxiety dissolve. "Something fit, something worked," she said. "He had a space where he felt comfortable. And I could feel that, and that was really neat." She showed me a photograph of Rafe draped across his bed, smiling, amid pink garlands and beaded curtains. He looked wholly at ease.

CISNORMATIVITY AND FRAGILE MALENESS

Most children display enough of a congruence between their biological sex, the social gender categories they are assigned at birth, and their gender behavior that adults take such configurations to be all but inevitable. This *cisgender*[12] alignment is a taken-for-granted expectation by most parents, so much so that it takes tremendous counterevidence to refute. *Cisnormativity* (or cisgender presumption)[13] leads parents to interpret most gender transgressions as exceptional, rather than constitutive. While parents took divergent paths toward conceptualizing their child as transgender, patterned responses mirrored parents' identities less closely than one might have imagined. Rather than family composition or social environment, parental responses had more to do with individual children's gender makeups than with the psychic or cultural makeup of their parents.

Most significantly, feminine boys—assigned male children who displayed female-typical interests, behaviors, or styles of self-fashioning—found themselves the targets of much stricter gender enforcement than masculine girls did. A related form of cultural sexism, the disproportionate value placed on normative masculinity,[14] allowed boyish girls far more latitude to display gender nonnormativity than it did for boys who display devalued feminine traits. Yet, while the gender assessments[15] being made by the parents I describe here may have resulted in disapproval or sanction, they also activated questions about the salience of gender categories themselves. Parents of feminine boys and masculine girls found themselves considering whether their child was "really" or "actually" better captured by the *other* gender category, whether their child was, in fact, transgender, in need of a "social transition" from male to female or vice versa. In this context, cisnormativity operated in conjunction with cultural sexism to produce a uniquely fragile "male" category, one more easily activated and questioned, and ultimately more porous, than the category "female" appeared to be.

As other sociologists who study childhood gender have found, families' race, ethnicity, and class backgrounds had little impact on either the reasons parents became concerned about their child's gender or the ways they discussed those concerns.[16] The salient difference was the directionality of the gender transgression. Parents questioned the gender identity of assigned boys for far more commonplace forms of feminine behavior than they did for assigned girls who exhibited masculine behavior. Assigned girls needed to assert fully a male identity, themselves invoking a categorical shift, for their femaleness to be in question. Some might call this sexism or homophobia, but for these families, gender categories themselves were activated. Maleness, as a social category, was brittle, called into question by smaller infractions that were not, in and of themselves, declarative. This may be due to the greater social disapproval faced by parents of feminine boys.

Overall, parents of gender nonconforming boys responded differently and at earlier ages to gender cues than did parents of gender nonconforming girls, though parents absolutely did label and pursue expert intervention and/or advocate support for extreme girlhood masculinity. While there was near parity in the assigned genders of the sample of children whose parents I interviewed and in my casual estimations of attendance at conference and support groups, the distribution of identity characteristics was noteworthy for several reasons. (See table 1.)

First, while parents sought support for cross-gender identities in both male and female children, they seldom sought support for masculine behavior in girls absent an extreme degree of emotional distress or a persistent male identity.

TABLE I

Identity Characteristics of the Facilitative Sample

	Feminine Spectrum	Masculine Spectrum	Totals
Gender Nonconforming	11 feminine boys	1 masculine girl	12
Transgender	12 transgirls	16 transboys	28
Total	23	17	40

TABLE 2

Mean Age at Interview and First Intervention

	Mean Age at Interview	Mean Age at Intervention
Feminine Spectrum ($n = 23$)	8.9	5.2
Masculine Spectrum ($n = 17$)	13.3	10
Gender Nonconforming ($n = 12$)	8.7	4.4
Transgender ($n = 28$)	11.6	8.4
Transgirls ($n = 12$)	9.3	6.2
Transboys ($n = 16$)	13.5	10

Second, children along the feminine gender spectrum (those children assigned male at birth whose gender-transgressive behaviors or identities were feminine or female) were significantly younger at the time their parents sought an expert intervention than were children along the masculine spectrum (children assigned female at birth, who exhibited masculine or male behaviors or identities). (See table 2.) Feminine-spectrum children were, on average, only 5.2 years of age the first time their parents began to think of their gender transgressions as problems in need of redress; masculine-spectrum children were ten, nearly twice the age. Likewise, parents had their initial interactions with me earlier in their child's life (8.9 for feminine-spectrum children and 13.3 for masculine-spectrum children). Some parents sought support for their feminine-spectrum children when they were as young as young as two and a half.

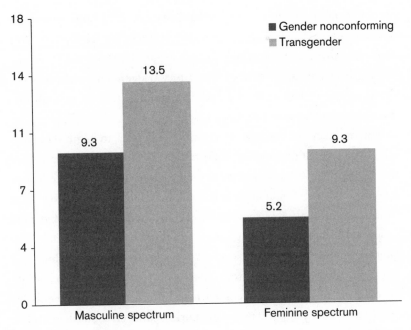

Figure 1. Mean age at first intervention.

Third, there was also a relationship between the identity designation that individual children were given by their parents and the age of the child at the time of our interview. The gender nonconforming children whose parents sat for interviews were by and large younger than the transgender children: the mean age for gender nonconforming children was 8.7 years at the time of interview, versus 11.6 years for the transgender children. This suggests, as does my interview data, that some of the children whose parents labeled them gender nonconforming may, in fact, assume a transgender identity later on. Gender nonconforming children were identified by their parents at an average of 4.4 years of age, whereas the sample of transgender children were identified at an average of 8.4 years old. (See figure 1.) Looking specifically at the transgender-identified children, transgirls were identified at a mean age of 6.2 years old, whereas transboys were identified at a mean age of 10 years of age. The interview setting captured parents at a particular point in a much longer trajectory of forging understandings of their children's identities. For some families, the labels they gave children will endure into adulthood; for others, they will shift.

Finally, evidence of boyhood femininity triggered different types of social sanctions, and more and earlier, than did girlhood masculinity. There were systematic differences in the types of events that provoked parents to reach out for support or, more generally, to begin the onto-logical process of questioning their child's identity. (See figure 2.) For the assigned-male/feminine-spectrum children, fantasy play, requests for girls' clothing, toy choices at school, and emotional volatility were the most commonly reported indicators that made parents seek expert support. Parents of masculine-spectrum children reported that it fre-quently (in nine of sixteen cases) took a disclosure from their child that *they were* male before their parents sought support. While seven parents of feminine boys reported seeking help after repeated comments by family members and parents of neighboring children about their child's gender transgression, no parents of masculine girls indicated that the opinions of others had a determinative effect (though several did recount uncomfortable interactions). Perhaps surprisingly, parents of masculine girls were more likely to report that their children's requests for short haircuts caused them significant discomfort, whereas only three parents of feminine boys said they found requests for long hair disturbing. This is particularly striking given the frequency with which parents of feminine boys recalled their children using shirts or towels to simulate long hair as toddlers, indicating, perhaps, that long hair on boys is more socially acceptable these days than short hair on young girls. For these reasons, the sample of children whose families I inter-viewed, while roughly split between feminine and masculine presenta-tions, includes many more transboys than it does masculine girls, who have much greater latitude to exhibit their masculinity without adults considering it a problem warranting attention or outside support.

In short, a cisnormative orientation leads many parents to ignore fairly substantial gender-transgressive behavior and even the identity

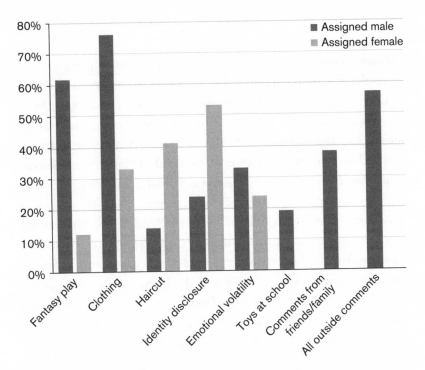

Figure 2. Precipitating factors for expert support.

claims of young children. When combined with the devaluation of feminine traits relative to masculine ones, however, feminine boys face much harsher scrutiny than their masculine female peers. Indeed, the category "male" reveals itself to be more fragile than "female" does; while masculine girls needed to assert fully a male identity, invoking a categorical shift, for their femaleness to be in question, maleness, as a social category, was brittle, called into question by smaller infractions that were not, in and of themselves, declarative.[17] While ample evidence exists in and beyond the sociological canon for the stricter assessment of masculinity,[18] this demonstrates that the category male itself is paradoxically both accorded high value and highly fragile.

CONCLUSION

Ethnomethodological theories of gender—which elaborate the ways we do gender as a routine accomplishment, and always at the risk of assessment[19]—employ a binary formulation of conformity and nonconformity, in which the latter category is the locus of scrutiny, social disapproval, and sanction. Certainly this is true in many cases, and with tremendous consequence. However, the families I interviewed demonstrate that there are ways to conceptualize and work with gender nonconformity that extend beyond the repressive, beyond theories of developmental delay, oppositionality, or psychopathology. Now, for the first time, adults have cultural tools at their disposal for interpreting transgression as a clue to underlying identity characteristics that are not neatly determined by the sex of the body. Gender is no longer merely the cultural overlay of biological sex. It is a subjectivity that is enduring, stable, and divorced from the body. Thus, we see that gender actually *requires* assessment, in both normative and nonnormative forms.

Male children might occasionally covet dolls, but if they coveted dolls *and* preferred the company of girls, parents began to suspect they might also be demonstrating a more general tendency toward femininity, and that that tendency might be constitutive of that child's emergent self. When attempts to socialize these children into masculinity appeared to fail and the episodes of gender transgression accrued enough density, or when adults outside the family commented on or criticized their child's behavior or their parenting, some parents shifted their framework from understanding their children as *feminine* to understanding them as *female*. This shift represents a fundamental transformation in the way we understand gender, from a set of interactional accomplishments to an enduring feature of the self. Parents of masculine girls often ignored fairly substantial forms of gender transgression, waiting until their children either exhibited extreme amounts of emotional distress or made ardent claims to a male identity. These systemic differences reflect the greater cultural value placed on masculinity relative to femininity and the fragility of maleness itself.

In order to link gender behavior to gender identity, parents had to find ways to ontologically extricate it from sexuality, or more specifically, from cultural notions of homosexuality. Because the idea of heterosexuality underwrites much of what we think of as gender—patterned ways of interacting, masculine/feminine complementarity, the expected coherence of bodies, behaviors, and desires—gender nonconformity often appears to signal homosexuality.[20] Indeed, it is the basis for many social assessments of homosexuality. Many of these parents initially interpreted their child's signals as incipient homosexuality, but something, often something they could scarcely articulate, led them to search for a construct outside sexuality to which to attach it. Thus began their ontological separation of gender from sexuality. Thinking gender as its own construct opened up a space for parents to begin to consider whether their children were, in fact, transgender.

Gender, the sense that a child was male or female, may have initially resided in the body. But gender fragments, desires, frustrations, movements, assertions, aesthetics, could accrue enough density that they surpassed the importance of the body. They became the locus of identity. Concluding that their child might have a problem at the level of core identity, rather than settling an open question, seemed to create a new one. Parents, realizing that their stylized ways of "giving gender" to their children had to change, considered whether they were willing to stand behind new and often uncomfortable interactional choices in front of others. This new gender was a relational product; it was identified, created, and ossified in interactions between parents and children. This relational work was emotionally fraught, introducing as it did new uncertainties, questions, and anxieties. This was typically the point at which parents reached out, first to the internet, then to advocacy organizations, support groups, pediatricians, and mental health professionals. There, they entered a new world of proliferating meanings, labels, explanations, and agendas.

CHAPTER THREE

The Gender Clinic

The lobby of the Gender Identity Clinic at the Centre for Addiction and Mental Health in Toronto (CAMH, usually pronounced Cam-H) had the feel of a hospital. I emerged from the elevator into fluorescent light and linoleum-tiled floors. The waiting room had a sterile institutional rug and couches and smelled vaguely of disinfectant, but it was adorned with the kinds of flourishes—construction paper mosaics, signs with balloon letters—that signaled an attempt to welcome children. I walked through a fire door and down a long hallway, past a large conference room and a photocopy machine, and arrived at the director Dr. Kenneth J. Zucker's office. His door was thickly layered with drawings done by young children: figures of girls with balloons, a dog, a portrait of him. He sat at his desk, typing furiously, but waved me inside. As I waited for him to finish, I inspected the cluttered piles of print materials on gender he had clearly been hoarding for decades, arranged along every inch of wall space on shelves and brackets. There were few places to sit. On a low shelf piled high with reprints of his articles, I noticed a box of toys. From it I lifted a small, yellowed, crumbling cardboard box containing four tiny figurines; the label said "Happy Family." Through the plastic window that covered the contents, I ran my fingers over a smiling white heterosexual nuclear family: Dad, Mom, Dick, and

Jane, all blond, blue-eyed, appropriately gendered, dressed for a party. It looked like the kind of 1950s remnant I might have found in my grandmother's basement. One of the first things Ken did when I got to CAMH was give me a stack of reprints of his work, the Happy Family toy, and a button with the phrase "THE Gender Identity Guy" printed on it. I suspect he knew that despite my carefully planned parent interviews, I was really there to study him.

It was 2012 and I was abuzz with nervous anticipation. CAMH—easily the most famous and controversial clinic for treating childhood gender nonconformity in the world—and Ken himself were lightning rods for cultural disagreement about psychiatric practice. Ken was the most published author on the topic of childhood gender identity disorder in North America; the editor-in-chief of the premier journal in the field, the *Archives of Sexual Behavior*; and the head of the committee to review the sexual and gender identity disorders section in the newest revision of the *Diagnostic and Statistical Manual of Mental Disorders* (DSM-5). His clinic was, by his account, the first in North America to begin using puberty suppression therapies for transgender kids in 1999.[1] In over thirty years of practice, he treated more than five hundred children and young adults with what was then termed "gender dysphoria"; some became transgender adults, others didn't. He was, in short, the leader of the field.

I spent a week at CAMH, interviewing eleven parents of ten children who used the clinic's services and sitting in on intake sessions and clinical staff meetings. Ken introduced me to everyone, facilitated private time with interns and staff, shepherded my administrative paperwork, and generally acted as a generous liaison to the institution. He never appeared conflicted or defensive about his work or his perspectives, though he knew that any number of his colleagues and many adult transgender people considered his methods rearguard, emotionally damaging, and tantamount to conversion therapy. Indeed, in November 2015, the Gender Identity Clinic at CAMH was shuttered and Ken Zucker fired in a spectacularly public ousting that drew the attention of international media and incited vigorous online debate among clinicians and near-universal celebration by transgender activists. Allegations by an external review committee that the clinic was "out of step with current clinical and operational practices"[2] mirrored the community lore about Ken.

How could it be that someone with such a substantial reputation for pioneering work in trans medicine was so universally reviled by transgender adults and many of the parents I met? How could a clinic be the first in North America to medically transition adolescent children and then, only fifteen years later, be shut down amid allegations it conducted reparative or conversion therapies?[3]

The answer lies in a rapid and dramatic shift in the landscape of psychiatry over the last two decades. From its origins in developmental theories that linked gender behavior and identity to dyadic heterosexual parenting (Ken's "happy family" model), psychiatric and psychological approaches to treatment increasingly de-linked gender identity from environmental etiologies and, instead, conceptualized it as a core feature of the self, potentially rooted in biology, with multiple divergent developmental pathways. In addition, trans activism altered clinical thinking in two significant ways, which rendered approaches like Ken's increasingly irrelevant. First, large-scale patient advocacy spurred a shift from regulatory to facilitative medicine; second, etiological explanations shifted from understanding gender nonconformity as per se psychopathological and tied to disordered social relationships, to formulating it as yet another form of benign variation, immutable and innate, akin to homosexuality. This does not mean clinicians abdicated biological or essentialist explanations for gender difference, though; quite the opposite. A rigorous research agenda on the complex interaction of biological and social factors influencing gender development continues, underwritten by a desire for the epistemological certainty that was lost with the relinquishment of theories of pathology. In a process that both mirrors and reinforces facilitative parenting, clinicians now view medical and social transition as appropriate responses to some forms of childhood gender nonconformity, installing transgender as a medical, as well as social, category of experience.

This is a story, on an institutional level, of how childhood gender nonconformity became a form of gender, rather than a label for its failure. The treatment apparatus that formerly intervened to transform atypical behavior into gender-normative heterosexuality was being redirected. The facilitative mental health practitioners, pediatric endocrinologists, and psychiatrists I met were no longer wondering whether disordered social relationships produced children's gender; they instead tried to parse which versions of transgression signaled an underlying, stable trans identity and what the appropriate psychotherapeutic and biomedical responses might be. Some clinicians lagged behind or, like Ken, mingled aspects of both approaches. But this was the character of the transition, and the frontier of medical practice. As the politics of trans recognition moved from the social to the biomedical,[4] the experience of treating (and, by extension, parenting) trans youth was an anxious encounter with the gravity of adult responsibility for children's corporeal present and future.

At the heart of transgender identity is a fundamental paradox: it both seeks recognition as a benign variant of human experience, and yet, in many cases, it also requires a certain form of medical intervention. So while diagnostic criteria increasingly liberated trans from the framework of psychopathology, clinicians themselves still adjudicated access to care, and there remained a tension between what some considered to be regulatory and stigmatizing therapeutic approaches focused on cure, on the one hand, and more consumer-driven, facilitative medical models focused on identity consolidation, on the other. Because transpeople and their allies continued to struggle against clinical and social barriers to accessing treatment, certain complex conversations proliferated, while others were quashed in the service of resisting the backward pull of regulatory medicine.

In a moment of profound sea change, tensions and emotions ran high. A category of persons long considered disordered had become a distinct class of medical consumers with a blinding new array of treatment choices. New facilitative approaches favoring social (and eventually medical) transitions for some children incited new sets of anxieties in parents and clinicians, each of whom faced grave decisions about life-altering medical technologies. How could they know which young children were likely to grow into trans-identified adults? At what point was it appropriate to facilitate medical gender transitions in children? What would it mean to allow a young child to make a social transition, who might later decide they wish to detransition? Who must hold the responsibility for these weighty ethical and emotional choices?

For many trans activists, Ken and CAMH represented the pathologizing impulses of past psychiatric practice. And indeed, some parents' stories appeared to corroborate their distrust. Parents reported being instructed to discard cherished possessions over the protests of distraught children. Some found Ken's very gaze injurious, stigmatizing or uncomfortable. But the full picture of CAMH appeared to me more complex. While many things about the place felt outmoded, both Ken and his staff clearly had deep investments in the health of their young clientele, and theirs was a clientele that presented with an array of complex intersecting issues. It was also the locus of decades of research, research that, along with activist and community pressure, served to shape the evolving clinical lexicon for facilitating gender transitions, research that in many ways paved the way for the very clinical and medical practices these activists desired.

I was surprised to learn that clinicians at the extreme regulatory and facilitative ends were asking strikingly similar questions about their most complex cases, only with different epistemological stances. Both yearned for secure and predictable ways to determine which children were likely to grow up to be trans, and which would be cisgender or gay. Those with a more classical orientation, like Ken, believed that short of psychologically damaging treatments, children should be encouraged to avoid transition if at all possible; more facilitative clinicians, influenced by decades of trans medical advocacy, believed either outcome to be desirable, so long as the child was well-adjusted. Both sides feared making "mistakes"; they simply disagreed on what the worst mistake would be. For more classical clinicians, the worst mistake would be to facilitate the transition of a child who might, even with struggle, plausibly live a cisgender life, or worse, a "regretter," a child who would eventually wish to detransition. Facilitative clinicians worried most about the trauma suffered by gender nonconforming children who might be prevented from fully expressing their identities, including the medical (or "psychopharmacological") forms of that expression. Both were vexed by questions of how to understand and disentangle the co-occurrence of gender nonconformity with actual psychiatric illness. The closing of CAMH and the ousting of Ken Zucker represented symbolic actions whereby the efforts of transpeople to capture and direct the regulatory apparatus of scientific medicine scored a significant win. Still, questions remain about what clinical practice with children will look like into the future.

OUTLAW DIAGNOSIS

Historically, the relationship between the psychiatric treatment of gay and transgender adults and that of children has been something of a paradox. In the moments when shifting social norms appeared to widen the space for psychology and psychiatry to adopt more liberal views on sexual and gender variation in adults, tighter restrictions and sharper clinical focus honed in on children displaying those very same traits. The relationship between the expanding clinical approach to gender and anxiety about gender instability in children dates back to the introduction of clinical engagements with intersexuality and transsexuality in the United States. In the latter half of the twentieth century, a theory of immutable gender identity came to replace earlier theories of "human bisexuality."[5] Pioneered in the mid to late 1950s by clinicians at Johns Hopkins working with intersex children, the notion that individuals have a deeply held, socially learned, psychological sex—which in the case of intersex children, could be more stable and dichotomous than even their bodies—foreshadowed our contemporary notion of gender. To explain the gender of intersex children, Hopkins faculty John Money, John Hampson, and Joan Hampson turned away from earlier psychoanalytic and biological models of gender in favor of a "behaviorist model of social learning."[6] They argued that for intersex children, the subjective sense of being male or female resulted not from their gonads, from physiology or anatomy, but rather from the sex the infant was assigned at birth and the subsequent interactions that comprised their rearing.[7] Perhaps most significantly, they argued that this sense of maleness or femaleness ossified in early childhood and that subsequent attempts to alter it would result in psychological harm. This last idea set the terms by which later psychologists could simultaneously argue for a stable transgender identity *and* also for the opportunity (and importance) of early intervention to prevent its formation in children.

Robert Stoller, who first coined the term *gender identity*, believed that cross-gender identities resulted from damaging psychodynamic processes in early childhood.[8] In his 1968 book *Sex and Gender*, he offered a psychoanalytic explanation for transsexuality; in his etiology, a depressed mother "beset with penis envy" overemphasized physical contact with her infant son,[9] while a distant father figure failed to protect the son "from the malignant effect of his mother's excessive closeness."[10] This excessive closeness prevented the infant from adequately separating from his mother, thus producing in him a core gender identity that overidentified with hers and misaligned with his biological sex. Conversely, Stoller argued, an overbearing father and distant or emotionally misattuned mother masculinized girls.[11] Parents, they argued, were the single most important socializing force in childhood gender acquisition.

At the same time, Stoller, Money, the Hampsons, and others were part of a cohort of psychologists working from a small set of university-based gender clinics that pioneered transsexual surgeries for adults in the 1960s and 1970s. In what historian Joanne Meyerowitz has called the "liberal moment," psychologists managed to cleave a domain free from the influence, on the one hand, of physicians and psychoanalysts who stridently opposed medically facilitated transition for adults and, on the other, of the burgeoning transsexual rights movement that advocated for a consumer-driven model of gender-confirming healthcare.[12] While we typically think of the 1950s as the "heyday of traditional gender roles," Meyerowitz argues, it was really the 1960s that introduced a conservative psychiatric clinical practice that instituted routinized treatments for cross-gender behavior in children, working from a theory that such behaviors were malignant signs of gender-identificatory processes gone wrong, of deficient parental gender modeling. As these university-based clinics became known for treating transsexual adults, they drew cohorts of child patients for treatment and study, whom they approached with very different treatment goals. Richard Green at UCLA, for example, directed what came to be known as the "Feminine Boy Project." Young boys who exhibited cross-gender behavior were presented for treatment to strengthen their masculinity, using behavior modification therapies. The goal, as he wrote in the 1987 book that resulted from these efforts, was to prevent so-called sissy boys from becoming the very adult transsexuals his clinic was founded to treat.[13]

While gender clinics managed the burgeoning demand for adult transition-related care, their child clientele was composed of kids whose parents felt uncomfortable with their gender nonconformity. Research emerging from UCLA and other places concluded that many of these children would grow up to be gay or lesbian adults, rather than transsexuals. At the same time, the political movement for gay and lesbian rights was successfully challenging psychologists on the idea that homosexuality was a form of psychopathy. In these years directly following the extrication of gender identity from notions of emergent sexual orientation, it seemed, once again, that the relationship between the two was in question.

The introduction of Gender Identity Disorder in Children (GIDC) into the 1980 edition of *Diagnostic and Statistical Manual of Mental Disorders* (or DSM-III) came immediately on the heels of the removal of homosexuality from the manual four years before. The deletion of homosexuality appeared, for many, a watershed moment in liberalizing rights for sexual minorities, perhaps "the first time in the history of modern medicine that a disease was eliminated by the simple proclamation that it no longer existed."[14] Many people questioned whether GIDC was included in the DSM-III as a "backdoor maneuver"[15] to replace homosexuality[16]—that is, to provide a mechanism, aimed at children, for continuing to pathologize the early indicia of homosexuality.[17] Many prominent psychologists, including Ken Zucker, have written about the relationship between the two vexed diagnoses. Some, like Ken, dismiss those connections;[18] others, like prominent feminist psychologist Sandra Bem, argued that "perhaps the psychiatric establishment still believed so completely in the pathology of gender nonconformity that if the politics of the times would not allow it to express that belief through homosexuality, then it would instead express it where and how it could."[19] Whatever the case, as clinical practice with adults liberalized, children found themselves the targets of new normalizing projects.

Since 1980, the DSM diagnosis for gender identity disorder has undergone three major revisions.[20] The most recent iteration appeared with the publication of the DSM-5 in 2013. The new classification, Gender Dysphoria, is overarching, though there are separate criteria for children, adolescents, and adults that reflect specific issues during each life stage.[21] Some of these criteria mimic older versions of the diagnostic outline: in adolescents and adults, a marked incongruence between expressed gender and one's primary sex characteristics, a strong wish to be the other gender, and desires for bodily change; for children, desire to "be" the other gender, strong preferences for toys, activities, clothing, and playmates consistent with the other gender, along with body dysphoria and desire for bodily change. There are, however, important differences in the classification that mark a substantial change in cultural understandings of gender diversity. For both children and adults, distress over one's gender is a key component to the diagnosis, allowing for individuals who appear content to escape its capture.[22] Further, the committee removed the sexual attraction criterion, acknowledging the small role played by sexual orientation in treatment models.[23] While many clinicians continue to argue for delisting gender identity–related diagnoses from the DSM altogether, or for relocating them to the International Classification of Diseases (ICD)—marking their status as disorders of the body, not the mind—many others argue equally strongly for their maintenance.[24] Ken Zucker was involved in many of these debates, serving on the committees for the last four revisions of these diagnoses and, most recently, chairing the committee that undertook the revisions for DSM-5. He feels these diagnoses have always been contentious, not the least because they've existed on the fringes of mainstream psychiatry. "These are not your bread-and-butter diagnoses," he once remarked. "In a sense, they've been outlaw diagnoses," always subject to debate and to a felt tension between clinical discretion and the personal self-concepts of the patients who bear them. While Ken said he believes it is the distress over the incongruity that makes gender dysphoria a mental illness, no amount of shifting nomenclature can change the essential feature of its phenomenology. The bottom line, he said, is that "it is in a manual that ends with 'mental disorders.' So, you can't sugar coat that."[25]

ANXIOUS TRANSITIONS

Today, a more consumer-driven model of trans healthcare dominates even adolescent trans medicine, but that doesn't mean treatment decisions come easily to doctors or families. The introduction of a framework for "early social transitions" in young children, the availability of puberty blockers for pubescent adolescents, and the increasing destigmatization of gender nonconformity in the DSM placed parents and physicians in uncharted territory. The question of whether a child's gender nonconforming behavior could be molded into a more normative form was no longer the animating concern of psychotherapy;

instead, parents and clinicians together had the task of determining which gender trajectory a child should take and what social and bio-medical supports that child would need. These decisions incited tremendous anxiety in both parents and doctors, each of whom longed for a kind of epistemological certainty that eluded them.

Although Jade was only eight years old when I met her parents, David and Lyn, they planned to take her to a pediatric endocrinologist at the onset of puberty. Since Jade had already been living as a girl for several years and felt comfortably situated and certain of her identity, putting Jade on puberty blockers didn't feel like a fraught decision. "It wouldn't make any sense to make her go through a painful male puberty, when we all know where this is going to end up," David said. "As a father, you want to place your child on the easiest path, the one that seems most in line with the self you see emerging. Jade is a girl. This is the way I treat her like one." David and Lyn understood medical transition to be a way to help Jade align her physical body with her psyche, to complete her process of gender transition. Making a medical transition would assist Jade in assimilating in a world that expects these things to be congruent.

Sam's mother, Sarah, felt certain that, despite his gender nonconforming childhood, Sam would never make a medical transition. Although his early childhood was marked by feminine interests and hobbies, female clothing preferences and friend groups, Sam's gender trajectory was not linear. Sarah said that she and Sam's father, Ian, struggled to discern whether Sam was a girl or whether he was simply a "boy who liked girl things." Sam liked dresses and dolls. Sam's mannerisms were feminine. However, Sarah felt something was missing.

We'd been thinking a lot about this because people on the listserv talk about this, when is your child transgender versus merely gender nonconforming? And we didn't see him being unhappy as a boy at all. He is quite fond of his penis. He talks about it all the time. He's happy with his body. He's fine being a boy. He just likes all the things that are feminine and he realized it was easier to get them if you're a girl.

Sarah noted that while many other transgender children made claims on identity, Sam never said to her, "I am a girl." He never expressed a hatred for or discomfort with his body. He merely asked for things—toys, clothing, and activities—that adults associate with girlhood. And indeed, as Sam got older, he began mixing more traditionally masculine toys and games into his collection. By the time he was seven, his room was a mishmash of swords and dolls, trains and tiaras. Although Sarah and Ian were active in the political community of parents with trans and gender nonconforming kids, they had no plans to transition Sam at puberty. They understood Sam to have a boy identity, a boy body, and a deep and abiding interest in "girl things."

I met Patti the night before her child, Avery, was scheduled to receive his first injection of Lupron. Lupron (Leuprolide or Depot Lupron) is a gonadatropin-releasing hormone agonist, one of a class of drugs that suppress the production of the hormones that incite puberty.[26] Patti told me that the recent few weeks had been especially difficult for her with regard to Avery's gender. During our conversation, she frequently compared Avery to other transgender children she knows. She described children who said, often with confidence, that they absolutely *are* girls, that there was some sort of mistake when they were born with the bodies they have. Avery used different language. She felt he was less confident in general, and that came across in his more reserved, less forceful responses about gender. But it also left Patti feeling uncertain about whether to proceed with blockers for him or, instead, to let him go through puberty just to "see what happens." She told me she spent a lot of time wondering if perhaps Avery was just gay—wishing it, in fact.

I feel like his life is gonna ... like there's gonna be lots of challenges in his life, Tey. So, for me, I prayed for years that he'd just be gay. [...] I just feel like it's not a big deal. You're gay, you grow up, you meet someone that you fall in love with. To the rest of the people in the world, you have a life together. If you want to have a family, you can have a family. You get a job. You do all these normal things. But if you're transgender, all those normal things aren't really so normal for the rest of the world looking in.

For some parents, the notion that their children might "just be gay" seemed the lesser of two evils. They pointed with a wistful longing to mainstream representations of gender-conforming gays and lesbians and to the type of normality they have constructed in their relationships and communities. It was often only after accumulating evidence of their child's body dysphoria or a persistent sense of cross-gender identification that they found themselves where Patti was, the night before the first doctor visit, anxious, rehearsing her options over and over again.

For parents whose children made successful early social transitions, blockers were often described as an inevitable rite of passage, a way station en route to a full medical transition. Avery had never transitioned and had few words for his gender discomfort, but he did express dread of his impending puberty. Patti was one of many parents who faced these medical decisions with uncertainty, feeling increasingly pressed for time, acutely aware that both action and inaction were affirmative decisions with important consequences.

> I worry a little bit about the pain for him and the shot, but that's not ... the bigger thing is, here he is fifteen years old still not even knowing what gender he identifies with. And having that be such an enormous part of his life. I mean, the gender. You know, the gender issue, his whole life is about this gender thing. You have to go into [the city]. We have to get shots. We talk about this all the time because he has to talk about it. He's got a year before a decision's gonna be made on cross-sex hormones if he wants to be able to present himself as female as an adult without any questions. Right? So I guess the worry is that we'll run out of time to make the right decision. And [our doctor] will say to me, "You can transition at any time in your life." And my answer is "Yes, but then you look like a transsexual," you know? You have this body and everyone can just tell.

Patti described a feeling of working against the clock while trying to determine what decision was best for Avery. She described her desire to "buy time" with puberty blockers, but also worried about keeping Avery in a perpetual holding pattern, the only prepubescent child in high school. She hoped he would come to a clearer understanding of his own gender and grow more able to express that to her. At the same time, Patti feared that denying or delaying his access to puberty blockers would consign him to a lifelong struggle to pass as female should that be his choice, trying to hide the masculine characteristics that come with male puberty. While he had told her he felt like he "lives pretty much as a girl anyway," for Patti, taking a step toward medicalizing those feelings seemed decisively different. She feared jumping the gun, but felt strongly that it was her responsibility to protect Avery from the kind of transgressive bodily appearance he would have if he went through male puberty and then tried to live as female.

Patti's physician, Dr. Dante Romero, headed up the gender identity service at a well-known East Coast children's hospital. While many families approached him after doing some amount of research, knowing that puberty blockers exist and thinking they are an appropriate intervention for their particular child, Dr. Romero conducted his own formal intake, personally assessing the suitability of each child candidate for the treatment. Dr. Romero had his own lingering questions and anxieties. He longed for a way to know with some certainty which children are likely to grow up with stable trans identities and which will likely be cisgender.

> That's a very complicated issue. Very, very complicated and very, very worrisome issue. What we try to figure out is, you know, if this appears to be something that is likely to remain the same, that is not driven by other things like severe anxiety ... which is of course a very difficult issue, because it's not always clear if the anxiety is driving the gender stuff or if it's in response to the situation.

Dr. Romero and his colleagues compiled a series of assessments, from standardized surveys for parents of recalled childhood gender behavior dating back to infancy, to measures of distress and social isolation, to children's self-reports of their feelings and identity. Ultimately, however, conversations with parents were the primary vehicle through which physicians got to know and understand individual children. "It's often ... an important part is the parent's sense of what is right for the child. Which is important, because it is ultimately the parent's decision about what is right for the child."

In Dr. Romero's experience, very few children went the route of taking hormone blockers, and then often only after repeated attempts by parents to find alternate means for handling their child's distress. He told me that each of these cases was difficult for him. He worried about his inability to know for certain how individual families decided to seek out blockers, particularly when parents contacted him having already decided for certain that blockers were appropriate for their child.

> It is always tough, because you don't know to what extent you're messing with a developmental process that may be ... um ... you know ... may change over time, and that you, by your intervention, you might prevent some change and precipitate another form of change, you don't know for sure. [...] In other words, what would have happened if I hadn't intervened? You don't know the answer to that. It's tough ...

The fear most commonly expressed by physicians and parents alike was that they would too quickly jump from seeing signs of distress in a child to moving toward a medical solution. Both parents and physicians worried they might forestall a developmental process that could resolve on its own, without a gender transition, or without the need for medical intervention. They struggled balancing a more hesitant approach against the task of weighing how much anxiety, sadness, or anger was too much to ask their child to bear. They struggled with their roles as adults in making decisions on behalf of children they believed were asserting a core identity while lacking the chronological maturity to consent, intellectually and emotionally, to permanent bodily changes.

Dr. Romero saw his role as, in part, to develop and understand a taxonomy of future identities, and to do his best to match treatments to the most predictable future outcome. He believed there were three kinds of children. There were children who did not assert a strong transgender identity, those who perhaps enjoyed gendered toys or fantasy play but who did not state that they were the other gender. For this group, which he said is quite large, prescribing blockers was excessive or premature. The second group were those for whom blockers were clearly necessary. "These are the kids that are saying, 'If I grow breasts, I'm going to kill myself.' Not just once, it's not a passing comment." These children presented with a level of distress that required redress. The third group was, for him, the most difficult to describe.

> It's the group that are in the middle, and I don't even know how to define them … is what is agonizing … I mean, you know, I can give you one example, which is the kid that this month is going to kill himself, and next month it doesn't seem to be an issue. And then the next month it's an issue. You know? It's agonizing, because you don't know what to tell them. There's not a clear, consistent presence or absence of that deep dysphoria. Or maybe there are conflicts in the environment, which muddles up things, because you don't know if a kid is sort of trying to run away from very unpleasant experiences, and we don't blame them for that. So, those are the ones that, you know, you lose sleep over, because you don't know what really is best for that child.

Avery would likely fall into this third typology. He was the sort of child about whom Dr. Romero and his colleagues would meet and discuss varied options. His case was complex. He presented with a sufficient amount of distress about puberty to justify intervention, but how much, when, and in what form remained unclear. Dr. Romero was eager to get answers to all of these questions.

> We are trying to find any kind of early predictors that would give us a more clear sense of where they might end up in the future, and that is, of course, particularly relevant to the question of puberty suppression, social transition, and all those very difficult issues. So, we're trying to figure out if there's a way to capture any kind of early signs, patterns, patterns of behavior that would somehow predict what's going to happen in the future.

This last question, in particular, motivated a growing number of treating physicians to engage in research on the long-term psychological and identity outcomes of gender nonconforming children.

Dr. Nicholas Cohen was a pediatric endocrinologist working at a large teaching hospital on the West Coast. He was part of a brand-new team of mental health workers, physicians, social workers, and community advocates working together on a comprehensive gender clinic to service the needs of these youth and families. Dr. Cohen was also a research scientist, who believed that a broad research agenda was needed to most effectively develop universal standards for treating these youth. He hoped the two projects would function in tandem.

I'm interested in trying to understand the biology of gender. And there's some really fascinating studies looking at brain slices and sexually dimorphic nuclei that are dimorphic in terms of segregating according to gender. And these are in addition to sexually dimorphic nuclei that segregate according to sexual orientation. It's completely separate. And there's certain gene variations or polymorphism that have been potentially implicated in gender and certain other phenotypic features that have been implicated in gender.

Dr. Cohen was describing and explaining a series of Dutch studies that suggest connections between gender and sexual identities and structures in the brain. He believed that there are likely such biological and/or physiological processes at work in the development of gender identity, and that isolating and identifying them might provide physicians with more predictable ways to forecast the longer-term identities of gender nonconforming children. He hoped that biology might serve as a means through which to minimize the epistemological uncertainty within which he operated. In fact, he believed quite strongly in a biological component of gender identity, but he didn't believe that biology worked alone.

I do believe that there's a biological, including therefore genetic and other factors that influence gender development as well as environmental things, but I just sort of wonder how much of that is really inherent, how much of it exists because we live in a society that says, okay, well, there are differences between males and females and therefore you have to see yourself, or that you *are* one or the other so which one do you see yourself as, you know?

Cohen and other doctors with whom I spoke worried about distinguishing biologically determined from socially imposed gender development. It made the task of guiding families more difficult. They looked to the closest correlate, treatment of children with intersex conditions, whose physiologies and/or body morphologies made less of a claim on psychological gender. Families of intersex children and adult intersex activists themselves have worked for the last three decades to increase awareness of these conditions and to assist physicians and families with making decisions about which gender categories to assign these children in infancy. Dr. Cohen viewed these cases as instructive.

> So, for example, if you have androgen insensitivity you can have—there's a whole spectrum of that where you can have complete androgen insensitivity, where your gender is virtually 100 percent female, to very minimal androgen insensitivity where your gender is virtually 100 percent male. And then if you're somewhere in between it's sometimes very difficult to predict. And so as practicing physicians, endocrinologists in particular are often put in the situation of guiding the family in how to make the choice of sex and rearing. And so you try to make the best possible decision based on your knowledge of what the condition is and how things have turned out in the past and how this person fits into all of that. And you don't want to get it wrong, because that causes suffering. So wouldn't it be great if there was a more clear-cut way of knowing what someone's gender was? [To be able to say] okay, well, this is how you should raise the child because there's a 99.999 percent certainty that this is how the person's going to be?

This desire for certainty led all clinics to require batteries of standardized tests from patients, often as a condition of their treatment. For the most part, the parents with whom I spoke were happy to comply. Patti was one of the parents who hoped this research would help parents like herself navigate treatment decisions. She also recognized that biological rationales worked to cement the claims to legitimacy that transpeople made when seeking accommodations from institutions.

> Wouldn't we like to know medically if our kids have anything in common, for tomorrow's kids? So that just like even school policies and discrimination

and all those things, you know, people are transgender, gay, there's no proof, there's just all these battles. You know what, if there was, so much of this would be so much easier for people in the future. And if at the end there's nothing, that's okay, but at least we've done that.

This focus on biological research, largely into the connections between brain structure and hormone levels and exposure in utero, signaled a belief in the connection between the body and gender identity, yet not in the way earlier psychologists thought. The sexed body, its anatomical structures, no longer determine the gendered psyche. The domain of physical sex has moved to the brain and endocrine system. Biology appeared to represent, for parents and physicians alike, not merely a way to understand the genesis of transgender identity, but also a stable, predictable, reliable way to stabilize and ensure that a given child's gender identity would endure. Perhaps most importantly, if gender could be located in the matter of the body, then one might say it is immutable, that social expectations should be revised to accommodate it, and that medical, hormonal interventions should become an inevitable adult response to the distress these children exhibit.

For parents whose children exhibited persistent, ardent, and unwavering insistence on a cross-gender identity, blockers felt like an inevitability. Trans childhood, once understood as such, has acquired a linear trajectory. It looks much like gender-typical childhood, only with a demand for biomedical intervention at the onset of puberty and, often, psychological support for the management of social responses to transition. This does not mean the decision to enlist medical help is easy. Parents know that a coherent gender relies on the body, but some medical interventions require parents to think about longer-term issues like preserving fertility, things they are often unprepared to confront with pubescent children. For parents whose children do not make ardent claims to trans identities or who do not exhibit body dysphoria, biomedical intervention seems unnecessary. They focus instead on how to support children who defy social expectations in a social climate that may resist such expression.

The children in the middle reveal most clearly the stakes of these anxious decisions. Parents and physicians understand the moment of puberty as a determinative bodily shift. Bodies become male and female anew in ways that can only be undone at great cost, if ever. Symbolically, the direction a child takes at that moment is declarative; they "are" trans, or they "aren't." A statement must be made, one way or the other. One cannot opt out of puberty. Parents and physicians ardently wish to make the "right" statement, believing that a mistake is tantamount to cruelty. The giving of gender extends to the body, and in these moments reaches beyond the relational and into the institutional. The institution absorbs this anxiety, as institutions do, by quantifying outcomes and instituting research agendas aimed at optimizing process.[27]

PERSISTERS, DESISTERS, AND REGRETTERS

Before the emergence of the trans child as a recognizable social category, psychiatry enlisted a binaristic understanding of gender development; on the one hand, there was normative gender, scaffolded by appropriate heterosexual dyadic parenting, and on the other, there was disordered gender. Disordered gender, whether underwritten by deficient parenting or psychopathology, was, in effect, a misperception on the part of the child about the relationship between body and psyche. It was a simple, dichotomous system. Children were either normatively gendered or psychiatrically ill. With the incorporation of trans children into the clinical lexicon, the episteme became more complex. Clinicians, once the arbiters of psychic health, were now also the arbiters of authentic claims to identity. The question facing doctors was not whether a child's gender was sufficiently normative to assimilate, but rather whether an individual child made an authentic, psychic claim to a particular gender. Adults now needed to adjudicate whether a particular child was normatively gendered, nonnormatively gendered, or transgender. And because gender transitions are considered major psychic and social events, such declarations were made with the utmost care.

Figure 3. Published peer-reviewed studies of childhood gender nonconformity, 1968–2015.

This transition to a trans-affirmative, patient-driven model of healthcare produced longitudinal research studies on the outcomes of gender atypicality in children, both to inform individual decision-making and to scaffold political arguments for the stability of trans identity. Between 2005 and 2015, the number of peer-reviewed published studies of childhood gender nonconformity increased fivefold (figure 3). These studies largely centered on etiological theories of transgender and the possible long-term persistence of different forms of childhood gender atypicality.[28] Clinical approaches to childhood gender were forward-reaching; they constructed gender as a static attribute, imagined an adulthood to which individual children aspired, and aimed their tactics to produce it. This forward reach required a certainty in the present of gender in the future. Parents and clinicians sought secure and predictable ways to identify the children most likely to be trans as adults, so they could be targeted with the appropriate clinical interventions.

These investigations into the biology of gender and longitudinal studies employed a tripartite typology of gendered subjectivity. Children might turn out to be *persisters*, those whose trans identities endure into adulthood; *desisters,* those who settle into cisgender hetero- or homosexual adulthoods; or *regretters,* the unlucky few who make social and medical transitions but ultimately decide later to detransition. These were not benign categorizations; they were normative and normativizing trajectories. When combined with a cisgender presumption—an ascribed preference for cisgender outcomes—the regulatory anxiety faced by clinicians was intense.

Much like those who engineered the explosion of studies into the "nature" of homosexuality in the late 1980s and early 1990s,[29] proponents of biological explanations for gender and sexual difference imagined that the "argument from immutability"[30] provided a political justification for accommodation. The logic goes something like this: if there is a biological basis for homo- or transsexuality, then gay and transgender people can't be other than what they are, and the majority has a social and legal responsibility to protect them.[31] Different concerns animate researchers investigating the etiology of transsexualism; many hope that biological origins for gender diversity might signal the possibility of better predicting long-term outcomes in individual children, who might then be targeted with reliable diagnostic tests.

As biological research expanded, the composition and theoretical orientation of the studies underwent a dramatic shift. Whereas prior to the mid-1990s almost all etiological studies of childhood gender nonconformity used small samples or single case studies, and presumed children's gender to be produced by parental modeling, by 2015 virtually all studies included some mention of the biological predetermination of gender identity (figure 4). Older studies with social explanations for gender atypicality linked it to deficient mothering (improper gender modeling, excessive symbiosis, absentia, or psychopathology), whereas later studies instead investigated brain structures, hormonal imbalances, and genetic factors. These changes represent the evolution in research practice from small studies to large-scale, experimental design, and in thinking from understanding gender as a singular developmental pathway that can be interrupted by poor socialization to an

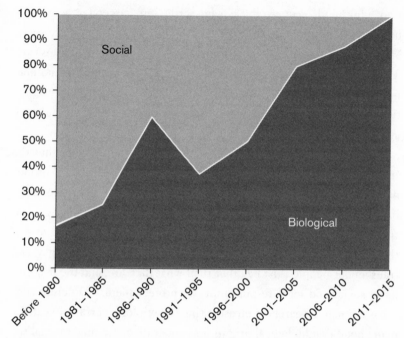

Figure 4. Etiological explanations for gender noncomformity.

internal psychic structure, potentially rooted in the body, less amenable to change.[32]

There have been only three major longitudinal studies of gender nonconforming youth, and several smaller ones (see table 3).[33] Older studies show an extremely low persistence rate, whereas the two most current studies show much higher rates.

The reasons for low persistence rates have been the subject of debate. Classical clinicians interpret them as evidence that the majority of gender nonconforming children are ultimately homosexual and not trans;[34] those writing on this topic now hypothesize that older studies reflect a cultural frame wherein gender norms were more restrictive, leading many parents to bring children in for treatment whose gender transgressions we might now consider insignificant.[35] And indeed, rates of persistence among children with gender identity issues are on the rise.

TABLE 3

Outcomes of Major Longitudinal Studies

Year/Study	N	Cis/Hetero/ Uncertain	Gay/Lesbian	Trans
1972, Liebowitz	16	62.5%	12.5%	25%
1978, Zuger	16	12.5%	75%	12.5%
1979, Money et al.	9	100%	x*	0%
1984, Zuger	45	22.3%	73.3%	4.4%
1986, Davenport	10	70%	20%	10%
1987, Green	44	98%	x	2%
1987, Kosky	8 .	100%	x	0%
2008, Wallen et al.	54	61.1%	x	38.9%
2008, Drummund et al.	25	64%	24%	12%
2012, Singh	139	87.8%	x	12.2%
2013, Steensma	127	63%	x	37%

*Some studies do not include data on adult homosexuality; others may have included subjects who dropped out in the "cis" category.

The general consensus among facilitative clinicians is that as norms around gender behavior relax, children referred for treatment have more extreme versions of gender dysphoria, and are subsequently more likely to be trans adults. However, as medical transition becomes an available option, social anxiety on the part of doctors about making the "wrong decisions" intensifies.

In early 2017, a handful of articles about "detransitioners"[36] appeared in the popular press, and while many interpret the regretter discourse as a smokescreen obscuring conservative, political, antitrans attitudes,[37] it's important to take these discussions seriously for a different reason. The regulatory anxiety[38] that characterized the orthodox psychiatric response in the 1960s, the notion that it is the clinician's role to enforce hegemonic gender roles and to diagnose the relational pathology (often familial) that impedes normative gender, still exists. A recent opinion piece by Dr. Michelle Cretella, the president of the American College

of Pediatricians, appeared to repackage an argument from the early literature; as she says, in normal life and in psychiatry, anyone who "'consistently and persistently insists' on anything else contrary to physical
reality is considered either confused or delusional."[39] In her estimation,
many children transitioned by adults might come to think their guid-
ance misplaced. But even facilitative clinicians have complex relationships to transition. As they struggle to adjudicate claims to authentic
gender, the regretter serves as a symbolic container for the notion that
they might fail at this task.

The regretter discourse serves as a proxy, in some cases, for arguments against early transition. Indeed, many see regret after gender reassignment as, in the words of psychologists Stig-Eric Olsson and Anders
Möller, "along with suicide, the worst conceivable outcome of SRS [sex
reassignment surgery]."[40] Yet a survey of the detransition literature, the
little of it that there is, reveals that only a tiny percentage of individuals
who make full social and medical transitions ever regret those decisions,
and when they do, it is often for reasons we might characterize as social.[41]
One study of 681 applications for sex reassignment surgery in Sweden
submitted between 1960 and 2010 included fifteen "regret applications,"
appeals to the National Board of Health and Welfare for insurance coverage to undo previous surgical and hormonal treatments.[42] There were no
reasons given for these requests, and the literature makes no empirical
distinction between dissatisfaction with the outcome of a particular surgical procedure and overall transition regret. Another study of 232 transgender women reported no cases of transition regret, yet some participants did report some dissatisfaction with the physical or functional
results of surgery.[43] Might the regret applications in the Swedish study
have come from some of the earliest surgical candidates, those whose
procedures were among the first ever performed and most experimental?
The other studies of regret were older, with very small samples, and had
unclear metrics for what constituted dissatisfaction.[44]

All regret studies appear to either conflate dissatisfaction with regret
or reflect normative biases among the researchers. These studies

mistake dissatisfaction with surgical outcomes for transition regret, when in fact little to no evidence supports that interpretation.[45] One study finding that 46 percent of a sample of transwomen (half of whom were in lesbian relationships) did not use their vaginas for intercourse[46] was used by another investigator to substantiate regret outcomes in another: "sexual orientation can indirectly affect regret rates when the functional result of SRS is a failure."[47] The conflation of surgical failure with the decision not to engage in vaginal sex is a classic example of the heteronormative biases that underwrite the idea of medical and social transition "success," even today.

The authoritative, empirical accounts of regret seem flat when compared to the complex stories transgender people themselves tell about detransition. For example, a recent article in the British newspaper the *Guardian* includes a first-person account of a childhood spent wishing to be a boy, disordered eating in an effort to prevent puberty, and an eventual suicide attempt by the age of fourteen. In college, the narrator began testosterone and had top surgery. The surgery was botched, leaving significant scarring, at which point the narrator began to think, "What am I doing?" They say, "I wanted to be male, but I was always going to be trans." While the narrator reports that being a man was easier, ultimately something didn't feel right. They wonder what decisions they might have made about transition had they had more counseling. Nonetheless, they reject the regret frame and feel generally optimistic, saying: "I've seen that I have an immense capacity to change and grow, even in very difficult circumstances."[48]

So, why the sudden focus on the regretter discourse? In some cases, it is a functional stand-in for archaic psychiatric theories that tie gender nonconformity to psychopathology. In others, it articulates the anxiety experienced by clinicians encountering the uncertainties of gender development. It's possible that we see few actual empirical investigations of regret because it is simply so uncommon. Ken Zucker himself noted that in his decades of work with hundreds of gender nonconforming children, he could remember only a single case of a child who fully transitioned, socially and medically, and then experienced significant regret.[49]

The explanations that tied gender nonconformity to inadequate parental role-modeling have been replaced by the anxiety of regulation; since we typically believe that children have limited capacity to consent, clinicians are in the position of adjudicating the authenticity of identity claims. The notion that adult clinicians might facilitate social and medical transition for a child who might then change their mind gets stitched to the construct of the regretter. Regret becomes the future accusation that one should have known better, that one should have seen through the gender behavior to a different authenticity that resided beneath. For some clinicians, authenticity still resides in the "body as bedrock" and nullifies claims to transness.[50] For others, it resides in questions of whether mental illness can trade in gender,[51] whether atypical gender behavior can be the visible marker of an underlying pathology (like autism) rather than evidence of an identity.

As treatment norms consolidate, the desire to taxonomize gender trajectories and to stabilize discrete categories of experience only grows. As psychoanalyst Oren Gozlan writes, "Studies of transsexuality often reflect a latent wish for stability and certainty manifested in the pinning down of categories of normative sexual development."[52] Taxonomies of gender development are "regulatory ideals";[53] strategies to resist uncertainty[54] that produce the outcomes they purport to reflect. In this framework, persisters are the "truly trans," for whom treatment concerns ought to focus on optimizing social integration in the affirmed gender. Desisters, in contrast, must be prevented from undergoing medical treatment that may encourage a trans identity when some other outcome remains plausible. Regret is to be avoided at all costs, presumably even erring on the side of prohibiting transition for children who might, in fact, be trans. This is a dangerous impulse, not merely because it risks collapsing into the phobic notion that trans is a worst case scenario, but also because it concretizes gender into an outcome that must always be stable, resistant to flexibility and evolution, that it must never be a place to visit, always only a place to rest.

INSIDE THE GENDER IDENTITY CLINIC AT CAMH

Most of what we know about childhood gender nonconformity owes its origins, in some way, to the CAMH Gender Identity Clinic. CAMH and the two other clinics that pioneered treatments for gender identity disorder, one in New York and the other in Amsterdam,[55] controlled both the clinical discourse and data production for decades. Ken Zucker, in many ways, steered both sides of the diagnostic process. He chaired the committees that revised the gender identity diagnoses for both the DSM-IV[56] and the most recent iteration, the DSM-5.[57] He is among the most published on the topic, authoring diagnostic tests, treatment protocols, and assessment measures used throughout the world. While CAMH was one of the most prominent clinics in the world actively facilitating gender transitions for some children, it was also considered by many to be one of the most highly regulatory.

The issue of childhood gender has defined Kenneth Zucker's career. In the 1970s, while still in graduate school,[58] he began working with Dr. Susan J. Bradley, a child psychologist, who had recently created the first child and adolescent gender identity disorder (GID) team, at the Clarke Institute in Toronto.[59] After a decade of Bradley's leadership, Zucker took over as director of the clinic in the 1980s. Fifteen years later, Bradley and Zucker copublished *Gender Identity Disorder and the Psychosexual Problems in Children and Adolescents*, the first comprehensive reference book on the topic, which they culled from the first two decades of clinical and research activities at the clinic.[60] In 1998 the Clarke Institute merged with three other organizations to create the Centre for Addiction and Mental Health (CAMH).[61] For the next fifteen years, CAMH, among the few clinics able to produce longitudinal data and comparative research, generated the most highly cited writing on the topic of childhood gender diversity.[62]

One feels the focus on standardization in the clinic atmosphere. Several of the parents I spoke with recalled feeling overwhelmed by the volume of initial assessments they underwent at CAMH. Janine and her feminine son, Connor, were referred to CAMH by their pediatrician when Connor was four or five, after repeated declarations that he was a girl. Janine describes her early months at CAMH as "very appointment-ish," full of questionnaires and interviews. Connor was interviewed and completed projective tests like drawing pictures of himself and of his family. Sabrina, mother of ten-year-old Lucien, reported that she initially felt alienated by the endless psychometrics and detailed assessments, questions about dissatisfactions, issues and struggles, what felt to her like "harping on the negative." Both parents reported feeling some relief at the individualized attention they were getting but also some discomfort with the intensity of the scrutiny.

I quickly understood their perceptions. On my third day at CAMH, I was invited to observe Dr. Zucker and one of his trainees conduct an intake on a new patient. I crowded into a small, dark rectangular room with half a dozen of the clinic's interns, who perched on high stools picking at their lunches or leaned against the back wall. Along one side of the room, a large tinted one-way window revealed the consulting room beyond, which contained a long sofa, a coffee table, and a handful of chairs. The room was fluorescent lit, and the walls were an institutional yellow. An intercom system piped the sound from that room into ours, and we spoke softly to avoid being heard through the glass.

That day, Dr. Zucker and an intern named Ashley were interviewing a twelve-year-old masculine girl named Steph and her mother, father, and older sister. (Steph, in fact, is an amalgam of several children I either met or heard discussed during my time at CAMH. She is the only child in the book about whom significant details have been altered.) To my knowledge, Steph and her family did not know an outside non-clinical researcher was in the viewing room, and were given no option to withhold consent to being observed or written about by me. I'm not even certain they realized how many people were sitting beyond the glass that day. This is the way CAMH functioned: patients were simply informed that interns and guests would be viewing their intake sessions. Ken told me that in his time there, only one or two families had ever refused the observations. It utilized an apprenticeship model not unlike that of some other clinics, with patients often being treated by trainees. But CAMH also did testing not directly related to the patient's care, and allowed researchers like me to observe clinical interactions. Dr. Zucker sometimes photographed his patients. These were presumably the conditions of treatment.

What struck me most poignantly about Steph was how desperately uncomfortable she looked. She slumped in a corner of the sofa, hugging a jacket to her body. She barely answered questions, apart from muttering "yes," "no," or "I dunno." Ashley, who did the initial questioning, quickly faltered, unable to coax even the smallest detail from her mostly inert patient. Dr. Zucker stepped in and began addressing Steph's parents and sister. The family was quiet and polite. Steph's older sister, a petite, blonde, carefully manicured teenager, barely spoke. She looked mortified. The family explained that Steph was having trouble in school. She was falling asleep in class. She had no friends. She found it difficult to interact with other children. She spent most of her time alone in her room. Steph's mother explained that they had called CAMH several months prior, when Steph grew even more noticeably depressed on noticing the first signs of puberty. Steph had always selected baggy, gender-neutral clothing, which may have been related to either her gender or her obesity, which hovered in the room but was never spoken about directly. Her hair was short and appeared unkempt.

After the intake session, Dr. Zucker discussed the case with the interns. He suspected that Steph fell somewhere on the autism spectrum. He wondered if she had an eating disorder. Most clinicians in the room agreed it was difficult to discern to what extent Steph's masculinity signaled true gender dysphoria, or whether it was a byproduct of Steph's weight, social anxiety, or some underlying trauma they had yet to uncover. Steph was unlike the children I met at the family conferences I attended. She appeared deeply miserable, lost inside herself, like a ghost. I thought about her for weeks afterward. Dr. Zucker told me they would work to unravel the threads of Steph's experience slowly over months.

Most CAMH parents I met came in times of desperation. They arrived at the clinic distraught, with children who were struggling socially, academically, and personally. They arrived with varying degrees of foreknowledge about gender, but most shared a sense that a complex constellation of social and emotional issues needed to be addressed, the gender issues perhaps, but not always, being the most fraught. Only one of the parents I met at CAMH thought initially that their child was transgender, though several indicated that they would have no trouble accepting significant femininity in their sons, so long as they could integrate socially. Most families engaged, at least for a time, in efforts to resocialize their children into more normative gender behavior. At the suggestion of Ken or one of the clinic's other psychologists, parents would remove some of the child's cross-gender toys and clothing and replace them with gender-neutral or male-coded objects. Two parents said their children seemed to take these decisions in stride. The dominant narrative, however, was one of pain and struggle.

Sabrina remembered her initial months at CAMH as "terrible." She and her husband, Charlie, brought then kindergarten-aged Lucien to CAMH after he was physically assaulted on the playground by a group of ten-year-old boys for playing with a Barbie doll. Apart from his obvious femininity, Lucien struggled to relate to other children. He started fights in school, had frequent emotional outbursts, and seemed generally unhappy. They felt desperate to find some way to help him connect.

Sabrina characterized the first year of treatment as "probably the most traumatic thing I think we went through as a family." At Ken's suggestion, she and Charlie began to systematically remove the female-coded toys Lucien had, along with his costumes, wigs, and dolls. For a while, she said, he was utterly miserable. He would beg, "Please, can I have just one more doll? Please, just one doll?" He began stealing toys from classmates, from stores. He would hide them in his room and, when asked where he got them, lie and say he "found" them. Sabrina said denying him those things felt awful, particularly because his older brother was able to get the toys he wanted. It didn't seem fair. She wondered if perhaps it was even cruel. For the first six months to a year under Ken's care, Lucien had trouble sleeping, and his volatility and difficulty with peers continued. Sabrina complained to Ken that she felt what she was doing was mean, that they were denying Lucien things that made him feel good, that they could never fully neutralize his environment anyway, since he continued fashioning towels into long hair and dresses. Ken told her to give it time, that the point was to help him to have more normal social relationships. Sabrina said,

> This is probably the only reason that Charlie and I continue is that I don't believe that anyone could ever really change him, ever. It was just about trying to make him happier. So it wasn't about trying to change him and make him a man's man. It was literally about trying to help his social skills and make him happier. The whole idea of having some measure of self-esteem around being a boy, that there's nothing bad 'cause he did behave as if being a girl is the best thing ever. And so, the way Dr. Zucker posed it to us was that what we want to find out from him is what is it about being a girl that he thinks is so much better. You know, what is it so we can help him still feel those things, experience those things, without hating who he is. Because that was my biggest fear is that he would go through adolescence hating his body.

Sabrina's explanation echoed much of what I heard from CAMH parents. All parents struggled with the behavioral treatments suggested by the clinic, even if the implementation wasn't always as traumatic. Yet this group of parents, for the most part, understood their child's originary gender as their "real" gender and, counseled by CAMH, searched for *the problem to which their cross-gender behavior was a solution.* They appeared to believe that there must be some intervening social mechanism generating the cross-gender preferences, and, while they figured out what it was and how amenable to change, the behavioral modifications might help the child interact more successfully with peers. The ultimate goal, they said, was to help their child inhabit their body with greater ease. For them, comfort with natal gender was the avenue through which to do that; the change they sought was internal, not external. When the social struggles that children experienced adhered to their gender behavior, presumably parents perceived their child to be more malleable than their body or their social environment. Or perhaps they, like Ken, felt the environment was less in need of change.

The range of ways parents understood their child's gender trajectory differed, but many took some responsibility for it themselves, even if they also resented that interpretation and resisted some of the treatment conditions that attended it. When Linda's autistic, feminine son Terence told her, in kindergarten, that he wanted to cut off his penis with a pair of scissors, their family's pediatrician referred them to CAMH. By the time I met Linda, Terence was eleven, and while he was still a patient at CAMH, they were no longer actively working on his gender issues. Linda described a very fraught relationship to Ken and to CAMH as a whole.

When the family first came to the clinic, Terence had problems at home and at school. He was volatile with his family and inattentive and inappropriate in the classroom, often getting up in the middle of activities to wander around, rip art off the walls, and try to eat classroom objects. Linda told me that her dislike of Dr. Zucker was immediate.

> My first impression over the phone was just he seemed like a cold fish. And, and I guess that, you know, you need a certain amount of that probably so that you don't, you know, rip your heart up into a thousand pieces in a job like this. But, but you know, it's weird. It occurred to me that if he hadn't become a psychologist he should have been a gossip magazine writer. 'Cause I think he has a bit of a prurient interest in other people's lives.

Linda attributed some of Terence's gender transgression to his home environment. She described his two older sisters who delighted in dressing him like a doll, her husband's general tendency toward conflict avoidance, and even some of her own parenting choices. Like some of

Terence's behavioral issues, Linda felt his gender should be addressed therapeutically and wondered if it would ultimately resolve.

Many parents, like Linda, reported a conflicted relationship with Ken. Most felt aligned with his skepticism of the push toward early transition, but struggled with the ways his ideologies constrained them, as people and as parents. Linda said,

> When we came here I didn't know that, that Dr. Zucker was associated with a certain ideological or political position on the whole debate. But I must admit that I tend to fall in the same camp, you know, I don't want to have my four- or five-year-old dictating the path for the rest of their life. Yeah, so I, I think I, I'm more, I'm more comfortable with the, yeah, fix-my-kid approach than the, okay, I'm gonna take the scissors and cut his penis off and let's just get on with this.

Linda quickly added that she was unsure what she would have done had Terence been actively suicidal or more insistent on being a girl. She also struggled with some of the implications for her own life of Zucker's treatment model. For example, shortly after beginning treatment, Dr. Zucker commented that Linda's style of mothering might be contributing to Terence's distress and suggested that she quit her job to devote her full attention to child-rearing. Linda's husband was quick to support that idea. Linda, however, felt railroaded.

> He's got this patriarchal kind of old style, at least that's how, that's certainly how it seemed to me. He has a certain view of your role, and his view was that, yeah, it's perfectly fine for me, I shouldn't be complaining that I had to give up my career and that I spend my life driving people around because that's really good for those people. And I said, "Well, yeah, it's good for them but it's not very good for me." And, and the thing is, he was not saying that to my husband. And so I mean he has some real sort of sexist biases.

Linda moved back and forth between expressing gratitude and discomfort. She resented what she perceived as Ken's sexism, but felt the family desperately needed CAMH's interventions in the beginning.

She said when they first came to the clinic, Terence was in a "death spiral." He exhibited repetitive behaviors like tapping his fingers constantly or running them around the rim of a glass, over and over. It would take them close to an hour to get him out of the house; he would make repeated trips to the bathroom before agreeing to leave. His anxiety was palpable and appeared to be gathering into these obsessive ways of acting that made their family life feel unbearable.

When they began treatment, Linda came weekly to meet with Ken while Terence spoke to another psychologist in the clinic. She would describe his symptoms and the family's struggles. She recalled one session in particular where her emerging discomfort with Ken hit a fever pitch.

> I remember being in a session with Dr. Zucker and saying, "Okay, [...] as soon as he comes out of the bathroom in the morning when we're trying to go to school, he goes back in again and we can't get him out of the bath-room." And Dr. Zucker said to me, "Isn't it interesting to watch Terence go from crisis to crisis?" And my jaw dropped. And I said, "No." I felt like saying, "It's not fucking *interesting.* It's tearing my heart apart and I can't believe you would say something like that." But of course I didn't say that. I just sucked it up.

Linda went home and thought about the interaction obsessively over the following week. When she went back into CAMH, she recounted her discomfort with the exchange to Ken. He replied, "Did I say that?" Linda said, "Yeah, you did." She reported that Ken looked at her in silence for a moment and then replied, "That's what we call an empathic breakdown."

Linda was shocked by this deadpan response. Though she attributed his dry tone to a professional distance she imagined was required by the rigor of his job, it also cultivated in her a strong distaste for him. She marked that moment as the beginning of a more instrumental engagement with CAMH. She began telling Ken only what she felt he needed to know to help Terence. She kept her own thoughts and feelings closer to the vest. Overall, Linda was happy they'd come to CAMH. Although

Terence's daily life was still rocky at times, and although she wondered if his gender dysphoria would reemerge at puberty, she thought he was happier than he had ever been. Things at home felt calm. CAMH played a role in that transformation.

The stories parents told about their involvement with Ken and the clinic were complex. Some felt objectified by him; some experienced him as stoic, judgmental, or shaming. Yet all of the parents felt their child derived some benefit from their treatment at the clinic. All were willing to come back, even months after a treatment had ended, to speak to an unaffiliated researcher (me) at Ken's request. Ken was a complex character. It was possible, they said, to dislike him intensely and yet to feel a kinship or connection. He was able to help troubled children attain greater psychic stability, even as some of his methods exacted emotional costs. It was hard, as Sabrina said, "to know just how to feel about someone who can do both of those things at the same time."

EMPATHIC BREAKDOWN

On my last day at CAMH, I invited Ken to dinner to thank him for so generously hosting me for those ten days, for the labor he did to shepherd my application through the center's arduous institutional review board process, and for reaching out to families and securing me interviewees. We sat at a café near CAMH eating cheeseburgers. He told me about his son, the front man for a political punk band called *Fucked Up*, who had recently gained some notoriety and was touring throughout Canada. He asked me about my gender for the first time that night—only a few tentative questions about my identity, about where I grew up and what my parents were like. I gave short but honest answers, then shifted the conversation and asked him about his treatment plan for Steph. For this particular child, he said, he worried that gender nonconformity might be a mechanism for coping with other issues—some possible underlying trauma, poor body image, social struggles, autistic traits. Her distress, he said, might be showing itself in forms that looked like gender. He would work slowly to unravel what might be precipitating her gender, rather than excavating her gender itself. The latter, he thought, would reveal itself in time.

I wondered anew if Ken operated this way because he understood most or all gender transgression to be a byproduct of trauma, or if he was merely saying that about this child. I thought for a moment as we sat in silence. I suspect he could see I was formulating something, because he didn't move to fill the space. I looked at him and said, "So, I understand that you think gender dysphoria can be an adaptation to trauma or other issues. Do you think it can ever be a positive adaptation?" As the words left my mouth, I was surprised to feel my eyes cloud with tears.

I was realizing, in real time, that neither Ken nor I understood gender identity as static. We both believed it to be emergent. Indeed, to take radical gender theory seriously, to eschew ontological certainty in the service of understanding gender as fundamentally relational, is to skate close to the edge of etiology, of thinking about what produces gender. If it is possible to understand gender as "an improvisational possibility within a scene of constraint,"[63] relational and produced through the interaction of individuals, it's not a huge leap to imagine that some forms of gender could be made of scar tissue, produced as much by trauma as by tenderness. But it's a quick and dangerous slide from thinking about gender deviance as compensatory and thinking it pathological. And if gender deviance is a maladaptation, then those of us with atypical gender presentations are, in fact, damaged goods.

I understood several things in that moment. When Ken asked me about my family, the field around us shifted. He became, once again, not my research subject, but a psychologist with an interest in *my* gender. At that moment, when he was asking me questions about my gender and my family, he was trespassing into my psychic life. It was not the condition of our exchange, but it was easy to collapse into that dynamic. It felt invasive. Again, my impulse to evade his questions was my impulse to resist being captured by the clinical discourse. I suspect I failed, and that when I asked him about gender as adaptation, it was difficult to distinguish whether I was asking as a sociologist or as a gender deviant. And Ken was not unaware of that; in fact, he invited it. I was surprised by how painful that question felt. Gender subjectivity is tender ground. It shifts beneath our feet, eludes easy capture, and impinges on emotional nerves. Sometimes we find ourselves seeking recognition in the most unlikely places. Even when handled with care, it is treacherous territory.

At the same time, his reply brought to the fore a question he and I share, an exquisitely vulnerable question that can easily dissolve into fear, defensiveness, or shame. How do we disentangle gender from the many complex interacting factors that produce it? And is there a way to take seriously the question of gender as an adaptation without understanding it as pathology? It may be on this last question that Ken and I diverge. All gender is an adaptation, a call for recognition. The mistake lies in thinking of it as somehow less real, less constitutive of selfhood, less central to psychic life.

Even after nearly twenty years of criticism by the adult transgender community of CAMH and its predecessors;[64] after efforts by CAMH to respond to community grievances against Ken and his clinic;[65] after community petitions, including one seeking to oust him from his position on the DSM revision committee (along with Bradley and Ray Blanchard, another notorious CAMH staff member),[66] Ken appeared all but impervious. But Ken Zucker no longer runs the Gender Identity Clinic at CAMH. In February 2015, community pressure resulted in another external review of CAMH, this one culminating in the widely publicized firing of Ken and closure of the child GID clinic.[67] This final standoff crystalized the general state of tension between the trans community and medical professionals in the field of GID research, but the level of publicity also reflected the particular symbolic and material significance of Ken Zucker and CAMH. Trans people took issue with the way Ken ran the CAMH clinic and also resented the income and prestige he had derived from his GID research and clinical practice. One trans advocate pointed out that because CAMH clinics are subsidized through taxpayer-funded healthcare payments, Ken's $155,500 salary in 2008 required "transgender taxpayers in Canada [to] help foot the bill for their own pathologization."[68] Ken was fired at the age of sixty-five,[69] after having built an entire career around the clinical treatment of children with GID. At the time of this writing, Ken Zucker had several lawsuits pending against CAMH and some of the activists influential in agitating for his dismissal. He continues to publish research and maintains a private practice in Toronto. We keep in touch via Skype and email. The last time we spoke, he invited me to come up for the CAMH trial, offering me a "front row seat." He tells me he looks forward to reading this book, and I find myself strangely hopeful that he sees the value in it. He has my respect and also my skepticism. It's hard to know how to feel about someone who has both.

CONCLUSION

As psychiatric practice around gender nonconformity moves from a regulatory or pathologizing stance to a consumer-based model of care, new clinical challenges emerge. What role, if any, should individual clinicians play in determining which trans-identified clients can access transition-related care? Does that calculus change in relation to child patients? Is it important to imagine that gender is a variable wholly separate from other parts of psychic life, from sexuality, from histories of trauma, from co-occurring mental health challenges? Must we understand individuals as fully self-knowledgeable subjects with a static, underlying identity in order to facilitate social and medical transitions? These questions belie the complexity of a process of great institutional change. Where once we understood all gender to be determined by the body, we now understand it to exist in tandem with the body, determined by and determinative of the body. Psychiatry now sees forms of atypical gender expression as signposts of a psychic state they are only beginning to grapple with.

Trans activists hope that the death of CAMH represents a more general transition among clinicians toward viewing gender nonconformity as a benign form of human variation, one with many possible developmental trajectories. Clinicians are generally more comfortable with uncertainty in relation to trans adults, to whom we impute greater agency and authority. As more children approach physicians and mental health practitioners seeking transition-related care, anxieties run high. Some clinicians take extreme positions on one end of the spectrum or the other, but most appear to be wading in the murky middle waters, navigating complex questions of autonomy, agency, self-knowledge, and clinical responsibility. These questions encourage desires for predictability and standardization, for a concrete break with psychiatry's injurious past, for a sense that we are moving forward into a new and better trans medicine. Parents and the clinicians I met are actively co-creating this new terrain as I write this.

CHAPTER FOUR

Building a Parent Movement

Kim Pearson's laugh was legendary. Something between a hearty cackle and howl, it often floated above the clamor of the crowd moving along the main stretch of hallway at the Philly Trans Health conference, a multiday, annual conference that takes over a large section of the Philadelphia Convention Center each June. Founded by a small group of transgender community activists in 2002, the conference has grown each year, from a fledgling group of a few dozen young adults to its current annual attendance of more than four thousand transgender adults and children, family members, service providers, and community advocates. In 2012, the conference transitioned from being an all-volunteer event to a permanent program of the Mazzoni Center, a Philadelphia-based, nonprofit that provides physical and mental health care to LGBT individuals. Today, dozens of families of gender nonconforming and transgender children are among those who gather each year to take part in workshops on a wide range of topics. For years, Kim Pearson and the organization she helped to found, TYFA, took the lead in planning and providing workshops for families on understanding, raising and advocating for youth.

That long weekend usually passed by in a blur of activity for Kim. She often ran at least five workshops per day for parents and allies, with titles like "Utilizing Existing Federal Law to Protect Your Gender Variant/Transgender Youth in School," "Creating Positive Experiences with the Media," and "Transition: What Is It and Is It Right for My Child?" Kim was mostly self-taught. She gleaned the materials she used from the dozens of meetings she had with parents, school administrators, attorneys, physicians, and others. Parents gathered to find new ways to understand their child's gender identity and how to negotiate that identity with institutions.

In between workshops, conference participants strolled up and down a long hallway where vendors and community organizations set up displays of products for sale and information about services. They perused the offerings and chatted among themselves. There was typically a crowd of parents surrounding the TYFA table, taking from the candy bowl and chatting with the two or three mothers who staffed the table at any given time, handing out brochures, talking with new parents, providing snacks to straggling children, and making runs to the nearby Starbucks. Some of them wore T-shirts emblazoned with the organization's logo. Kim was often there in between sessions, surrounded by a gaggle of animated women, most of them mothers. She engaged each one in turn, listened intently to their individual struggles with school administrators, extended family members, or doctors, and offered advice or referrals. Now and then she would step aside with an individual parent who exhibited particular distress. Her days ended with a rambunctious dinner with other volunteers at the local Maggiano's Italian restaurant, where they would post to Facebook group photos of themselves laughing and holding martinis. She appeared tireless.

Anyone entering the hallway where the TYFA table stood might think this was a conference solely for adolescents and adults. The kids were most often secluded in a guarded "child" section of the conference, with its own staff and programming. They had little contact with the larger conference and with the transgender adults who created it. While new families would enter the conference together, children clinging shyly to parents, it wouldn't take long for most children to recognize the unusual opportunity for community the children's programming offered and to disappear into the back, leaving their parents to wander the hallways and workshops.

Kim Pearson was an accidental activist. She was, perhaps, the most visible of a growing group of (mostly) mothers of transgender and gender nonconforming children, whose own experiences of parenting and advocacy led them to create organizations, online message boards, community-based support groups, and an increasing body of knowledge on raising children who depart from gender norms. Less than a decade ago, a parent wanting to find positive trans imagery would most likely have needed to search for a transgender adult, or in urban centers might have found an LGBT community center or a lone message board or online support group. By the time I sat with Kim at Philly Trans Health, there was a burgeoning group of websites, conferences, and organizations, along with individual blogs, media articles, and YouTube videos, children's books and pamphlets, all of which combined social networking with broader projects of social and institutional change. These parents took important cues from (and, in some isolated cases, were instrumental actors in) earlier efforts for LGBT visibility and equality. Yet whereas previous generations of gender outlaws came of age as adults, and formed cultural and political institutions on their own behalves, today it is parent-activist energy (and money) that fuels the youth movement. As a result, it was often parents, rather than transgender children, who become the figureheads of efforts for institutional change, and the logics they mobilized were parent logics, and often cisgender, heterosexual logics. At times, they stood in stark contrast to the rhetorical and political strategies crafted by transgender adults. Parents fashioned the "best gendered selves"[1] they thought would empower their objectives, and the ways in which they did this differed across social locations. The construct of "transgender" they mobilized combined identitarian politics and a sense of acute social vulnerability. Their advocacy work and the outcomes it produced suggest that this new group of young transgender people will have distinct identities, social trajectories, and political objectives from those who came before them, ones that align more closely with those of their parents than with the meanings of transgender produced by trans adults.

Parent advocates played a dual role. They were the primary mobilizing force behind efforts to change the institutional practices of places like schools and churches, sometimes on behalf of their own children, sometimes paraprofessionally on behalf of other families. To create change in these varied settings, they became "radical translators"[2] of the gender order; they leveraged gender expertise gleaned from the fields of education, psychology, medicine, and politics to convert their child's subjective self-understandings into socially sanctioned forms of identity and personhood. At the same time, they engaged in tremendous emotional labor[3] to present themselves, the primary conduits of expert knowledge, in ways that were culturally assimilable to the people who ran institutions. Some secured the sympathies of others by presenting themselves as typical parents in exceptional circumstances and their children, at times, as exquisitely vulnerable to death by violence or suicide.

All parents doing this work engaged in efforts at impression management and negotiated what they described as a tension between representation and privacy; however, there were vast differences in the orientation of organizations toward understanding gender diversity in general, and in methods of engagement with outsiders (including adult transpeople), which suggests that this fledgling movement was actively working out the terms of its investments. What the relationship will be between today's gender nonconforming youth and previous generations of gender outlaws, what the predominant message to institutional actors struggling to accommodate gender nonconforming children should be, and who can be an effective representative for transgender children in hostile or resistant environments were critical issues under active debate.

Gender Spectrum, an organization founded on the West Coast, had clear ties to previous LGBT activist struggles and foregrounded its members' professional credentials and experience working in educational contexts to leverage political and rhetorical capital; TYFA, in contrast, traded heavily on the cachet of the heterosexual, nuclear family, the notion of benign tolerance, and rhetorics of precarity to forge more affective ties with their audiences. Each organization took deliberate pains to differentiate itself from the other, and parent participants, some of whom traveled back and forth between the two, became engaged in this process of organizational differentiation. Both were working out their own place in the emergent marketplace for expertise on this issue, through developing concepts of which children were best served by each organization and what each organizational self-concept would be. In their methods of self-presentation and rhetorical strategies, they took starkly different positions on the role of personal identity in child advocacy projects and on the extent to which the emergent movement to affirm childhood gender nonconformity should be grounded in concrete identity politics and a heteronormative rhetoric of family. Neither camp espoused many of the political approaches taken by adult transgender activists to increase the visibility of post-transition transgender lives or larger political efforts to fundamentally destabilize the institutional architecture of gender. Although more recent public policy recommendations have taken small steps in the direction of disestablishment, the question of where the movement will settle remains wide open.

A PARENT ACTIVIST MOVEMENT DEFINES ITSELF

Even in 2013, organized parent activism around childhood gender nonconformity was still brand new. Both of the main national organizations providing advocacy were less than a decade old. Yet while this novice movement was only just getting its bearings, a tremendous amount of work had already been done by individual activist leaders to shore up the boundaries of the movement, to compete for positions in the marketplace for expertise on gender, and to promote a very particular set of goals for their public advocacy efforts. The stakes, at that moment, were clear: either this would be an identitarian movement organized around gaining institutional access for children who transition from one category to another, or it would be a broader push to expand the constellation of options for childhood gender overall. It would be a movement for and about transgender children, or a movement about gender itself. While we might understand these divergent rhetorical perspectives as political choices, they reflect diverse parent self-understandings as well.

The frames parent activists used were deliberately aimed at recruiting supporters, inspiring a sense of solidarity, and demobilizing opposition to trans inclusion.[4] The three organizational leaders with whom I spent the most time, Stephanie Brill, Joel Baum, and Kim Pearson, encouraged parent participation in the work of their organizations. They fostered in the parents they met a sense of collective identity, shared injustice, and the possibility of effecting change; in so doing, they served instrumental needs, while also engaging in a tremendous amount of expressive work.[5] They each counseled other activist parents on how to tell two distinct sets of stories in their negotiations with other adults in their child's life. One set was pedagogical: they explained gender diversity conceptually, encouraging others to broaden their constructs of what gender is so they might better accommodate the needs of individual children in particular social contexts. The other set of stories was about the self, as parent, expert, or activist. In both community and larger social settings, these latter, more personal stories did emotional work, clearing an affective space in which their larger messages about gender could be heard. These stories of personhood and parenting resonated because they were familiar; and yet, while shared interpretive frames allowed an audience to assimilate new information, like other important social movement revolutions, they also fundamentally disrupted the existing social order: they were, by definition, "moments when agency explodes structure, the taken for granted becomes precarious, when 'old words lose their meaning.'"[6] Their stories had the power to "turn the anomalous into the new."[7]

These two emergent organizations and their leadership were proto-typical examples of "activist mothering," the culturally specific ways mothers intervene in their communities to maximize the chances for the success of their individual (or, in some cases, all) children.[8] It's no surprise that both advocacy organizations were started by activist mothers. Mothers often shoulder primary responsibility for managing the institutional lives of their children. While all parents want their children to be healthy and happy, the sociological literature tells us that middle-class mothers are more likely to view their children as a project and more apt to have both the time and financial resources to develop their children's talents and skills through organized activities.[9] These mothers—whose class backgrounds ranged from working class to wealthy—felt their child's gender was a project that presented itself uninvited, a project to which they needed to attend with some urgency.

Motherhood, some feminists argue, is structured by cultural imperatives to foster not just the preservation and growth of individual children but also their acceptability to the social milieu in which they live.[10] The parent activism I encountered focused instead on transforming the existing social arrangements to accommodate a child's obvious and challenging difference. In this particular case, accommodation could be complex. Some children sought access to the very narrowly bounded gender categories that transgender identities appear to resist.[11] It was often the goal of individual interventions to have a transgender-identified child integrate fully into the other gender category, without significantly disrupting how the category itself functions. For gender nonconforming children, however, there was no gender category into which they could fully and unproblematically assimilate. The goal, in those cases, was often to minimize the significance of gender distinctions overall. Yet even in the most complex cases, there was an impulse among parents of trans children to normalize the particular form of deviance their child exhibited, both as a means of improving their child's social experience and deflecting the stigma attached to the parent themself.[12]

The ways parent activists told their life stories, particularly their entry into activist work, informed the development and differentiation of the organizations they founded. Each parent entered the movement from a different vantage point, understood their child differently, had different reasons for distancing themselves from some transgender adults, and consequently, each parent developed different discursive strategies and different orientations to their advocacy. They mobilized their life histories and personal identities in divergent ways, understanding their own subjectivities to be intricately connected both to the reception they received from audiences, but also just what precisely their audiences understood them to be saying about gender itself.

The Accidental Activist

Kim Pearson joked that she always enjoyed having a soapbox to stand on. Yet she never would have anticipated that an episode of depression her youngest child suffered during his middle school years would lead her to radically transform her own daily life from that of a stay-at-home mom suffering from a variety of mental and physical ailments to a career as a tireless figurehead for the nation's largest advocacy organization for transgender youth. Depression was something that Kim understood. She suffered from debilitating bouts of it for most of her life. Kim grew up on the West Coast and described her family upbringing as "very disjointed." Both of her parents divorced and remarried multiple times during her childhood, and she had many step-siblings and half siblings from those marriages; she remembered protracted custody battles between her parents, instability, and "just all the things that come with having divorces and remarriages and all the strife that goes along with that." She recalled an unsettled childhood, punctuated by episodes of verbal and physical abuse from the adults in her life, several of whom struggled with alcoholism and other forms of addiction.

Kim herself married young and divorced young. She lived with her second husband, John, in a small Southwestern city, and together they raised three children, their youngest, Levi, a transgender boy. As an adult, when her children were still at home, she was diagnosed with diabetes and fibromyalgia. She spent years coping with chronic pain, exhaustion, and the debilitating effects of her depression. She went on and off psychotherapeutic medication and in and out of therapy. After her physical health began to deteriorate, she realized she could no longer serve as her family's primary breadwinner. The financial and emotional strain on the family was overwhelming, and Kim entered a brief period of several short hospitalizations. She quit her job, went on public disability, and she and John decided to relocate to the small town in which the family now lives.

For several years, Kim said, her primary focus was on improving her health. "When we moved, I literally came here feeling like I had no skin on my body, like every nerve was exposed. And it was a process to grow the skin back on my body." Kim described that time as one of intensive introspection. She listened to motivational tapes about self-esteem, and tried to improve her diet and physical health. Over time, she began to think about reentering the workforce, but knew her continued struggles with poor health made conventional employment impossible. She still had good days and bad days and said she needed a flexible schedule for "self-care." She wasn't quite sure what to do. She described sitting in her car one afternoon and having a conversation with God.

> I just literally asked the universe for what I wanted. I said I wanted a job that would let me have a lot of flexibility. I said I wanted a job where I could teach people. I said I wanted a job where I could travel a lot. I said I wanted a job where I could become an expert about something, be respected. I just asked for all these things, having no idea what kind of job it would be.

Her child Levi had come out as a lesbian several years prior but continued to struggle. He became increasingly withdrawn, silent, and solitary. "I saw him disappearing into himself," Kim said. Kim began attending therapy with Levi. A short while later, Levi told his therapist that he was really a boy. Kim said she knew Levi would be gay years before he came out, but she knew little about what it meant to be transgender. So she did what most parents these days do: she went online in search of support. This was in 2006, when there were only a tiny handful of websites even mentioning transgender children and one lone email listserv for parents.

It was through this initial foray online that she hooked into a small group of parents with gender nonconforming children who connected over email. Over the course of the next year she traded stories and met with a handful of women from different parts of the country, and together they decided to form an organization to develop resources for supporting families. "Basically, we were all learning as we went along, and then in would come a new parent, and we just didn't want them to have to reinvent the wheel all over again. We wanted to find a way to tell them what we already knew." TYFA was born in January 2007. Kim laughed and told me it began with an initial $10,000 startup fund she won when she deposited a quarter into a slot machine on a lark, after stopping to use a bathroom while driving through Las Vegas. (Kim had a lot of stories that involved Vegas "bathroom breaks" and slot machines.) In the beginning, Kim functioned as the organization's treasurer and said she had no intention of being a visible leader. When one of the initial cofounders left the organization, however, she stepped in to fill that role.

Kim spoke frequently about her complex emotional life and her struggles with physical illness; yet it was almost two years into our relationship before she gave me permission to write her individual story. We were sitting together in a rental car, and she was driving us from an event in a suburban New Jersey church back to the home of a TYFA board member in Manhattan with whom she was staying. She was in the sixth week of a seven-week stint on the road doing advocacy work. It was difficult to believe that someone who kept the kind of travel log she did once struggled to get out of bed each morning and move through simple tasks like picking her children up from school. At that time, TYFA was the largest nonprofit trans youth organization, working on projects that ranged from education programs targeted at individual schools, churches, and other organizations to media advocacy. Kim said she spent some forty weeks a year on the road, traveling to LGBT conferences, to provider workshops, to professional seminars, to media appearances, and to the individual communities where families and children lived. She appeared on national television and radio and in more print media articles than she could keep track of. And although all of her personal and travel expenses were covered by individual donations (mostly from families), she did not receive a salary for her work. While few would make the personal sacrifices necessary to do this kind of advocacy, it was clear that Kim's activism animated her life in ways little else had.

During the hour-and-a-half drive, I asked her why she hesitated to publish details about her life. She spoke freely about herself with parents, made occasional reference to her marital travails in workshops, shared openly with me over coffee. She routinely narrated in detail her own son's transition and his emotional experience. Having her life in print, though, felt different to her. She feared that small details might impeach her credibility, risking injury to the families and children who depended on her work. Kim described her presentation of self as if it was an essential component of the education and advocacy work she did. And I myself found that my initial impressions of Kim did not match what I eventually learned about her upbringing and worldview. I saw her coiffed and highlighted hair and carefully applied makeup and thought she was a Midwestern maternal archetype: the avowedly Christian, no-nonsense, protective nurturer who never gave a thought to gender or sexual nonconformity until she had a clinically depressed child on suicide watch. I heard her say enough times, to enough effect, that after some struggle she'd finally decided she'd "rather have a live son than a dead daughter" to imagine she'd been brought into the fold of postmodern gender formations under some duress. Yet I came to learn that Kim grew up in Sacramento, California, and, although her natal family was religiously and socially conservative, Kim herself had always been somewhat liberal. Her first marriage was to an African

American man, she explained, and the intolerance of her own family and friends solidified her resolve to both resist discrimination and take an active role in educating those around her about difference.

This was not the image she projected when she entered a school to advocate for a child. Although Kim's identity as the parent of a transgender child was both real and accidental, it was one she mobilized in strategic ways to persuade individuals to engage in conversations in which they might otherwise refuse to participate. In parts of the country where religion was a primary organizing force, Kim described herself as a lifelong Christian confronted by a painful faith issue: how could she not love her child through his layers of difference? In politically conservative environments, she relied on her conventional appearance and peppered her conversations with references to her middle child's military service in Iraq and her oldest daughter's newborn twins. In all of these settings, she appealed directly to a heteronormative sensibility and an ethic of empathy, and it won her support in unlikely places. All of these things were, in fact, true, but they were not a whole truth. The "self" Kim employed was the product of a thoughtful process of sorting out which parts of her story, her emotional experience, and her life history would encourage a particular audience to identify with her.

My initial impression was that much of this "mom habitus" was unintentional, a simple dividend of hegemonic femininity. And then I saw her outline the mission of TYFA and its work to a roomful of affirming parents at a liberal, progressive church in New Jersey. She joked about her "sensible shoes" (Dansko clogs), the gender trouble provoked by her short haircut, and her own tomboyish girlhood. Shadowing Kim as she moved through different social locations, in and out of groups, and spending time with her individually revealed that her fashioning of self was itself the central feature of her advocacy. For Kim, being a parent advocate was far less about espousing a particular political worldview (though she certainly had one) and importing that into different settings; rather, it was a way of cultivating an intelligible and relatable self, in a context where she might then exert influence over the behavior of others. She was keenly attuned to the ways her gender presentation and life history, and those of her associates, saturated her message and determined its efficacy.

The Rainbow Pioneer

Stephanie Brill was *not* an accidental activist. When we met, she had been a pioneer on the cutting edge of queer family life for close to two decades. Among LGBT adults of child-bearing age, she was probably best known as an expert on lesbian and transgender pregnancy, conception, and birth. She was the parent of four children, had formal training as a nurse midwife, wrote books on pregnancy and queer parenting, and for nearly a decade operated a successful midwifery practice in Seattle and San Francisco. In the 1990s, she was a visible part of the beginnings of institutionalizing services for lesbians wishing to conceive children.[13] As her practice grew to meet the demands of contemporary family arrangements, she encountered transgender individuals also looking for hard-to-find resources on conception and pregnancy. She was the primary resource for media outlets when the story of Thomas Beatie, the pregnant transgender man, headlined prime-time news.[14] Although she had left her midwifery practice several years before to start an organization for families with gender nonconforming children, Gender Spectrum, she still received numerous requests each month from queer people around the world seeking support on issues of family planning.

Stephanie Brill and Kim Pearson couldn't appear more different. Stephanie was tall, very thin, and had close-cropped brown hair, peppered with gray. She had a casual presentation of self, often appearing in jeans and a button-down shirt. I first met Stephanie on the evening she and Gender Spectrum's director of education and training, Joel Baum, led a meeting for parents at a small urban charter school, where a middle school child was transitioning. I had spoken to Joel on the telephone several times in preparation for that evening. He quickly agreed to put me in touch with families he thought might be willing to be interviewed. He was slower to put me in direct contact with Stephanie, and I arrived on the scene with some trepidation about how she would respond to my presence and to the project itself. We finally came face to face in a small classroom. As we stood surrounded by a disorganized collection of diminutive chairs, desks, and tables, I was struck by several things.

Stephanie Brill had a commanding presence. Almost from the moment of our introduction, I lost control of the conversation. I began asking her about the program for the evening and the history of the school, and before I got halfway through my first sentence, she interrupted to fire a string of questions at me about who I am, how I envisioned the frame of the project, and what sort of things I'd want to know. Although both Stephanie and Kim described conflicted relationships with media and research, Stephanie's distrust was immediately palpable. I found myself in that initial conversation utilizing trans vernacular far more than I did in my initial interactions with Kim. She asked me what I teach, and I described my transgender studies course rather than my survey course on law and society. I felt myself trying to use my queer cultural capital to position myself as an insider, and it seemed imperative that I do that if I wanted access to the families she so keenly guarded. Later that evening, alone in my hotel room, I encountered my often-present hesitations about how and when to claim an insider identity, and how it might serve to filter my access to certain ideas and relationships. It was clear from the start that Stephanie wanted to control not just her message, but mine as well.

I also noticed that Stephanie wasn't just thin, she was *very* thin. The first night we met, she was wearing loose-fitting pants and an untucked button-down shirt, and the clothing seemed to hang off her narrow frame. It was early evening and as we talked, she sipped from a large Styrofoam container of Thai soup. I didn't examine this impression carefully until later on. Still, there was something striking about the ferocity of her persona paired with a kind of physical frailty that was also clearly visible. I spent the better part of the remainder of that trip out West trying to nail down a time to get together for a one-on-one conversation. She evaded my attempts, finally sending me a one-line text message on the very last day of my trip to offer up an hour-long window. I jumped at the chance, and boarded a train and headed forty minutes outside the city to meet her near Gender Spectrum's office. We sat together at a picnic table in a nearby park, and as Stephanie huddled against the fall chill, she made her first shadowy reference to ongoing health problems.

Stephanie's affect, her rhetoric, indeed her entire approach differed starkly from Kim's. Rather than focusing in on a specific group of children with bounded concerns, she talked in broad terms about the larger system of binary gender, presumptions of heterosexuality, and the unique concerns faced by queer parents and parents of queer children. She also made reference to a long history of working collaboratively with mental health care providers and physicians on a range of issues. She advocated for "expert parenting," the necessity to understand children from a developmental perspective, how gender fluidity fits into that, and how parents must become conversant both with their child's inner sense of self and with how that self maps onto continuing and incremental development in other areas.

Through her midwifery practice, which maintained a particular focus on same-sex parents, she created and ran several support groups in the late 1990s, including one for lesbians raising sons. She explained that it was an attempt to carve out a space for parents to talk together about gender and parenting and to confront and think through the stereotype that lesbian parenting was deficient without a male role model (a stereotype she was quick to dismiss with a wave of her hand). During this time, she and her partner were also grappling with the fact that one of their own children (assigned female at birth), then only a toddler, was communicating to his parents that he was absolutely, positively certain he was a boy. Through discussions in the lesbian parenting support group around whether and how rigidly to enforce gender roles in their children, Stephanie learned that another parent in the group was facing similar concerns with her child. It was, she says, the first time she'd given any serious thought to a child of any age, but especially a toddler, knowing that they were transgender.

I had done a lot of work in classrooms and staff trainings around issues of gender bias in the classroom—how girls are treated, how boys are treated—and issues of sexual orientation and family structure. I was really comfortable with that. But I didn't really understand gender to the extent that I understand it now. I certainly didn't understand transgender emergence as a child. I still, like everyone I knew, thought that was a grownup kind of thing, that was when people came to an awareness of this.

She realized they couldn't possibly be the only families facing these concerns, so she decided to begin a support group for families whose children had struggles around gender. "Starting groups was easy for me. Whenever I see a new social need out there, my first instinct is always, 'Oh! Let's start a group!' It cuts the loneliness and isolation. It helps people connect and cope." She made a strategic decision not to host the group through her midwifery practice, reasoning that housing the program in a non-LGBT- focused space would make it more accessible to a wider range of families. Instead, she used her personal and professional connection to a well-regarded local psychiatrist to get space at a children's hospital. Word of the group's formation spread quickly, and within a few months there was a steady stream of families coming to meet monthly to discuss their children and parenting. The size of the group and the rate with which it was growing demonstrated a larger need for services and interventions for families dealing with these issues.

As she spoke, drawing connections between her evolving understanding of children and gender and the swell of demand for family services, I thought about early LGBT organizing and its role in transforming social and emotional alliances into concrete social and political projects. Of course, today's culture is a psychotherapeutic culture, and Stephanie moved very quickly from running a single support group to approaching personal and professional contacts to fundraise for the formation of an organization that would institutionalize these kinds of services in a bigger way. With close to $150,000 in hand, Stephanie contacted several prominent transgender rights organizations, including one whose own organizational structure included a program devoted to resisting childhood gender stereotypes. Nobody was interested in taking on the politically explosive issue of transgender children.

> People thought I was crazy. "Kids are not transgender; you're condemning them to a horrible life." And these were, like, my friends who are transgender! Initially I lost all my transgender friends! [...] And I'm sure now they'd be horrified to admit that this was their initial stance. But it was truly, "Kids can't be transgender. Yes, we may be, and we all knew at that point in time, but you don't let them live that way. You're going down the wrong path, Stephanie, like, this is dangerous stuff." And I knew in my heart of hearts that they were actually wrong.

Stephanie described a tense set of exchanges with older transgender activists, who said it would be politically damaging to publicly support transition for children. She characterized these conversations as painful. Queer and transgender communities were those within which she functioned both personally and professionally. The notion that she might hurt larger efforts for encouraging acceptance for gender and sexual diversity by finding ways to support and affirm her child and others like him felt anathema to her. And at the same time, she was also guiding her own child through his early transition and watching him blossom.

These early conversations were my first glimpse at an emergent set of tensions between this new generation of gender nonconforming youth and adult transgender activists. They also signaled a particular vulnerability felt by queer adult activists when faced with the question not merely of affirming transgender identities in youth, but of actively advocating for and enabling the development of those identities. Because the cultural conventions around childhood position children as uniquely vulnerable, transgender adults feared accusations of child corruption. These concerns sat in an odd juxtaposition with the way Kim Pearson and TYFA mobilized that very same vulnerability to argue for the facilitation of gender nonconformity.

After her failed attempt to develop a partnership with established transgender organizations, Stephanie decided instead to focus her energy on developing a conference where families could go to meet one another and seek support. She met Jordan Scott at a large, annual West Coast adult transgender conference he had organized for six years. For Stephanie, it felt like she'd met a "soulmate." Jordan was a major figure in trans political organizing in the Pacific Northwest; he knew how to do outreach and how to run large conferences. She invited Jordan to the Bay Area for a weekend to discuss the possibility of partnership in an annual event for children and families, to be held in conjunction with his conference.

The ways Kim and Stephanie came into activist work matter. Kim had little experience with LGBT political advocacy, whereas Stephanie's life was, in many ways, defined by it. Kim's family appeared from the outside fairly normative, until her son began to transition. Stephanie's family life was innately and self-consciously queer. She had long cultivated a political relationship to her parenting, and this would inform the direction of her advocacy efforts. Kim's organization, TYFA, focused on the integration of specifically transgender children into their social surroundings, normalized children's identities as boys or girls, and used the threat of anti-trans violence often to mobilize support. Stephanie's organization, Gender Spectrum, embraced a broader agenda of gender diversity, aimed to change large-scale social discourse on the fluidity and multiplicity of gender, and mobilized its own professionalized expertise to establish authority. As a result, we might expect Gender Spectrum to look more like trans advocacy of generations past, but as we will see, both organizations took pains to distance their kids from the political choices of older trans adults.

ORGANIZATIONS AND CULTURES CLASH

Kim, Stephanie, and many of the families who worked with both TYFA and Gender Spectrum took pains to differentiate the two organizations.

Both Kim and Stephanie themselves described their first meeting in 2006 as an absolute disaster. Although both were actively networking with other parents of transgender and gender nonconforming youth, and both had assembled communities of activists that included other parents and adult transgender activists, their personalities and perspectives clashed mightily. A fateful weekend at Stephanie's house sealed an enduring animosity between the two individuals and organizations. Kim Pearson received a call from Stephanie inviting her to come out for a meeting with her and Jordan, to discuss combining their two nascent efforts into a formal, national organization. Kim arrived with her son and spent the weekend at Stephanie's home. She says she felt that Stephanie condescended to her and treated her as if she knew nothing about the subjects of gender and youth. In fact, Stephanie understood Kim's singular focus on transgender youth and concern with medical and social transitions to be a worrisome and limited frame for a political agenda. She worried that Kim might encourage parents to transition their children too early, that the idea of making a full and undetectable move from one gender category to the other might seem like an easy fix to parents who feared the social repercussions of having a gender-fluid, gender nonconforming, or gay child.

Stephanie and Kim told different versions of this story, and I heard several inventive interpretations from parents as well. One thing seems apparent: parents viewed these organizations as fundamentally different, even as they themselves moved between the two communities. They described TYFA as a "transgender" organization, one whose core goal and constituency was children who make full transitions from one social gender category to another. They thought Gender Spectrum, in contrast, focused more broadly on issues related to gender diversity and gender nonconformity ("variance" in the terminology of the time) for all children, but particularly for those whose nonconformity created obstacles in their social environments. TYFA was an organization run by "Midwestern moms"; Gender Spectrum was far more closely aligned with a West Coast queer political sensibility that focused on norm challenging. Parents allied with TYFA accused Gender Spectrum of being ineffective and alienating in many more conservative parts of the country; those allied with Gender Spectrum accused TYFA of homophobia and a restrictive focus on medicalization.

The parents and caregivers I met were surprisingly savvy about these interorganizational tensions and had done their own investigative work to determine which group most effectively served their needs. Some families aligned themselves closely with one organization and debased the other; others made strategic use of both. The parents (again, predominantly mothers) who donated time and resources to keep these organizations afloat also faced strategic choices about how and where to donate and volunteer. As these two organizations developed, their different leaderships, targeted demographics, and ideologies led parents to begin to separate out which children were best served by which group.

Hunter's mom, Nan, thought that the Gender Spectrum conference historically focused too much on gender nonconforming youth and not enough on the particular needs of transgender children.

> I think the conference this year at Gender Spectrum, the family one, I did think it was better. It was a little more trans-identified this year than it was last year here. Although definitely there's still more room for variant [than trans]—but last year I felt it was totally gender nonconforming, with not enough trans in it for me. Whereas the Philly one is totally trans.

Nan participated on both TYFA and Gender Spectrum's online listservs. She said she attended Gender Spectrum's parent group mostly because it was located nearest to where she lived. But she volunteered with TYFA, staffing the information table during Philly TransHealth. She did not volunteer to help at Gender Spectrum's conference. She began speaking with a conspiratorial tone, her eyes downcast, when she explained her deeper affiliation with TYFA. They just felt more comfortable to her, she said, more aligned with her sense of who Hunter was and what he needed. She looked up at me and paused thoughtfully for a moment, then continued:

But this year in the conference I saw a very big change with the Gender Spectrum approach, and Stephanie, even in her ... and the speech at the end of the first day where we were all in there in the auditorium—she very much spoke more to transgender as opposed to just gender nonconforming. And I have seen a difference in our support group because in our support group realistically everyone has a transgender child except for [one parent]—for her really the decision is, do I let my kid go out of the house in dresses and interesting girl stuff or do I not? For the rest of us it's okay, well, we just need to know these ... I keep my child stealth,[15] should she go to school stealth or should he be out. So it's a very different situation and I think Gender Spectrum shines with the gender nonconforming children. Don't you agree?

It was an awkward moment in the interview, and I felt a desire to disavow any connection to Gender Spectrum. I sensed she was editing her commentary to fit some perception she had of me. Perhaps it was my own presentation of self, far more like Stephanie Brill's studied androgyny than Kim Pearson's soft, maternal femininity. Perhaps it was merely that we were sitting in a hotel room in a major West Coast city, as opposed to one in Philadelphia. But I managed to evade the question and instead asked her about the types of families that were drawn to TYFA. She replied,

I am fully aware that in the bylaws we include gender nonconforming as well as transgender children, but realistically, even down to the name, people who would consult TYFA are the people who think, "I have a transgender child." That's my opinion.

Nan's mother, Sue, who joined us for the interview also volunteered with TYFA, conducting intake interviews with new parents who called to join the listserv. Sue thought that although parents of gender nonconforming children often contact TYFA for resources, its organizational mission was focused more squarely on working with families whose children were or might be transitioning fully.

With all the ones [parents of gender nonconforming children] I've done intakes on, I'm thinking maybe one, maybe two ... most of them don't participate. They don't need the services of TYFA, and when they contact TYFA, it's many times just to get on the listserv. Because it's kind of the only listserv for parents of young children. And I think that once when I talk to them, they do understand that we have other parents on there who have children who are gender nonconforming, but for the most part realistically ... I mean, I think TYFA is very, very clear, that for the most part it's the transgender children.

I asked Sue to explain how that difference mattered when fielding intake calls for TYFA. She explained, "They make it very clear to any parent of a transgender child from the get-go, and when I do intakes I know I have to—I have to and I want to—tell that parent about a safe folder. You have to stress the safe folder, and Gender Spectrum doesn't do that." (Sue was referring to a particular dossier of documents, discussed in more detail in the next chapter, that TYFA encourages parents to assemble for self-protection, in the event that another family member, health professional, or state agency questions their parenting choices around their child's gender.)

Nan thought that each organization and its leadership possessed concrete, practical strengths; still, she said, TYFA presented an image that was far more relatable to the average American than Gender Spectrum's more hip cosmopolitanism.

> NAN: Well, I think this: I think if I had a gender nonconforming child, I would absolutely be cool with Stephanie or Jordan coming into my school and teaching about gender variance, absolutely. I love Jordan and I think Stephanie is wonderful and I think that is their forte, explaining gender to all and educating everyone about gender. I think they're fantastic, and I think they would shine more than TYFA as far as gender variance. But when it comes to a transgender child, I want TYFA behind my back.
>
> TEY: Tell me why?
>
> NAN: I'll tell you exactly why, and I can say it because I'm gay, so I'm not being prejudiced. I want a straight female going into my school. I mean, I'm passionate about that—I do. But if I weren't gay, it would sound like maybe I was being prejudiced, but I'm not. It's that those teachers, the

way I saw ... the way that I saw them identify with Kim as a mother ... you might get that one person who is going astray to get roped back in because of their connection with Kim or with another mother.

Nan was talking about more than Stephanie Brill's sexual orientation. She worried that Stephanie's gender, her presentation of self, the likelihood that an observer could impute her sexual orientation, affected the ability of an audience to relate to her, to incorporate and accept her point of view. Sue added,

> I think that everyone who has a child ... when someone comes in to speak, I think they can relate to someone who could be their neighbor, who could be a friend of a friend, who might live in their area. [...] I think women who are mothers in particular, I think they like hearing from another mother, and not just another mother, because Stephanie's a mom and she's a wonderful presenter. But I think that [...] outside of Seattle, outside of San Francisco, outside of New York City, basically the whole country is country, it's not city. And I think that people can relate to a Kim. I think when Stephanie goes in, I think they see someone different than their neighbor. Now, that doesn't mean that they don't have a neighbor like that, but I think ... there's no agenda. I think that people ... feel like we have an agenda. There is no chance in that being an issue for them, and I think that benefits the child and the acceptance of the child.

Nan and Sue voiced openly what I heard other parents affiliated with TYFA imply, that the personal characteristics of the parent advocates who intervened in institutional settings often mattered as much as the intervention itself. Both Kim and Stephanie were conscious of this, and that consideration informed the way each organization framed its expertise, its connection to the issues being raised, and its leadership.

TRANSGENDER ACTIVISM, CISGENDER LOGIC

In my fieldwork, I witnessed complex processes of identification and disidentification with what activist parents perceived to be the meanings of transgender created by previous generations. Both Kim and Stephanie presented elaborate explanations of why the children with whom they worked differed from older transgender adults and engaged in efforts to manage the exposure gender nonconforming youth had to older transpeople. Yet adult transpeople also become deeply symbolic in a variety of conflicting ways for many of the parents. They functioned as floating signifiers for the hopes and fears parents attached to their children's uncertain futures. For some parents, the deep pain and pervasive discrimination faced by transgender adults was too much to bear emotionally; for others, the primary concern was the notion that their child might cultivate an oppositional identity, one that radically departed from social norms. These parents attempted to disassociate their child from what the transgender adult has become. For still others, constructing taxonomies of different forms of adult gender allowed them to exert more careful control over precisely what *sort* of influence connections to the adult transgender community might have on their children's self-understandings. It was around these issues of identification and disidentification that I felt my own gender presentation become most salient for my interview respondents, and navigating those moments proved treacherous, both methodologically and emotionally. Adult transgender theorists indeed write about their own struggles to navigate competing desires for self-determination and legibility to others.[16] In my conversations with parents, those competing tensions were evident in the ways they discussed interactions with transgender adults.

Jerri, the guardian of a six-year-old transgirl, expressed concern that the dominant media representations of transgender people—and in fact, the dominant self-representations she saw them present in some community spaces—emphasized points of difference from the norm, rather than similarities. Jerri worried this would be the sole representation her granddaughter, Phoebe, had access to and that she might therefore grow up thinking she had to form an oppositional identity herself.

> You know, I'll be really blunt with you. I don't want to offend you or anyone else, but the truth is a lot of trans people, a lot of trans adults, are fringe, right? They're not fully accepted in society. A lot of them present

themselves as being different and wanting to be different. Some of them present themselves as being freaks. And if that's their path and they're happy, good for them. And if that's Phoebe's path and she's happy, good for her. But I want her to know that she has many possible paths. And so I don't want her to go into the trans community and just see the fringe people and so that's [her] only path. I want her to know that she can be an Olsen twin if she wants to! Or she can be a freak if she wants to. You know, she can have any of those paths.

Jerri was one of many parents whose representations of transgender adulthood seemed to foreground their transgressive qualities. Many expressed the outright desire that their children live relatively normatively gendered lives. Others indicated a greater openness to transgressive gender, but still hoped their child would have the opportunity to participate in normative forms of gender, if they so chose.

For some parents, strategic exposure to certain forms of gender nonconformity functioned as a way to manage anxiety about the uncertainty of their child's future. Parents of masculine girls (generally of middle school age, and generally those who had yet to fully make a social transition) approached me during my fieldwork at conferences and asked me to spend time with their child. I was particularly struck by Eve, who had an unusual stillness of presence for a twelve-year-old. Her mother and I talked for a long time about her newly emerging gender identity and her own sense of isolation as she struggled to cope with her feelings about it. She asked if I would talk with Eve and her husband during the lunch break at the conference. I agreed to, and she replied, "Oh, that's great. Because here you are, smart and successful and writing a book ... *and you're not a man.*" She seemed then to pause as if looking to me to confirm my identity. I smiled at her but didn't reply.

When I met Eve later that day, she was wearing a striped boys rugby shirt, crisp white shorts, and impeccably clean running shoes. The burnt embers of her red hair were cropped short around her ears, longer and disarrayed around her forehead. She had disarmingly bright blue-green eyes, and she seemed at once shy, quiet, and self-possessed. We sat on the floor of the Philly convention center lobby with her parents, and she played with her shoelaces as she described what she'd learned that morning about blockers at a workshop on medical transition for youth. We discussed some of the older youth at the conference who left behind unsupportive family to attend. At one point, she leaned in conspiratorially to whisper to me, "I feel so bad for them. They couldn't get blockers and had to go through puberty, and now, they don't look so good." I saw her parents glance at one another out of the corner of my eye. They were watching us carefully, as if prepared to witness something important, revelatory. And then, in unison, both parents looked down at my chest.

My gender entered the frame in any number of other interactions with parents: some treated me as a potential role model; others appeared to view me as part of a larger transgender imaginary that they found provocative or worrisome. As I sat at a conference table at Philly Trans Health during my first attempt to recruit families for interviews, the father of a middle school–aged transgirl I'd seen running by with a pack of other children approached me warily and began asking questions about the study. He was quick to say that he had no intention of participating, but he still wanted to understand the project. As I explained that I wished to learn about the experience of parenting gender nonconforming children and negotiating gender with schools, he cut me off abruptly and demanded, "But what's your *story* about these kids? Because these are just kids. They're not mini-activists or troublemakers. They're just kids." I explained to him that I had no intention of depicting the children, or families' choices about supporting them, in any particular way, but rather that my intent was to look at the negotiations between parents and institutions around gender (which reflected my emergent understanding of the project at that time). It took several minutes and many questions to uncover his underlying concern, which was that I somehow wanted to use these children to help further some larger transgender political agenda. To this father, and to several other parents I met, the primary goal was to fully assimilate their children into their chosen gender category, for his daughter to be merely his daughter, a girl, and

not a transgirl. To some of these parents, what they read of my own gender complexity aligned me with a set of competing interests and politics,
ones they believed threatened their children's chances for assimilation,
for conformity.

These fears were compounded by the lack of transgender adults in
positions of visibility within advocacy organizations and at events. This
was particularly true for parents of trans-feminine children (feminine
boys and transgirls), since it was rare to find adult transwomen among
the cadre of adults in caretaking positions at conferences or local groups
and meetings. Though some conferences targeting kids and families
happened in tandem with adult transgender conferences, the child and
adolescent programming was always held in a separate, controlled
space, to which entrance was restricted to people vetted by the organizations. Many activist parents reasoned that the dissonance between
the experiences of transgender adults and this new generation of gender nonconforming children caused pain for some transgender activists
who try to participate in providing support to families. There was a
kind of disidentification with many of the meaningful and hard-won
self-concepts older transgender people forge. Stephanie explained,

> If you talk to most of these kids, they never would call themselves trans-
> gender. Other people have called them that, so they take it on because it's
> lingo. But they are very clear. "I am a girl." "I am a boy." They don't have a
> transgender identity. They're not going to be able to relate necessarily to
> older transgender folks after a certain point in time. This is gonna become
> like they're one breed, they're another breed of people. The have unique
> issues. The closest we can come is to look at what transgender issues have
> been, but that's very different than a child who has these issues, who maybe
> transitioned at four or five or six, you know.

Stephanie was signaling a concrete difference in the childhood experiences of transgender adults, most of whom grew up in one gender category and made a transition into the other as adults. Their identities as
transgender adults drew from that experience of category shift, of the
complexities of living in a liminal space. This differs significantly from

the life experience of children whose families allow them to transition at very young ages. They won't necessarily have to endure their natal puberties, nor will they have childhood memory books filled with images that don't match their sense of selves as adults. Stephanie continued,

> Teenagers who come out as trans, you know, or genderqueer, or anything like that . . . in this point in time, or young adults . . . they often have a very complex understanding of sexual identity and gender identity, that's greatly inspiring, you know, it's—that's where a lot of the change is actually happening around gender, is in that age group. Because they are discovering themselves and gender and they're thinking in their minds in all these ways. Now these young kids, they're just telling people who they are. But they are still being raised within the standard gender system.

Stephanie spoke further about the differing developmental trajectories of trans adults and children. Kim Pearson used more direct language about her fears that transgender adults may carry residual trauma that might affect the children or their own emotional well-being. She described the risk of allowing transgender adults to work with kids as one largely borne by the adults themselves. She imagined that seeing the kind of familial support and acceptance some of these children are receiving might be deeply painful for adult transgender activists who were rejected or repressed by their own families.

> There was this one transwoman who just really underestimated the impact being with these kids and their supportive families would have on her. She found herself breaking down, because she just kept thinking, "Why didn't I have these supportive parents, and this access to medical care and these sorts of social supports?" It was just too much for her. She ended up spending forty-eight hours in the psych ward.

While both Kim and Stephanie described the tangible benefits of positive role modeling by trans adults, both also took great pains to filter precisely which transgender adults had access to the youth and families who came to their conferences. During the planning process for Gender Spectrum's teen program in 2010, Stephanie and I discussed bringing in some transgender musicians or performers from San Francisco to do a show for the teens on one of the evenings. Stephanie expressed some hesitation, given that "so much adult transgender performance has tremendous pain and anger in it." Stephanie said she labored to create a space where transgender representations were visible, yet the appearance of trauma was muted. In this way, access to transgender adults was structured around presenting an image consistent with what this community hoped for the futures of these youth, rather than, in fact, representing the visible social dis-integration in some of the community art produced by transgender adults. What hovered beneath the surface of these exchanges, spoken more directly by parents, was that older transgender people did not have the same kinds of transitions as contemporary trans youth. Parents believed that transwomen who transition as adults often don't pass and, as a result, live in social circumstances they don't wish their children to emulate. Those narratives would not assist Stephanie and Kim in assuaging the worries of new parents. The image they were working toward was one of political and social belonging.

While activists and parents alike expressed reservations about intergenerational mixing, I also witnessed some amusing and heartwarming moments of positive identification between transgender youth and adults. Seven-year-old Hunter's realization that twenty-two-year-old Tommy also had a vagina made him feel a kinship with an older, in his words "so cool," representation of himself. The day Chaz Bono came to Philly TransHealth, kids and parents alike swarmed him seeking attention and offering gratitude for his visibility. Many of these connections, however, happened in private spaces, when parents reached out to adults, like they did to me, extending invitations and cultivating friendships and support networks.

MOURNING JACK

TYFA's rhetorical focus on risk prevention was born of a catalytic moment in their consolidation as an organization. It was the day that

Jack died. Often through tears, the three founding members of TYFA described and discussed the story with great frequency. In fact, I never once heard Kim Pearson speak publicly without mentioning Jack. It was usually in the middle of a program, once she had generated some sort of rapport with the audience. She always began the same way: "When we started, we were three moms with three kids. Now we're three moms with two kids." Jack was a teenager when he took his own life in October 2007, ten months after TYFA began their work. His mother was one of TYFA's founding members. He had a loving, supportive family, a community that allowed him some measure of space to figure out his identity. He didn't face homelessness, eviction from his family, or horrific harassment. Yet, his mother says, living the reality of his identity in a society that didn't understand him was simply too painful to bear.

Jack's name came up often in informal conversations with TYFA's founding members Kim and Charlotte. (Jack's mother, Carla, the third of the cofounders, is the organization's treasurer, and while she did still attend conferences, she preferred to have a less visible role.) For Kim, his death felt like a deep personal loss. "We began this organization together, you know? We were the moms; they were the kids. And when Jack died, it felt like losing one of my kids. And it just reminded me that these children's lives are fragile."

Most of the parents I met could cite a statistic that close to half of all transgender youth attempt suicide.[17] Some of them learned this statistic from TYFA materials; others found it online. It was a fear parents mentioned often, that, apart from the social isolation and institutional discrimination, the most dangerous place for their child might be within their own inner life. Some parents intentionally sought suicide prevention information, because it took a threat of suicide for them to understand the gravity of their child's distress. Many reported learning about the high rates of suicide when I asked what they found in their initial attempts to locate information on transgender children. These statistics also functioned as powerful tools in advocacy contexts, and both organizations used them frequently. Jerri explained it this way: "Phoebe is just a high-risk kid. She's going to be high-risk for [substance] abuse, self-harm, possibly suicide. She needs a lot of protection." For Jerri, any successful advocate for Phoebe must know and understand these sets of concerns, and she often mentioned them during her negotiations with schools and social services. Ann, mother of fourteen-year-old transboy Patrick, said:

> Some of my friends totally don't get it and then I try to explain to them, look, you know, trans kids are much more likely to commit suicide. You know, the most important thing for any child is to feel loved and accepted, and so I can't just keep telling Patrick he isn't what he says he is.

Ann found mentioning Patrick's inherent vulnerability also served to lessen tension in social situations when faced with peers or other parents who question her choice to affirm Patrick's gender.

Older transgender people, however, voiced concern that these statistics might prove costly in the long run. Jackson, a thirty-one-year-old transmale advocate, worried that the foregrounding of these statistics, which he thinks reflect the more strict social environment faced by older transpeople, might actually increase the incidence of self-harm among trans youth. By providing them with a visible, articulated option for coping with distress that brings with it attention and grief, he thought suicide contagion may be a real issue.

> Look, you know, the day after Donald Trump was elected, there were these parents of trans kids saying that half a dozen kids killed themselves the night before. Like that this was what trans kids do in response to political crisis. And nobody can demonstrate that those numbers are at all true. So, if you're a kid who feels fragile and you go on Facebook and see this, what's that going to tell you about how you should handle your trauma or, like, even your sadness?

The suicidality frame, often used in political advocacy for gays and lesbians, is based on a range of dubious metrics. From the trans surveys that conflate ideation (thinking about something) with attempt (actually trying to accomplish something), to those that simply rehearse the infamous "Gibson Numbers" (a faulty paper that hypothesized without demonstrating that 30 percent of suicides were performed by gay youth), there are no reliable statistics on suicidality for this group. The repetition of these numbers, some warn, may serve more to teach youth that suicidality is a correlate of their trans identity,[18] ultimately exacerbating the problem the numbers are meant to reflect.

The death of seventeen-year-old Leelah Alcorn in 2014, for instance, traveled the internet like wildfire. A transgirl from a conservative Christian household in Ohio, she took her own life by walking out into interstate traffic, after months of rejection by her family.[19] In a suicide note posted online, Alcorn described the rejection and judgment she faced from her parents, who removed her from school, cut her off from contact with the outside world, and sent her for religious conversion therapy.[20] Within forty-eight hours, her suicide note, posted on Reddit, had been shared more than two hundred thousand times.[21] Online petitions emerged urging her parents to use her chosen name on her tombstone[22] and urging politicians to ban conversion therapy.[23] Allies held vigils and memorials across the country and in Europe. Transgender celebrities Laverne Cox, Janet Mock, and Andreja Pejić issued statements about her death.[24] Jill Soloway dedicated her Best Television Series Golden Globe award to Alcorn's memory.[25] For a moment, she was, perhaps, the most famous transperson on the internet.

Jackson worried that the media attention paid to cases like Alcorn's may have the effect not merely of spreading the message of parental acceptance that Alcorn outlined in her suicide note, but also, and unintentionally, of promoting a deadly solution to the trauma that rejection produces.

> I just think that some lonely kid in the middle of nowhere might look at that and say, "Hey, this is one way to connect to other transpeople." Like, if you feel that nobody cares about you, nobody sees or celebrates who you are, this is one way to both be really really seen and to publicly punish the people who hurt you.

Jackson and I talked at length about how complex the issue of suicide has become. Jackson, who lost a close adult transgender friend to suicide several years before we spoke, said he certainly doesn't minimize the very real, very violent cost of social stigmatization. He tries, he said, to hold both in mind at the same time—the losses and the need to project different imagery for the youth who still remain.

FRAMING THE ORGANIZATION, FASHIONING THE SELF

It was sometime in October 2009 when I first realized Stephanie had disappeared. In the months that followed my first experience at Gender Spectrum's annual conference for youth and families, we kept in close touch by email and telephone. She allowed me access to the teen programming during my visit, something she denied other researchers, after which she requested I share some general thoughts on what content might be missing, impressions of how the youth were reacting to different facilitators, or whether I'd heard from children or parents that additional programming was needed on specific issues. These conversations marked a turning point in our relationship; without sacrificing my still fragile and emergent impression of the organization, I was able to contribute something that felt useful to them. We established a sense of reciprocity through my willingness to provide some skilled labor that further cemented their sense of me as an ally. I could tell them that one of the facilitators' overuse of profanity seemed strange, and that some of the youth asked for more programming related to athletics. I could offer my impressions about which presenters were particularly charismatic and which seemed boring.

I felt, finally, that I had earned Stephanie's trust in earnest, and that I was beginning to form some understanding of the internal dynamics of the organization, its self-understandings and the ways it attempted to operationalize them in practice. Mostly what I observed was that the organization took form around Stephanie Brill's charismatic persona, as well as her honed expertise in child development and parenting. As the fall wore into winter, however, she seemed to recede more and more into the background. Joel Baum was taking over the daily operations and conducting more and more of the trainings in schools, utilizing the model they had developed together. Eventually we spoke and she revealed that she had been living with a chronic and degenerative vascular disease for most of her life, which caused her bouts of debilitating illness. She was in the downswing of what would turn out to be the worst episode she'd ever had, and for the remainder of my fieldwork period she would play no more than an occasional advisory role in the daily operations of Gender Spectrum. I felt a tremendous sense of loss in her absence, and these feelings were shared and discussed by the families who had coalesced around the organization. Parents mourned her absence at the following year's conference.

My relationship with Joel Baum developed and deepened as Stephanie receded from the helm of Gender Spectrum. She told me she had handpicked Joel to direct the organization's education efforts the year before. Joel appeared to be in his late thirties. He had an easy, affable demeanor, and I sensed upon meeting him that he was the kind of guy kids love. He was short and stocky, with a long ponytail and thick brown beard. He often wore wrinkled khakis and a T-shirt emblazoned with some sort of political graphic; his favorite depicted a line of Native Americans seated together, bearing the slogan "Homeland Security." I liked him instantly. Both he and Stephanie at different points identified his particular brand of solid yet gentle masculinity as an asset in the work of the organization. "He's relatable to the kids and to the teachers and parents," Stephanie said. But it wasn't merely Joel's presentation of self that suited him to do the work of Gender Spectrum. He had built his prior career in educational contexts, first as a teacher and later as a school administrator. And he had a unique and long background in social justice education. This combination of his gender presentation, experience and expertise in understanding the institutional contexts of schools, and keen sensitivity to social justice aligned closely with Gender Spectrum's focus on professionalization. As I began to shadow Joel, I realized that even though he employed the same sorts of conceptual frameworks and educational tools as Stephanie, his presentation of self transformed the delivery of those messages, as well as the relationship of Gender Spectrum to TYFA and the larger world of organizing around childhood gender nonconformity.

Joel and Kim approached education work in radically different ways. They were not merely different sorts of people; they used different language, explained things differently, cultivated their public presences differently, and ultimately advanced different political arguments for inclusion.

One Saturday afternoon, I looked on as Kim Pearson stood before a roomful of parents and mental health professionals in the meeting room of a church in suburban New Jersey. The space was bright, full of ornate windows, with a tall, domed ceiling. Folding tables lined one wall, with materials, bottles of water, coffee cups, and scattered belongings laid out on them. Members of the congregation and the larger community assembled in rows of pews for a diversity education workshop, organized by the parent of a local middle school child who was beginning transition. Some were there, it seemed, to learn generally about the issue. Some were there to support the family. A few parents sat anxiously in the back, clearly concerned about the presence of the child in their school. When Kim took the stage, she launched into a description of TYFA's organizational mission and the scope of their work. She flashed the organization's vision on the screen behind her: "A world free of suicide and violence in which ALL children are respected and celebrated." She paused and described the breadth of what they're trying to do, using the universalizing language of supporting and nurturing children in their vast diversity, and read aloud TYFA's mission: "TYFA empowers children and families by partnering with educators, service providers and communities, to develop supportive environments in which gender may be expressed and respected." She then described their varied role as experts in childhood gender, their work on behalf of families around the country, and their recent role as consultants for a National Geographic documentary on gender. Finally, she shifted gears into a description of herself. She said, "I am Kim Pearson. I'm a wife and a mother. I've got three kids, nineteen, twenty-one, and twenty-nine. My oldest just completed his second tour of duty in Iraq and is now home safe and sound." There was scattered applause in the room. She continued, "I'm also the grandmother of eleven-month-old twins." She continued to list out her many advocacy roles, as a director of various PFLAG projects and a board member of various LGBT organizations.

Kim oriented herself toward her audience by establishing the credibility and generosity of her organization, which funds its work not through charging fees but through private donations, and by constructing a self that was both relatable and accessible to her intended audience. That image of self was anchored in the work she did as an advocate, but also in her personal roles and wife, mother, and grandmother.

Being with Joel was different. Walking together through the front doors of the Village West School (not its real name), we were greeted by a massive flow of bodies and backpacks wending their way into the crowded corridor and up the stairs to the various classrooms. As we signed in at the front desk we stood watching school-wide announcements and photographs of students from recent plays and sporting events flash across an LCD monitor affixed to the wall above. Beneath the monitor, the wall housed a giant corkboard. A sign pinned across its top read, "Diversity at VWS," and it was scattered with writing and drawings illustrating this idea. Some students described the geographic diversity of their extended family; others described their family's religious affiliation and the foods they consumed in observance of particular holidays. Desserts featured prominently: colomba pasquale, or Italian Easter bread, dense and topped with sugar and almonds; honey cake eaten by some Jews during Rosh Hashanah; kheer, a South Asian sweet rice pudding.

A few minutes later we were greeted by Jess, the school's diversity coordinator. At first I was surprised by the fact that there was a staff person in a small school whose entire charge was creating and maintaining diversity programming for the school, but I soon came to understand that there was much for Jess to coordinate. The West Village School was founded in the early twentieth century by a pioneering feminist educator, steeped in the most radical strands of progressive-era education reform. It considers itself to be a continuing experiment in progressive education, melding community-building projects with classroom instruction. WVS had interest groups for different subcommunities within the school, including meetings for students of color and for parents of students of color, a gay-straight alliance and a group for lesbian and gay parents, as well as parent-run committees charged with creating programming for adopted children, children whose parents have divorced, Asian American families, and many, many more. The school had installed a rigorous diversity curriculum into all of its varied age groups, which it executed through special assemblies, in-class programming, and curriculum-based instruction. Each year, Jess selected a theme for the diversity programming. After doing year-long programs on racial identity and lesbian and gay identities, Jess decided that the current academic year would be devoted to gender diversity. To Jess, gender was one of the many axes along which individual people can vary, and she felt it especially important for students to develop a thoughtful understanding of how stereotypes about boys and girls inform their social interactions.

Jess described to us the rigorous day ahead, which included a workshop for parents, an assembly with several classes in the middle school, and a full high school assembly. At the end of the school day, Joel would run a two-hour continuing education program for teachers and administrators from across the school. Joel wasn't thrilled about the schedule. Typically, he said, he preferred to do multiple visits to a single school, moving from the top of the authority schema downward. First, he liked to talk with school administration, then conduct teacher trainings, then offer a workshop for parents where we can answer questions about his classroom curriculum, and then meet with students in small, classroom-sized groups. He said it cut down on the incidents of parent discomfort and complaints about the material. It became clear fairly rapidly, however, that this was no ordinary school, and these were not ordinary parents.

By 8:45, close to forty-five parents had gathered in the small cafeteria of WVS's middle school. As one might expect, the group consisted of mostly mothers and about three fathers. Some carried paper cups of coffee and breakfast snacks, obtained from the teacher's lounge. Jess greeted the group and introduced the theme of the workshop. Part of an ongoing series called "How to Raise an Ally," this workshop would complement their year-long series of conversations exploring diversity and gender. Joel began by introducing himself. He described his professional experience as a teacher, a school administrator, and a frequent trainer in educational settings throughout California and around the country. He posted a summary of the organization's mission, which read: "Gender Spectrum provides education, training and support to create a more gender-inclusive environment for all children and teens." He outlined his work within a variety of professionalized settings, including educational contexts, medical and mental health provider professional trainings, academic research and policy development, along with parent and family support and Gender Spectrum's annual conference. That morning, he said, they would develop a basic understanding of gender diversity, learn key concepts and terms one needs to fully understand it, and take a look into the perspectives of gender-diverse people and families.

From the start, Joel Baum mobilized a far more professionalized persona than Kim did. He made no mention of the composition of his family or his personal investments in social justice education. During the workshop, although he occasionally shared stories from his work experience, they were never connected to his identity or his personal life. He made frequent mention of his experience in schools, his advocacy in professional contexts, and the work Gender Spectrum does within the medical community. These are his expertise, and the primary way he connected with the materials he taught.

Kim and Joel approached audiences from very different subject positions. Kim mobilized her status as a mother to accrue emotional capital. Joel presented himself as an expert on early childhood education and projected a professional persona that relied less on affect. These were not merely rhetorical tactics: they mirrored differing political priorities, value systems, and ways of talking about gender.

BUILDING A GENDER LEXICON

The interface between advocacy organizations and social institutions was an important place where transmission of evolving cultural understandings of sexuality and gender complexity occurred. Both TYFA and Gender Spectrum directed their varied audiences to develop a nuanced lexicon for identifying and communicating the various components of gender. Kim Pearson called this "learning the lingo." Both organizations constructed tasks to help the audience forge conceptual distinctions between gender and sexual orientation, and between the micro components of social gender: biological sex, gender identity, and gender expression. Kim connected these concepts to personal examples; Joel didn't.

Much as with the ontological distinctions proffered by feminists to delineate social from biological gender, both sets of activists believed that separating out bodies from identities and practices represented a crucial interpretive task for both understanding and accommodating gender nonconformity. It is within this complex gender schema that they placed their initial definitions of transgender and gender nonconforming identities. Yet while both organizations provided their audiences with a more complex gender lexicon, the details varied (see table 4).

TYFA provided a kind of bare-bones ontology, delineating the boundaries between the components of identity and body that require separation for transgender to become a possibility. Kim flashed a set of definitions on a screen before a roomful of parents and social workers and said, "First of all, if we're gonna talk about this stuff, we need to

TABLE 4

Gender Lexicons

Trans Youth Family Allies Gender Lexicon	Gender Spectrum Gender Lexicon
Gender Identity: Who you are	*Binary:* A whole composed of two
Sexual Orientation: Whom you like	*Spectrum:* A broad range of varied but related ideas or objects, the individual features of which tend to overlap so as to form a continuous series or sequence
Gender Expression: What you do, what you wear, and how you act	
Gender Nonconforming: When you run into resistance because you don't fit the expectations of others	*Biological Sex:* Physical anatomy, especially genitalia, typically used to assign gender at birth
Transgender or Trans: An umbrella term used to describe those who challenge social gender norms	*Gender Expression:* Presentation of gender externally to the world (clothing, hairstyle, mannerisms, etc.); roles that individuals play or expectations placed upon them that are associated with assumed gender (behaviors, interests, jobs, styles of play)
Affirmed Female: An individual who was assigned male at birth but identifies as a female	
Affirmed Male: An individual who was assigned female at birth but identifies as a male	*Gender Identity:* Internalized, deeply felt sense of being male, female, both, or neither; who you know yourself to be; may be same or different from gender assigned at birth
	Sexual Orientation: Who do I think is hot? (Attracted to men, attracted to women, bisexual, pansexual, asexual)
	Trans Boy: Child born biologically female but living as a boy.
	Trans Girl: Child born biologically male but living as a girl.
	Gender Nonconforming: Refers to individuals whose behaviors and/or interests fall outside what is considered typical for their assigned sex at birth

SOURCES: Trans Youth Family Allies, "Understanding Through Education" (Presentation, 2011); Gender Spectrum, "Gender and Children" (Presentation, 2011).

know what we're talkin' about. Gender identity is who you are; sexual orientation is who you like. So, I'm Kim, and I'm a woman. That's my gender identity. I like my husband, John, so that's my sexual orientation." Heads in the room nodded in understanding. She continued, "Gender expression is what you do, what you wear, and how you act." She pointed to various pieces of her attire. We were in suburban New Jersey, at a liberal church, so she pointed to her comfortable shoes, her loose-fitting dress, her short and spiky hair. She described the ways in which some parts of her attire are conventionally feminine, yet, particularly in some parts of middle America she visited, elements like her haircut seemed more unusual or out of place. Gender norms, she explained, are contextual. She then offered up definitions of gender variance and transgender. In theory, she made little distinction between gender variance, which she defined as behavior that provokes resistance in others, and transgender, which she situated historically by describing people who, over time, have challenged gender norms and, in some cases, shifted the gender category in which they live.

Gender Spectrum's approach was broader and more ideologically expansive. They, too, utilized particular definitions of biological sex, gender identity, gender expression, and sexuality, but they situated these terms both ideologically and historically. In one presentation for educators at the Village West School, Joel asked participants to think about when and how they knew what their gender was. Explaining biological sex assignment, he then offered up contrasting definitions for the ideas of binary and spectrum, and asked the audience to consider moving from a binary to a spectrum view of gender. The Gender Spectrum glossary included a tripartite scheme, comprising biology, identity, and expression. Understanding how the spectrum works, Joel explained, required an ability to see the three major indicia of gender as variables that can occur in various combinations (see table 5).

Joel described these various permutations by bringing in cross-cultural examples. He screened a short film for middle schoolers about Indonesia, depicting a culture with five established gender categories.

TABLE 5

Gender Spectrum Model of Gender Diversity

Biological Sex	Gender Identity	Gender Expression	Label
Male	Male	Masculine	Traditionally gendered boy
Female	Female	Feminine	Traditionally gendered girl
Female	Female	Masculine	"Tomboy"
Male	Male	Feminine	"Sissy," "girlyboy," "homo," "faggot," brave
Male	Female	Feminine	Transgender girl
Male	Female	Masculine	Also transgender girl
Female	Male	Masculine	Transgender boy
Female	Male	Feminine	Also transgender boy

He also presented examples from different animal species: red and gray kangaroos and wallabies, which have both boy and girl parts to their bodies; male bighorn sheep that act like females for the sake of group harmony; hermaphroditic snails; pregnant male seahorses; and clownfish that actually change their gender.

TELLING FAMILY STORIES

Both organizations used the stories of individual families to humanize and concretize the intellectual work they did with their audiences. But they did this in vastly different ways. Kim Pearson peppered her theoretical remarks with stories about her son and the other families for whom she advocated. Joel and Stephanie, who rarely made use of themselves as referents, partnered with a filmmaker to develop a series of short films they routinely screened in their workshops. One, *I'm Just Anneke*, follows a Canadian family through their first visit to receive hormone blockers. Another, *The Parent Journey*, profiles parents of several gender nonconforming and transgender children, who discuss their respective processes of realizing, coming to terms with, and eventually facilitating their child's identity.

I'm Just Anneke profiles twelve-year-old Anneke and her family as they describe their process of coming to understand her gender. Anneke's mother, Nicole, speaks about her daughter's inexplicable depression as a young child of four, her adamant rejection of dresses, the way she identified with and played with boys throughout her childhood, only to be ostracized by them as they approached their teenage years. Nicole exhibits a sense of certainty that Anneke's gender is different, even if the family remains unsure how precisely she will identify as an adult. Nicole recognizes Anneke's ability to resist the conformity pressures of adolescence, which was very different from her own experience. "I wanted to wear the clothes everyone else wore, to listen to the music everyone else listened to. It was all about fitting in. […] And for Anneke, it's never been about that. She lives the consequences of not fitting in." Anneke herself is soft spoken and upbeat. She plays hockey, has a sturdy frame, and dresses like a typical athletic kid. It would be easy at a quick glance to assume she is a preadolescent boy. Early in the film, Anneke and Nicole arrive at British Columbia Children's Hospital to receive her monthly Lupron shot. Her mother explains, "It buys Anneke time to decide where she is in that fluid place, whether it's a male place or a female place." Anneke herself appears unsure what the outcome of that process will be, but the audience is left with a sense that her parents will welcome and honor whatever self-realizations Anneke has.

The Family Journey is an assemblage of interview footage of ten parents, two siblings, and one gender-fluid child as they discuss their challenges, acceptance, and celebration of gender nonconforming children. The film begins by depicting many of the same sorts of struggles the parents I interviewed related, including emotional distress and misdiagnosis by psychiatrists. One mother explains of her trans son, "It always felt like he was fighting something. Fighting life. Fighting, fighting. Never quite able to fit in. He was bullied. He was rejected. He was marginalized." These parents mention attempts to discuss their child's gender, to mitigate the severity of it, to understand. Another mother describes looking on the internet and finding the term *gender variance*. Her eyes become visibly misty as she says, "That gave me so much peace. You know, like yeah, this is something that's out there, that other kids actually experience." Parents describe relief at finally being able to identify the source of the distress their children experience, tinged with worry about the reception they will get from family and friends. One African American father relates his concerns to his own experience growing up in a predominantly white neighborhood and not wanting his child to have those same feelings of difference.

Another father, clearly in pain, says, "We gradually evolved to accepting that the change was as profound as considering our son ... might now be our daughter. I still ... have a hard time saying that word .... in relation to her. It's easier to use a female pronoun than to use the word *daughter*." These are clearly parents in struggle. "In every other relationship there are conditions. The parent-child relationship is the only one in which you must have unconditional love." Yet while there is struggle, tolerance, and acceptance, there is also celebration. The father who struggles with the word *daughter* says, "My child is a pioneer. She didn't choose to be, she just is. [...] My child is going to be some sort of force in the world. And I'm lucky enough to be connected to that. And this may be the most important thing I do in this life ... is to be parent to this child."

These films did significant political and discursive work for Gender Spectrum. First, they projected a vast array of parents puzzling and struggling through the same material they ask the audience to grapple with, but from a personal perspective. They allowed for the kinds of identificatory processes to emerge between the viewers and those parents whom Kim Pearson actively cultivates with her presentation of self. They also allowed for those identifications to happen, while still maintaining distance between Joel as expert and the real people whose lives are the topic of discussion. They had a humanizing power. Anneke is a tremendously compelling protagonist, navigating the cringe-worthy minefields of adolescence, friendships, and changing bodies with a sweet, quiet awkwardness. The parents depicted in *The Family Journey* display a vast range of emotions, from delight, to love, to deep sadness, worry, and fear. The audience, in turn, is invited to share their uneasiness, to struggle or test the material along with the parents, while still being in the discussion. Rhetorically, these films function in concert to provide both an opportunity for the audience to imagine themselves confronted with the challenge of supporting a child like Anneke and a diverse set of models for what facilitative parenting can look like in all of its emotional complexity.

CONCLUSION

When I first encountered them, Gender Spectrum and TYFA were young organizations in an active process of self-invention. Both had charismatic leadership, well-honed expertise, and demonstrated efficacy in bringing the realities of life for children and families into public view. Yet they were formed from and functioned within vastly different personal, geographical, and epistemological frameworks. Gender Spectrum had clear ties to LGBT and queer organizing; TYFA emerged from the accidental activism of a group of mothers with little or no preexisting relationship to issues of sexual or gender rights. The families they worked with formed alliances to one organization or the other, sometimes moving between the two as they labored to determine which framework best suited the needs of their child and their unique social environment.

The divergent origin narratives and intellectual orientations of the two organizations connected in meaningful ways to the individual identities and life histories of their founding members. Stephanie's long history of queer activist work, along with her failure to obtain the active support and participation of mainstream transgender rights organizations, influenced her organizational approach. Gender Spectrum framed its expertise in the language of social justice education more broadly, rather than positioning itself as an organization founded by a parent. Stephanie, in the handful of public speaking events I witnessed, never once mentioned her child or family. This presentation of self also influenced the way Joel communicated with the audiences to which he spoke. The clear ties Gender Spectrum had to LGBT communities and social movements framed their expansive vision for uniting the work of advocating for gender nonconforming youth to larger goals of transforming and loosening the restrictive gender system as a whole. The nuanced lexicon they offered for understanding and communicating about gender reflected the expansiveness of this vision. They did the emotional work of communicating family stories not through personal narrative, but through screening videos of children and families with whom they had worked. In this way, they were able to shore up their professional authority without the risk of losing the efficacy of their message to concerns about their presentations of self.

Kim Pearson foregrounded her son's transgender identity and her process of coming to understand, support, and advocate for him. She frequently took the temperature of the room around her, looking for cues about the identities and subjectivities of her audience, and whether they were connecting or rejecting her message. She fashioned a presentation of self that, while always based in the facts of her life, tailored closely to her perceptions of the social context she entered. In this way, she was able to create an emotional and relational container for the challenging work of helping audiences to understand what transgender is and why a parent might choose to affirm the transgender identity of a young child. Her own subjective experience of pain around the loss of cofounder Carla's son Jack informed discussions of suicide and the danger faced by these youth. But hers was a story anchored in gender normativity, that of a parent of a child who just wanted to be a boy. It was a story that entreated its audience not to abandon their categories, but merely to open the gates to allow a few more members inside. This was a cisgender perspective on transgender rights.

This was not accidental. TYFA was trying to gain recognition for trans kids *as boys or girls.* The end goal was assimilation into dyadic gender categories. The plea was for a kind of normality, a world in which transgender children were boys or girls just like other boys or girls. Gender Spectrum was aiming for something different. Joel and Stephanie both wanted to expand gender options for all children, to create room, on an institutional level, for newer forms of gender to proliferate, to degender structures and curricula and to erode the entrenched distinctions between boy and girl. The stakes of this difference felt high to each activist. They believed that one could only argue for one worldview a time. In a zero sum game of social change, transgender and gender nonconforming children were placed on opposing sides of a common problem.

But before we conclude that Gender Spectrum was fundamentally different, it's important to note that they, too, had a conflicted relationship with adult transgender organizations and activists. Both Kim and Stephanie communicated that they understood today's transgender children to be having fundamentally different experiences of their identities than those had by older transpeople; and I observed both of them, at different times, make deliberate efforts to edit the exposure the children had to the forms of adult transgender identities with which they assumed children would disidentify. In some ways, the very idea of transgender to which these youth were exposed was a sanitized version of an adult community's history, whitewashed of some of its traumatic and painful past. Echoing the efforts individual parents made to model specific forms of gender nonconformity to individual children, these activists and organizations labored to present their own normative models for the sort of transgender community into which they hoped these children would emerge. This work, and the intergenerational tensions it signaled, suggests that this new movement for gender liberation may have more normative investments than prior iterations have had.

Older transgender adults initially resisted the efforts of the parent activists and advocates who first began agitating for support from schools and doctors in the late 1990s and early 2000s, fearing political repercussions from the public endorsement of social transition for young children. While many have since come out in support of gender nonconforming children and their families, trans adults must cope with the deeply different trajectories and life chances of the smallest gender outlaws. Some of these children may elect to be stealth as adults; some may never identify openly as transgender; many will never go through their natal puberties or retain childhood memory books filled with pictures that don't mirror their gender identities as adults. For these reasons, this new generation may have wider latitude to disidentify with transgender history, and with those who came before them.

If the work of social change is indeed embodied in "moments when agency explodes structure," then TYFA and Gender Spectrum were doing the work of social change. They lobbied for the inclusion of transgender children into the gender categories with which they identified, and insisted that institutions like schools and churches accommodate their gender in the daily course of their routines. And they were often successful. Because adults speak on behalf of children in the realm of politics, because the gendered gaze always expands beyond a singular object, because we believe that adults determine much of who children are, Kim, Stephanie, and Joel all mobilized the best gendered selves they imagined would legitimate their credibility. This movement for transgender children is innately a movement by non-transgender adults, aimed at non-transgender adults. What of trans culture as adults know it will be lost to this discourse remains to be seen.

CHAPTER FIVE

Anxiety and Gender Regulation

Yvonne thinks she began disappointing her mother the moment she was born. She's never been much like her seven siblings, all of whom, according to Yvonne, are pretty typical, "straight-arrow people. [...] And then there's me." Yvonne stands about five feet nine inches tall and appears younger than her twenty-eight years. She's incredibly striking—a thin, African American woman with an immaculately rendered Mohawk haircut, multiple piercings, tattoos, and stylish, offbeat clothing. When she began allowing her four-year-old child, Raine, to wear dresses and skirts at home, she explained to her mother, a devout Baptist, that she had done a great deal of research and was beginning to think that Raine might be transgender. The conversation didn't go well. Her mother began to scream, asking Yvonne how she could "do that" to her child. She told Yvonne that Raine's gender confusion was clearly a result of Yvonne's poor parenting. "She said, 'You have pretty much murdered your child. You are a murderer.'"

For Yvonne, these comments were painful, but she was even more heartbroken to learn that her mother proceeded to discuss the matter with Yvonne's brother, sisters, and father. Although they all initially voiced support for her parenting choices, over the next weeks she began to feel increasingly isolated from her family. Conversations were tense.

Phone calls stopped coming in. One afternoon, not long after the conversation with her mother, Yvonne received a phone call from Child Protective Services informing her that her mother had called the police and reported Yvonne for child abuse. They immediately launched an investigation. On the day the children's services liaison arrived at their house, Raine was running around, prancing and playing with her brother, dressed in full princess regalia. Ironically, Yvonne reports, her mother didn't specify the nature of the abuse she was reporting, so the liaison just assumed the child dressed as a princess was a biological girl. She scanned Yvonne's modest but well-ordered home, watched her children interact for a few minutes, and then left without incident. Not so easily deterred, Yvonne's mother hired a private attorney and sued Yvonne for custody, alleging "coercion to brainwash a minor." Aided by interventions from other family members and with the support of Kim Pearson and TYFA, they eventually settled the matter privately, and Yvonne retained full custody of her children. Still, she remained both incredulous and very frightened that what she saw as an insignificant, everyday parenting choice, allowing Raine to wear a dress, could be framed as of the kind of poor parenting against which the state offers safeguards. She remained sad and angry about her mother's betrayal and the risk it posed to the continued unity of her family. She felt less certain now about whom in her life she could trust.

Yvonne's experience was not unique. When parents decided to facilitate public expressions of gender nonconformity in their children, be it by providing them with the clothing or toys of their choice, openly discussing their child's evolving identity with peers or professionals, or even seeking gender-confirming medical care, they opened their families up to social disapproval, ostracism, and, in extreme cases, interventions by the state. While stories like Yvonne's traveled through social networks, precisely how and when these formal and informal sanctions occurred was unpredictable. What one person considered a private, individual parenting choice, a neighbor or teacher might consider evidence of abuse. And it took only one anonymous telephone call to trigger an investigation by children's services. In a context of fear and uncertainty, acutely aware of their vulnerability to both institutional and interpersonal sanction, parents engaged in affective and social practices to mitigate the risk of intrusion by others. These efforts created a climate of hyperalertness within families, leading some parents to enforce versions of normative gender expression in children they would otherwise, and in private often did, allow far more leeway for transgression. Parents became proxy regulators of their children, simultaneously reproducing the logics of social institutions while attempting to insulate their families from actual formal regulation.[1]

While parents largely voiced disapproval of the social gender norms against which their children's identities pushed, and while many took active pains not to enforce those rules in private, a good number of parents constructed different sets of rules for their child's public life than they maintained within the walls of their homes.[2] Some children had different sets of clothing for home and school; others were instructed by their parents not to speak about their gender identities with others or to keep portions of their histories private. Parents did these things not because they believed them to be valid or even desirable actions, but rather because they feared and wished to protect their children from the negative consequences of visible deviance, which they imagined might range from simple social disapproval to major legal sanction. Because parents perceived the threats to be multiple and shifting, they also worked to become experts in defending themselves against the state. They compiled formal records of their child's gender history and documents evaluating their parenting practices, and sometimes they even left or abandoned particular institutions, communities, or social environments altogether. Formal institutional regulation didn't affect families with equal force. Only a minority experienced direct policing by the state, interventions into their family life, or removal of their gender nonconforming children by social service agencies. Yet in a context of tremendous uncertainty, many families feared and prepared for such forms of regulation, even when they seemed unlikely.

A PECULIAR VULNERABILITY

Kim Pearson didn't introduce me to Christine right away. It wasn't until we'd established a close rapport, in my second year of interviewing at Philly TransHealth, that she walked up to me in the lobby looking sober and said, "You know, you really should interview Christine. We had to smuggle her out of town in the middle of the night." I sensed when I approached Christine to introduce myself that she was walking a difficult path. She was lingering at the back of the pack of mothers that surrounded the TYFA table. She seemed nervous to meet me, shifting her weight back and forth between her feet as we talked. But she also said right away she felt that telling her story would be important. "And," she added, "if Kim thinks you're okay, that's all I need to know. I'd do whatever Kim asked me to do."

Christine was working as a special education teacher in a remote rural area in the Deep South when she adopted three children five years ago. Emmy, the middle child, was three at the time. The very first day they spent with her was in her special education classroom, and she remembered a co-teacher commenting that Emmy (who was at that time living and presenting as a boy) would be gay. Emmy chose only girls' toys and dress-up clothes; she colored everything pink. Although her gender behavior seemed extreme to her co-teachers, Christine gave it little thought. There were other issues that seemed far more pressing. Christine was told by children's services that the three children had suffered serious abuse at the hands of previous caretakers. They arrived at school starving, with giant potbellies swollen from lack of food. They suffered from emotional problems, their language was underdeveloped, and they struggled to communicate. They hoarded food, hiding it in every conceivable place in the house. They lacked basic skills like toilet training and eating at a dinner table. And they looked and acted terrified.

Christine said she fell in love with them instantly because despite their many hardships, they had "fighting spirits." They were sweet and endearing one moment, mean and demanding the next, which

Christine interpreted as a sign of resilience. Her first months with the children were spent trying to make them feel secure. After finding left-over macaroni and cheese hidden beneath the couch cushions, she began giving them packaged food to hide around the house. She took each of them for psychological testing and therapy. She enrolled them in school. Within a few weeks, Emmy's gender behavior became an issue in preschool. Christine was called into school by a teacher who insisted she explain to Emmy that princess costumes were for girls, pirate costumes for boys, and that the expectation in the classroom was that Emmy make the correct selection. Christine said Emmy simply stayed away from the dress-up corner from that point forward.

Over the next two years, while Emmy seemed able to conform her gender behavior to the preferences of her teachers and peers, she also became increasingly sullen, angry, and oppositional. She withdrew from activities and relationships; peers began targeting her for teasing and bullying. Christine assumed the shift in Emmy's behavior was just another byproduct of her traumatic past. She worked with Emmy in many different ways to help her assimilate socially. During this time, Emmy would often tell Christine she thought she had "girl hands," or that she wished she was a girl. It wasn't until Emmy was eight that Christine realized just how great Emmy's distress actually was.

There was one day in particular Christine would never forget. Christine and her family shared a home that sat carport to carport against Christine's sister's home, on a plot of land that had once belonged to their father. Christine's sister had four children, and the rambunctious clan of cousins played together regularly. That day, Emmy came home from school unusually upset. From what Christine could glean from her conversation with the children, Emmy told one of her cousins that she didn't understand why she couldn't be a girl. She recounted:

My sister has one daughter who's just [...] there's no boundaries on this child. She said, "I know why you can't be a girl!" And she pulled her pants off, lay down on the floor, spread her legs out wide, and said, "You see? Boys have a penis. Girls have a big black hole, and you don't have a big black hole, so you can't be a girl." And apparently up until then Emmy had thought everyone on the planet had a penis. Everybody. And so part of the confusion was why are you making me be something different when I'm exactly the same as you and I'm exactly the same as her and I'm exactly the same as that one. That's why the, you know, "I have girl hands, I have a girl voice." All that stuff, just trying to express herself.

Later that afternoon, Christine noticed that Emmy had been locked in the bathroom for a long time and went in to check on her. She was shocked by what she saw.

I went to check and I knocked on the door and she had gotten a big kitchen knife and hidden it under her clothes and had gone in there and she was going to make herself a big black hole so she could be a girl. Fortunately, she's very squeamish about blood, so she didn't get but just a couple tiny little cuts in, not a lot, enough to make my heart drop and die but not enough to really hurt her any—it bleeds a lot down there. Anyway, that was a moment, and I knew that if someone wants to be a girl that badly, a child who's scared of pain, who's scared of blood, who can't get the least little boo-boo without climbing on my lap for two hours . . .

In that moment, she said, everything changed. She took the knife from Emmy and locked it away in a cupboard. She sat down, pulled Emmy into her lap, held her, and began asking her questions. Emmy replied, "Mom I'm just really a girl . . . I have a girl mind, and I have a girl heart. I have girl hands and a girl voice and I draw girl pictures and I play girl games, but I can't ever be a girl because I have a penis." Christine asked Emmy if she wanted to be a girl. Emmy replied immediately, "Oh yeah."

It was as if she had opened floodgates. They sat together for hours that afternoon, and Emmy confided to her mother all the things she'd been hiding—her pain, confusion, desires. Christine was completely overwhelmed. While she noticed an almost immediate shift in Emmy's behavior and mood, virulent tensions erupted with her husband as she began to allow Emmy to dress in more feminine clothing. Christine made frantic calls to mental health facilities across the state, and finally received a referral to a doctoral student studying gender development. Although this woman wasn't licensed to see patients clinically, Christine drove over an hour and a half to meet her at a fast food restaurant in the closest large city.

It took Christine several more meetings and phone calls to find a therapist who would work with Emmy. She began driving four and a half hours each way weekly to meet with a psychologist referred by a member of the TYFA online list. Christine and her therapist felt certain that Emmy was in a delicate psychological state, and Christine felt she needed to allow Emmy to continue to dress in girl's clothing. She set up a meeting with the principal, under whom she had worked for over a decade, to strategize about how the school would manage Emmy's gender going forward. The backlash was swift and severe, and it caught Christine by surprise. The same day they met, she received her first harassing phone call. The next day, she began noticing that fellow teachers weren't answering the phone when she called. Later that week, she forgot her keys at home, and the school janitor ignored her request that he unlock her classroom. She drove home that afternoon and noticed missed calls on her answering machine. A moment later, the phone rang. A voice on the other end called her a sicko and told her that Emmy was "going to hell." Over the next few days, the calls became more regular, and more specific. Voices on the other end threatened physical harm to Christine and to Emmy. They threatened to abduct her other two children.

> I must've been out of my mind, because at this point I'm still convinced that we can do this. It's gonna be rough, we might have to go to a different school in the county, but we can still make this work with some training and appropriate enforcement of the no bullying policy.

Christine's next move was to set up a meeting with the school superintendent, a woman who once described Christine as "the best special education teacher she'd ever seen." She felt certain their long professional relationship would predispose the superintendent to support Emmy. As she entered the building, she noticed a line of other parents outside her door, none of whom would look at or speak to her. She realized they were also there to discuss Emmy. She began fearing not only for her job, but for her safety. Over the next three weeks, a kind of "mob mentality" took over the small town. The phone kept ringing. Cars would idle outside the house for hours at a time. Christine wouldn't let the children play outdoors. She began keeping an unloaded shotgun beside the front door and a magazine of bullets in her pocket. Although Christine hated having it in plain view of the children, she quickly realized her instincts were correct. One night, as the children slept, a neighbor broke into Christine's house, and she chased him away with the shotgun, petrified he would discover it was unloaded.

The following day Christine received a call from an acquaintance she trusted asking her to come over. When she arrived, he sat her down, begged her to listen carefully, and told her that he'd been privy to a conversation among a group of men in the town, some of whom she thinks may have been part of a local chapter of the Ku Klux Klan, in which they planned in some detail Emmy's abduction and brutal murder. Christine says she was dumbfounded. "I just couldn't accept what he was saying. [...] It wasn't real. I mean, this can't be real. This is America! It was 2009! These things don't happen!" She left his house and drove to her church. When she confided to her pastor what she had been told and by whom, he advised her to go home, pack quickly, leave, and never return. As she departed, he handed her some money.

Christine drove home in a daze, packed a few boxes of clothing, loaded her children into the car, and drove away. For the next month they stayed in a succession of motels. Christine barely slept. She kept watch over the children at night and drove during the day. She occasionally stayed with relatives or close friends who lived out of town. A chain of trusted people would pass messages back and forth between Christine and her increasingly estranged husband. A week or so after she left town, her husband found the family dog, a beautiful standard poodle, strung up on wires from a tree outside their home. He had four broken legs and had been gutted and left to bleed to death. Attached to the body was a written warning that a similar fate was planned for Emmy. Over the next weeks, he reported the constant surveillance of their house by townspeople. She simply couldn't return.

When we met, over a year later, Christine and her children lived in a trailer park on the outskirts of a major U.S. city. Christine had been unable to work as a teacher since she left home because she feared that potential employers conducting background checks might disclose her location to her former employers. She struggled to find a dentist and pediatrician willing to treat children with no medical records and a school willing to enroll students with no school records. She thought she was in trouble with the Internal Revenue Service because she was unable to acquire tax paperwork on some rental properties she owned in her hometown. She buried her face in her hands and sighed, "I own a dozen houses, and I live in a trailer. [...] I was salutatorian in high school. I graduated in the top 5 percent in college, and I'm living in a trailer park doing nothing. It just kills me."

Christine suffered from terrible insomnia. Her heart raced when her phone rang with an unfamiliar number. She had been diagnosed with PTSD. She and her husband had separated. While he denounced her publicly so he could maintain a life in their town, he did transfer to her the monetary allowance provided by the state for her children, and occasionally drove to visit them. She and her children had acclimated to their new life, even though it was radically different in almost every way from everything they knew. Emmy remained totally stealth in school. Only the principal and assistant principal knew she was transgender. Christine said, "I wonder a lot ... I hear about other families where the kid can be out, and they can be free, and they can be themselves, and I want that so badly for Emmy. But I'm just scared to death that something is going to happen to her. I'm scared every day."

Only a few people in the TYFA network could pair the story of Christine's exile with Christine herself, but many spoke about it in generalities. Spread from person to person in vague references to the mother of three who was chased from her hometown at gunpoint because her child was transgender, Christine's was one of several such frightening accounts that circulated among the parents in support groups and at conferences. Kim mentioned the story in trainings for mental health providers and sometimes in conversations with people she hoped would support TYFA monetarily. Her introduction of Christine to me was somewhat hyperbolic, I came to realize. Kim and TYFA did not squirrel Christine away; she had done that hard work herself. But that didn't change the sense of importance Christine placed on that connection, or Kim's sense of investment in Christine. They understood themselves to have a common project. Kim spoke of Christine often and with great emotion. Christine, however, stayed largely silent in family gatherings. While she desperately needed both emotional and material support, she let very few people know who she was or where she and her children lived. She never spoke publicly about her experiences, fearing that men from her hometown were still hunting for her family.

Christine didn't carry her fear alone. It became dispersed throughout the community with each successive retelling. In moments when parents ritualistically indoctrinated new families into the community, or when growing close to other parents whose children shared experiences or identity characteristics, the telling and retelling of stories like Christine's cemented certain affective bonds between parents, a sense of shared vulnerability and tenacity. Some parents used these stories to impress upon their extended family and community members the severity of their need for support. Others measured their own smaller rejections against more catastrophic tales, taking comfort that things in their lives weren't worse. Storytelling was one of the ways communities of parents first transmitted, and then collectively managed, the trauma suffered by some of its members.[3] It also made clear the risks attendant to facilitating a child's gender nonconforming expression in public. And while many families moved through their children's transitions with only minor incidents of social disapproval, others faced formidable challenges.

I quickly came to understand that the single most pernicious residue of traumatic experiences, most particularly those that involve the state, was a persistent sense of always being watched, forever at risk. It took very little to trigger an investigation by children's services. A single anonymous phone call was often enough. And indeed, a surprising number of families I met faced administrative inquiries by the state into their parenting. From my first efforts to recruit families to participate in this project, parents pulled me aside to describe their interactions with social services agencies, local law enforcement, and Child Protective Services (CPS). I spoke in depth with over a dozen families who faced investigations by CPS related to their child's gender. Most of these families declined to do formal interviews, for fear that any recognizable detail of their case that appeared in print might open them up to further scrutiny. Two families who sat for interviews (one who had had physical custody of their child terminated by the state for a period of time) later apologetically withdrew their consent for the publication of interview material at the urging of attorneys representing them in suits against schools or the state child welfare agency. Both of these families were multiracial, poor, and living in rural areas. The shuttering sense of precarity these parents experienced made it nearly impossible to speak publicly about what they felt to be unjust, injurious intervention by the state. Even those whose investigations resolved quickly were muted by concerns about protecting their child's privacy. Indeed, the more violent they felt the intrusion was, the stricter their silence. Christine was a notable exception.

The legal and social privileges we commonly associate with the heterosexual nuclear family (which include the right to be free from state intervention into the private sphere) were unevenly distributed.[4] Formal state regulation was more prevalent among families with black children, those with a gay or lesbian parent, and adoptive families with preexisting relationships of surveillance with the state. While predictive measures or prevalence estimates are impossible to generate in this community,[5] a striking number of the gay- and lesbian-headed households I met faced direct interventions by child welfare agencies. The nature and extent of the follow-ups differed by family composition in noteworthy ways.

Sean Murphy, a forty-four-year-old single gay father of adopted siblings Michael and Alessandra, was among the few parents willing to share his experience of a formal investigation with me.[6] Two years before we sat down to talk, Sean and Michael had begun discussing Michael's gender issues with their family therapist, although Michael had been adamant about his clothing and pronoun preferences for some time before that. Their many conversations over the next twelve months, along with the increasing certainty on the part of both Sean and Michael's therapist about the persistence of Michael's male identity, led them to seek information from a local LGBT health clinic. It was there that they first learned about Lupron and puberty suppression.

Sean described that moment as a paradigm shift in his understanding of what Michael's gender demanded from him as a parent.

> I was just sort of living with it, right? "This is how [she] is; she's more like a boy than girl." Okay. I didn't really think about it terms of, "This is a process we now have to manage." Right? And then after meeting with [the doctor] I started to get the idea that it was. But even then I didn't fully get it. Like, "What do you mean, you want to inject my kid with something called Lupron?" And, "Why would we do that?" It's one thing to help her psychologically; it's another thing to start injecting her with something that might alter her body.

Sean spent time with his physician and psychiatrist working through his complicated thoughts and feelings, and in the fall of that year he made an appointment with a pediatric endocrinologist at the local children's hospital to get general information about medical options, in anticipation of Michael's impending puberty.

His appointment was scheduled for January. Sean and the children spent their holiday with their extended family. Sean recalled feeling exhausted that winter. It had been a difficult fall for both children, and the depth and consistency of the emotional work that parenting and therapy had demanded from Sean had taken its toll. At the insistence of his family therapist, he scheduled a few days of child-free relaxation time in Mexico during the first week of January. The children stayed at home, watched over by Sean's sister and his closest friend.

Sean was headed back home the day before their appointment at the university hospital when he received an email message from Michael's school advising him that Child Protective Services had removed Michael from class to interview him. Sean was shocked and terrified, and he immediately flew into action. He called the school, his friend who was watching the children, the social worker involved in his case, and the family therapist. Nobody had any information about why children's services was at Michael's school or why the interview was happening.

Sean's first clue came in a message from the pediatric endocrinologist at the university hospital, confirming that "no matter what [Sean] may have heard," his appointment for the following day would take place. Both the message from the doctor and the content puzzled Sean. He finally reached the CPS investigator, who told him that he was under investigation for forcing his child to undergo a sex change operation. "It was incredible," Sean said, becoming more animated.

The conversation went like this. I said, "First of all, how is that physically possible? Like, how could you force a child to have a sex change operation? What surgeon in the United States is gonna perform a sex change operation on an eleven-year-old kid? At all!" And I said, "Second of all, I'm in Mexico. Third of all, if I were trying to surreptitiously force my child to have a sex change operation, why would I make an appointment at [a university hospital] to come in and find out about how this all works? Like, wouldn't I try to hide it?" "We don't know; we just know that a mandated reporter made a report." "Well, who made a report?" "We can't tell you that." I said, "I don't get it, all we did ... " I said, "We didn't even make the appointment at [the hospital], a health clinic doctor did. They're the ones that suggested we go." I said, "Did you pull her out of class and ask her about her gender identity?" "Well, yes, sir, we did." I said, "You are telling me you yanked my child out of class," and I said, "you know what, I don't mean to be rude, but I didn't fall off a truck yesterday," I said, "You're picking on the wrong guy." I said, "I don't know what you think you're doing. But I'm flying back tonight, I will be in there tomorrow."

Sean became increasingly agitated as he recounted this story. He paced back and forth as he spoke. Realizing he had begun to shout, he paused, took a deep breath and sat down again. He explained that for Michael, the interview itself was likely a traumatic event. Michael had lived with several foster families before Sean adopted him, and interviews by CPS typically preceded his formal removal from one family and transfer to another. So Sean was acutely aware that being pulled out of class to be interviewed by CPS likely signaled to Michael that he was about to lose his family. And Sean was hundreds of miles away.

Sean boarded the plane a bundle of nervous energy. When he arrived back in the United States, there were several new voicemail messages from the pediatric endocrinologist. The story was becoming clearer:

"Mr. Murphy, we just found out one of the older doctors here who wasn't even assigned to your case found the fax that you were coming in for gender identity issues and potentially Lupron for your daughter and made some assumptions about you as a gay man, and he reported you to CPS. You have to understand, we don't treat transgender children here, so maybe he didn't know what was going on, but he didn't even understand the referral, and he's reported you to CPS. But don't worry, we put a kibosh on the whole thing."

Sean shook his head. "So I get back and I'm like, well, at least the head of pediatric endocrinology doesn't think that I'm some gay guy trying to change his kid into a boy so that I could have sex with him. I mean, this is what this doctor [who made the report] thought! We're talking about an educated endocrinologist in [a major city], okay?" In subsequent conversations, Sean learned that the endocrinologist who had reported him somehow discovered that Sean was gay, and on the basis of his homosexuality and the fact that he had gone to Mexico had conjured up a fantastical image of Sean's promiscuity and propensity for child sexual abuse, the only explanation for deviant gender behavior that doctor could imagine.

Of the eight gay- or lesbian-headed families who remained among my interviewees, half faced some inquiry into their family life. (Three were the targets of actual investigations, and one parent inadvertently learned a formal complaint had been filed but never received notice of any investigation.) This is a notably high proportion. Far fewer of the heterosexual parents had these experiences. These numbers suggest that lesbian and gay parents face increased scrutiny when their children depart from gender norms. Homophobia in their surrounding communities expresses itself in accusations of abuse, linking abuse to both the parent's sexuality and the child's gender.

For Sean, the following days passed in a blur of phone calls to the Transgender Law Center, the ACLU, and the entire team of experts Sean had so meticulously assembled to aid him in caring for Michael. He instinctively knew that the more expert power he had behind him, the more likely he was to successfully defend himself against the mounting investigation. He secured the legal representation of a national advocacy organization. He interviewed the CPS worker. He contacted the hospital and was able to secure a letter of retraction from the physician who initially incited the investigation. He threatened a lawsuit. He had his children's teachers, their principal, their other doctors and therapists all calling the CPS worker to defend Sean. The university hospital responded quickly, retracting the complaint. The accusing doctor called Sean and apologized.

By the following week, Sean had managed to get the CPS ombudsman involved. They agreed to halt the investigation. Sean realized fairly quickly, however, that a great deal of information about Michael's gender identity now resided in the electronic database monitored by the state in which they live. When we met, Sean was still, months later, struggling to have the investigation expunged from his family's record. Sean says he never expected he'd have to fight this battle: "I figured I'd have to protect him from bullies at school, not from doctors and social workers! It's a peculiar kind of vulnerability." He paused. "I think that while I will never ever, ever say that I'm happy that what happened with CPS happened, *ever,* it certainly prepared me for how much I was going to have to protect my son and people like him in ways that I had never even dreamed of." Sean said he thinks his family's experience had some payoff. He concluded, "I think [that doctor's] life will be forever different. I think that department of pediatric endocrinology will be forever different."

In our five-hour interview, and in my subsequent communications with Sean (most of which involved my attempts to deepen our relationship and Sean unceremoniously blowing me off, telling me he was too busy), I was struck by his no-nonsense demeanor. He never minced words or lubricated conversations with unnecessary commentary. Even as I felt his agitation, it was clear that he felt both entitled to and effective at fighting state bureaucracies. Many other parents lacked his assertiveness and, I suspect, had more trouble deflecting complaints by others. Yet even with the armor and artillery his entitlement provided him, the affective echo of fear pervaded the room. It was palpable.

Penny had less of a sense of entitlement, so she enlisted some help. Penny and I had several telephone conversations before she agreed to be interviewed. I could hear in her voice, from the start, the tension she felt between fear for the safety of her child and family and the desire to participate in the project. She wanted to talk, and believed that her story would be instructive for potential readers. I remained fairly passive in our early conversations, inviting her participation without exerting any pressure, and tried to reassure her that I would protect her family's anonymity as best I could. After our third conversation and some subsequent talks with her two co-parents, Penny agreed to go on record.

Penny was a thirty-three-year-old white lesbian living in a suburban community on the West Coast. Penny, along with her then partner, Pam, and her ex-partner, Sophie, raised and cared for their nine-year-old transgender child, Delia. Delia always required special attention; she had a significant hearing impairment and multiple serious food allergies. School had always been a fraught environment for Delia. Penny recounted years of daily struggle to coax Delia to get dressed in the morning, arguments and protestations over leaving the house, and urgent departures from her classrooms at the end of the day. Penny described Delia literally tripping over her own feet and falling to the cement in the parking lot, in her efforts to propel her body away from the school building as quickly as possible. When Delia began talking with her mother about feeling like a girl, what Penny previously understood as separation anxiety and a dislike of school came into focus as something entirely distinct.

> [Delia] would say things like, "I don't want to be the dragon. I don't want to be the daddy. I don't want to be the king. I don't want to be the uncle. I want to be the princess, and I want to be the queen, and I want to be the sister, and I want to be the mom." And she would just come home like this everyday, saying the same thing and crying, "Nobody understands!"

Although Penny had adult gay and transgender friends, she found accepting Delia's gender challenging. "It was just one of those things, like, this is my child!" She struggled through initial clothing purchases and Delia's first ventures into the world wearing them. But when Penny allowed Delia to present as a girl at home and on weekends, she watched her formerly sullen and introverted child begin to smile and to engage with other children. Dressing in boys' clothing for school became nearly impossible. Penny knew it was time to talk with the school about allowing Delia to attend as a girl.

Delia began attending a new public school at the start of her kindergarten year. From the start, they were resistant to even discussing her gender. The hard-of-hearing specialist who was working with Delia was the first to use Delia's new name and pronouns, but the teachers and administrators uniformly declined to follow suit. Penny made phone calls to Delia's teacher, the school director, and the staff psychologist, all of whom refused to use Delia's female name or to allow her to use the girls' bathroom. Penny contacted the school district, only to be told by their staff psychologist that Delia was too young to be transgender.

Penny grew anxious that Delia would again become depressed, so she removed her from the local public school and reenrolled her at a private school she had previously attended. Although Penny was concerned that even the administration of that old school seemed "wishy-washy" about supporting Delia's gender transition, they were at least open to being trained. She contacted TYFA and scheduled Kim Pearson to come out to conduct workshops for the school administrators and staff. The week before Kim's visit, the owner of the school called Penny to discuss the possibility of moving Delia to a sister school forty-five minutes from their home, where she suggested Delia remain stealth. She also expressed concern that Delia was too young to make such a transition, insinuating that Penny's lesbianism might be the cause of Delia's gender distress. She confessed to Penny that she worried she would lose business from other families if Delia's trans status was known. Penny persisted and urged they continue as planned with the scheduled trainings. The school reluctantly relented.

Kim Pearson arrived the day before the first scheduled training and met with Penny at her home to discuss Delia's needs and the school environment. Early the following morning, the day of the first school training, Penny's phone rang. When she answered, she was greeted by a representative of children's services, who requested they meet. Penny asked if there was something to worry about; the CPS worker told her they would discuss the matter in person. Penny hung up the phone, sat down, and had her first panic attack. She immediately called Kim, and at Kim's insistence, over the course of the next several days they compiled a "safe folder," an arsenal of documents Kim hoped would insulate her from whatever arguments CPS might devise to challenge her parenting choices. It included a letter from a pediatrician explaining Delia's condition; testimony from Delia's therapist about the longevity and persistence of her gender identity and attesting to Penny, Pam, and Sophie's competent parenting; letters of support from friends, family members, even the pastor of the local church; information from TYFA and the American Academy of Pediatrics on transgender children; and finally, a collection of photographs of Delia that spanned her life, an effort to prove that her gender nonconformity had remained consistent over time. Penny also retained an attorney. She recalled riding a wave of panic through the week and into the interview.

Her panic, as it turned out, was unnecessary. Penny was met in that meeting by a CPS supervisor who had received training in transgender issues and immediately put Penny at ease. She said, "I'm not really sure why I'm here, but I have to be here, so let's sit down and talk." She requested that one of the parents take Delia out of the room. Penny told her the story of how she came to understand Delia's gender, about her distress at school, and about Delia's unfettered joy at being allowed to express her female gender identity in public. The CPS worker read the doctor's letter and took a copy of it. Then she turned to Penny and said, "Make sure that your daughter has a lot more opportunities like these, to be who she is." And with that, the investigation was closed. Later that evening, Penny received a hysterical phone call from one of the teachers at Delia's school. Barely audible through her tears, she said, "I'm so sorry. I'm so sorry. I was wrong. I'm so sorry." Kim Pearson had by that point trained the teaching staff at Delia's school, and it was during that training that the teacher who called CPS realized the harm she had done.

Penny said she felt incredibly lucky the meeting went as it did, but she retained emotional scars from the experience. "I think it heightened my sense of a lack of security. It heightened my sense of . . . almost paranoia. It made me feel really unsafe." She felt betrayed by the school community, despite having a relationship with them that spanned several years. Although it was almost Thanksgiving, the middle of a school term, they never returned to that school. Penny was hypervigilant and frightened for months. "I felt like everywhere we went, we had to hide." She avoided situations that required her to disclose information about Delia's history. "We were trying to do the right things, and that's what felt really violating. It felt like I just didn't know who I could trust." She worried that other people thought Penny's sexual orientation was the cause of Delia's gender identity.

When I met the family, Penny was driving forty-five minutes each way to shuttle Delia to and from a charter school that supported her gender identity. Delia remained mostly stealth in school, and all of her paperwork had been altered to reflect her affirmed gender and name. Even as the hypervigilance began to ebb, Penny struggled actively with anxiety whenever she encountered acquaintances who knew Delia before she transitioned. Because she didn't tell coworkers about Delia's transition, she kept most colleagues at a distance. She couldn't display photographs of her family on her desk. Yet she found one use for the residue of her experiences with CPS.

> I just sort of use it as protection now. I mean, I feel like it's almost empowering in some ways, that I can use it. Other people can't call; we've been there and done that. I can say, "Yeah? Do you want their number?" You know? It's like a defense.

She paused, then said: "Still, some people are safe, and others aren't." It was difficult to tell the difference, so she often prepared for the worst. She teared up as she recounted one neighbor's response to Delia's transition that she found particularly surprising:

> I told him she was living as a girl. He just simply said to me, "Well, how is she doing?" And I thought that was probably the most beautiful thing anybody could have said to me. You know? I cried. I really did. I cried. And I just said, "Thanks for asking. She's doing really well."

It's impossible to know how many gay or lesbian parents end up targets of false allegations of child abuse. Paula, another lesbian parent, found out accidentally, while submitting paperwork for a second-parent adoption,[7] that her family had been the target of a CPS investigation. All adoptions require extensive background checks by social service agencies to ensure suitability to parent. When Paula and her partner, Rhonda, initiated the second-parent adoption of their second child, she was informed by the agent in charge of her "home study"[8] that her investigation had revealed an allegation that Paula was harming her child by allowing her to cross-dress at school. Paula was not permitted to see the formal complaint and was unsure how it was resolved, but she was permitted to complete the adoption. She now volunteers as a book-keeper for an organization that does gender advocacy work for families. She says she wonders how many other families she knows have hidden files in the children's services archives.

Why was Michael pulled from class and interviewed, and Yvonne paid a surprise, intrusive visit by CPS workers, while Penny received both advance notice and an individual meeting? Why did both Sean and Penny face full investigations into their parenting, while the complaint against Paula sat untouched and unmentioned? Sean is a gay man, who built his family through an interracial, state-mediated adoption. Paula and Penny are both white, both lesbian co-parents of biological children with no prior dealings with the state. These stories raise questions about the effects of formal relationships with state agencies and the interplay between gender, race, and biology on the scope of parental autonomy. Multiracial and nonwhite families (particularly those with black children), gay and lesbian families, and those with prior relationships—even good ones—with the state were more vulnerable to interventions than other families.

Something about gender nonconformity gets knitted to sexuality, even to sexual aggression.[9] The susceptability of gay and lesbian parents to accusations of abuse from within their communities demonstrates that in the imaginations of some, gender transgression can be the result, as well as the cause, of sexual transgression. The implicit accusation is that the sexuality or sexual behavior of the parent produced this gendered outcome in the child. And the state, for its part, becomes drawn ever more intricately into scrutinizing the gendered dimensions of parenting.

Paula's story also suggests that there may be many more reports levied against parents of gender nonconforming and transgender children than there are actual investigations. What accounts for the differing outcomes is unclear. The CPS worker who arrived at Penny's home had training in transgender issues; Sean's did not. Yet homophobic fears incited complaints in both cases, and those complaints and the ensuing investigations had lasting emotional implications for the children and parents in both families. Sean busied himself, focusing his nervous energy on parenting his children and trying to clear his family's record. Paula poured her energy into volunteer work. Penny seemed more profoundly shaken by the experience; she found it hard to trust people and avoided building new relationships.

MANAGING RISK AND STIGMA

Few families I interviewed hadn't heard of either Christine's story or another one like it. Almost every parent with whom I spoke, at some point in our conversation, grew solemn, took a deep, heaving breath, and began to talk about fears for their child's safety. Parents knew that their child was at increased risk for emotional and physical harm at the hands or words of others. Many families described the school environment as a source of constant worry, a minefield of potential microaggressions or, in some cases, a patently dangerous yet compulsory routine of daily humiliation and disregard. Christine's and similar stories often left parents feeling powerless, vulnerable, distraught; they prompted conversations among family networks and activist groups about how best to prepare for and protect their children from emotional and physical harm.

When parents of gender nonconforming children came together to share strategies, the anxiety in the room was palpable. While much of that anxiety attached to medical and social decisions made on their child's behalf, parents spent a great deal of time discussing what constituted safety. Parents, particularly those with activist orientations, saw themselves as moral entrepreneurs;[10] they understood that they and their children were doing the work of shifting social gender norms and that individuals and institutions might resist those efforts, sometimes violently. As a result, parents devised a range of risk management strategies to control the intense uncertainty. Some families, like Christine's, left communities of origin entirely and found more accepting social environments; some determined their children would be safest remaining stealth; some closely controlled their child's behavior in public. Most scholars approach quotidian parenting decisions as indexes of internal belief systems;[11] for these families, however, many routine decisions, like the choice of school shoes and coats, haircuts and dance lessons, were made through a process of weighing potential disruption[12] to peer or familial relationships and monitoring[13] the expressive resources children had when they left home and entered the outside world. Many parents who, at home, facilitated atypical modes of dress and self-presentation expected that their children do a fair bit of "covering,"[14] or minimizing the obtrusiveness of their gender nonconformity, in public. Finally, parents in most social contexts learned to use the language of law and the state to protect themselves from the interference of others.

Going Stealth

Van never liked going to school. From the time he was very young, his mother, Faye, remembered fighting him into his clothing, into the car, and into the building. Van endured teasing all throughout his schooling. From the time he entered middle school, other children called him a "he-she," "dyke," or "faggot." Some of the parents in the community joined their children in baiting him. When he attended school as a girl, he was routinely questioned and harassed by peers in the bathroom. Other children threw objects at him and tried to trip him in the hallways. One student even stabbed him with a pencil; when Van responded by punching the student, the principal suspended Van. Verbal harassment, taunting, and physical aggressions were a daily part of his educational experience. For Faye, one of the most striking things about allowing Van to transition and attend school as a boy was watching him wake, dress, and scoot out the door easily, eager to go to school. His mood at home improved dramatically. His grades went from Ds and Fs to As and Bs. But she soon realized that was only the beginning of a new set of problems.

Once Van transitioned, the bullying intensified. One child in particular made his experience at school so terrible, so frightening, that Van eventually confided to Faye that he was afraid for his life. Another child in his class, whose father was among the parents who occasionally taunted him, began threatening to kill Van. When Faye approached the school to complain, the principal told her that a school official would need to witness the bullying in order to take action against the other student. Faye decided to pull Van from the school and enroll him in a larger, nearby high school. To do so, she needed a different address. She found a listing for an empty house for rent in the school district, copied the address, and filed registration papers for Van. She told the school he was male. Van finished high school mostly stealth.

For families who encountered routine, daily harassment, most particularly in educational contexts, having children remain stealth in at least some parts of their lives offered the best protection from harm. Christine needed to share Emmy's gender history with school administrators in order to convince them to allow her to enroll Emmy without most of the standard paperwork required of other children. But she still ensured that teachers and other families did not know that Emmy was transgender. Faye simply enrolled Van as male and made no mention of his history to the school. It was only several months later, when a conflict with her ex-husband threatened to expose Van's secret, that she eventually met with the top administrators at the school to discuss the matter. Even after that meeting, most of Van's classmates and teachers simply assumed he was a cisgender male. Many parents told me that almost nobody in their schools, churches, and communities knew that their children were transgender, and that they lived with a constant hum of worry that some unintentional disclosure might upset the balance of their lives.

Because parents worried that the very idea of a secret implied shame and dishonesty, they clarified that being stealth is distinct from "lying," "hiding," or even what sociologists call "passing."[15] Passing implies making calculated daily decisions about whether to disclose a stigmatized identity to significant (and insignificant) others—in Erving Goffman's words, "to tell or not to tell, to let on or not let on, to lie or not to lie, and in each case, to whom, when and where."[16] This constant negotiation of truth management means that individuals "must necessarily pay a high psychological price [for living] a life that can be collapsed at any moment."[17] Transgender discourse on stealth frames the issue differently. Transpeople presenting in the world as a particular gender contest cultural claims to the naturalness of those categories themselves; if a transgirl is a girl, the logic goes, she is not lying by failing to disclose her gender history. Instead, parents argue, maintaining stealth is akin to not disclosing prior medical conditions, information that may be relevant to various relationships but is the province of individual privacy.[18] They suggest there is a distinction between privacy and dishonesty, that a gender history is not the same thing as the truth of gender in the present.

Of course, parents were acutely aware that small children have remarkably bad information filters. Advocates and parents collaborated to form a language with which to assist children in understanding how to protect the confidentiality of their gender histories, while still insulating them from fear that others might disapprove. In one small, closed-door workshop for parents, Stephanie advised parents to discuss the secrecy/privacy distinction with their children, likening it to more general discussions other parents might have with cisgender children about discussing their body parts in public. She said, "We don't tell our children that our genitals are a secret, but we do tell them they are something we keep private." She urged parents not only to educate their children about the need for privacy, but also to use that distinction as an explanatory tool for working with schools and camps when discussing the disclosure of a child's medical information to potentially disapproving staff.

When, how, and to whom to disclose transgender histories dominated many conversations among parents. For the children who fully transitioned at young ages, and who will navigate the social world as adults in bodies that do not betray their complex gender histories, the "coming out" process will never fully end. The sole models available to parents around disclosure were riddled with potential dangers—movies like *The Crying Game* and *Boys Don't Cry*, which portray adult transpeople who are murdered once their transness is known to others; stories of youth suicides following disclosures gone awry. Dating and sexuality produced particular anxiety. Each conference for children and families I attended had at least one workshop devoted exclusively to the topic of managing dating and disclosure. In these workshops, parents learned that denial of adolescent sexuality was an unacceptable parenting strategy for these children. Rather, managing their safety required a nuanced vocabulary for bodies and desires that could facilitate complex discussions about negotiating sexuality with others, communication, safety, and risk. Ironically, this is one area where parents of heterosexually-identified adolescents felt they had it hardest, imagining that queer life offered a more open orientation to sexual negotiations.

Deirdre, for example, mourned the fact that her son, Colten, wouldn't have an opportunity to experiment casually with sex.

I don't want him to have to disclose to every single girlfriend that he gets. I want him to be able to have, which you probably don't hear many mothers say this, I want him to be able to go out there and have casual sex, but he can't do that. He can't experiment around. Every relationship that he's in is going to have to be meaningful, which some people say, "That's a good thing. Having meaningful sex shouldn't be casual." Then I think about my own history. I had a lot of really fun casual sex. I didn't get hung up about any of it. I just don't want to deny my kid that. He's not going to be able to have that, unless he gets in a group of people where there are enough of those people, like if he gets in a genderqueer crowd and he comes out.

Deirdre imagined that immersion in a lesbian and gay (or even better, queer) community might empower Colten to be more open about his identity, which would, in turn, lead to greater opportunities for casual sexual encounters. Parents of stealth children initiated long discussions about when and how to disclose to potential dating partners. Parents, particularly of transgirls, described fears that potential sexual partners would feel duped or coerced if disclosure happened after physical contact; yet they also suspected that premature disclosure might lead potential mates—particularly straight-identified boys—to discount their children before getting to know them. They worried that their children would struggle to manage themselves well in intimate encounters, that out of immaturity or lack of forethought they might even unintentionally disclose. Stephanie warned parents in a support group session for parents,

> Children don't necessarily know how to think ahead. Or they think they can control the disclosure in most circumstances. Teenagers, especially, don't realize that in the heat of making out, hands can wander unexpectedly. They may not be able to control, they may not *want* to control, who touches precisely what part of their body and when.

Parents were compelled to develop an unusually nuanced language not only about gender, but about sexuality. And that language was not merely used to explain identity to others; parents developed a sophisticated lexicon for exploring relational issues with children, issues of trust, boundaries, and communication. This is a far cry from the "birds and bees" conversations, marred by discomfort, that parents often joke about in other contexts.

The paradox of stealth is that it becomes necessary in some cases, to argue that an individual child is, for example, just a girl. Yet if we had truly achieved a cultural frame in which a transgirl was just a girl, stealth would no longer be necessary. Parents knew this, interacted with it, thought about it, devised intricate language to manage it. They planned for their child's social and sexual future, imagined it in detail, and worried over how best to equip them to feel entitled to and secure in an identity while preparing for the inevitability of social rejection.

Leaving

For Christine and Emmy, the choice to leave their town was obvious. They were in immediate and clear physical danger. Faye similarly pulled Van out of school to ensure his safety. For other families, leaving was prophylactic. They chose to remove their children from places where they *might* face sanction or disapproval. Tom and Sandy were active members of their local Christian church. Before Alexander was born, Sandy worked for the church, running the early childhood ministries weekend programs. She pulled back to have more time to spend with her children, working part-time watching children in the mid-week drop-off program. Eventually she began volunteering to assist in the Sunday school programs. She and Tom felt they were well integrated into the community, and Alexander grew up attending all of these programs. They found themselves in a moment of profound struggle and anguish when Alexander, who had always been extremely masculine, began using his male name. Fully expecting they would receive the supportive notes and prayers other members of the community received when they encountered difficult moments in their family lives, Tom and Sandy emailed their pastor to discuss the situation. The response they received, while not negative, was eerie silence. Sandy said:

> I have not felt supported by the church. Haven't gotten a phone call from the head pastor, who you would think, especially in this church, this is such an opportunity to show compassion and acceptance, or what have you, and it's just ... I don't see it. I think what this church and the support group that I thought we had, it's just not there.

Sandy spoke first to the children's pastor, for whom she had worked. He had known Alexander for years. Surely, she thought, this wouldn't come as a huge surprise; surely he would have some wise counsel. And he had, in fact, encountered another transgender person: he told Sandy a story about a transwoman who worked at an affiliated church. This person, he told her, decided she had to express her female identity, but she also concluded that abstinence was the virtuous path, given the church's stance on homosexuality. He told Sandy that he would pray for their family, but other than that he had nothing to offer her. When Tom and Sandy decided to allow Alexander to transition, he advised that the church would support the name and pronoun changes, but that Sandy should never allow Alex to change his body.

Sandy grew increasingly uncomfortable. Alexander was about to start church camp, and she felt he was psychologically fragile and that he needed a safe, supportive environment. When she went to discuss Alex's gender change with the close friend of hers who ran the camp, she realized the support she lacked was not just emotional, it was material and logistical as well. They expressed concern he might wish to use the boys' bathroom. They asked if he intended to join them for swimming. Most basic activities at the camp were somewhat gender segregated, and it became clear that Sandy would need to do substantial work to establish Alex as a member of the boys' group. The three pastors affiliated with the camp scheduled a meeting to discuss how to proceed with Alexander's participation in the church's programming. For Sandy, that meeting was the final straw. She decided to leave the church shortly thereafter. The emotional neglect she experienced during a time she saw as pivotal in their family life convinced her that Alexander was at risk for social ostracism, or worse. It wasn't a chance she was willing to take.

The stakes of social disapproval were very high, particularly for families who interacted with rigidly gendered social institutions. As Sandy confronted the structural barriers to Alexander's participation in activities, she calculated that severing their social ties and beginning anew in a different environment would be preferable to trying to get the old one to adapt. This kind of break was heart wrenching for families, who walked away from sometimes vital social supports that had accrued during many years of participation.

Monitoring

Leaving and going stealth were practices families used to reduce social sanctions by avoiding the acknowledgment of a child's transgender status.

Remaining in place and allowing children to transition openly, in contrast, opened families up to scrutiny in a variety of contexts. Rather than experiencing support for a child's transgender identity as a singular event, parents engaged in an almost constant process of weighing potential harm and managing their children's self-expression. Parents functioned as membranes separating their child from the outside world, filtering out unrealistic or damaging social expectations and providing their children with gender options that conformed enough to cultural norms to ensure their safety. This meant sometimes allowing their children to control their engagements in the outside world, and other times, limiting choices they feared might expose them to negative sanction. This routine "monitoring"—controlling expressive conduct to conform to social norms[19]—functioned like a "covering demand,"[20] or an effort to "restrict the display of failings most identified with [an individual's source of stigma]."[21] Even the most affirming parents in relatively supportive environments engaged in some forms of monitoring from time to time.

Luciana and Raymond had a difficult time determining how much to restrict their son Sebastian's feminine clothing and toy choices around their families and neighbors. Each parent found these choices painful and confusing, and struggled to reconcile their desire to affirm Sebastian with the conservatism of their cultural backgrounds. Raymond watched his brother struggle to come to terms with his homosexuality throughout his adult life. Chronically depressed, his brother suffered from an addiction to drugs, and eventually contracted HIV. Luciana, who was Latinx, felt her family's ethnic culture was similarly unforgiving when it came to gender-norm violations. While she and Raymond were both supportive of Sebastian, she recalled the small ways that, over time, they began to monitor and set limits on his cross-gender play: "We reached a time when my husband was saying he was okay; however, [...] we started setting some limits about when it was okay to dress up, where it was safe to dress up." I asked her if she recalled when they decided to begin putting limits on Sebastian's dress-up play. She replied,

Yeah, it had to do with, you know, we live in the suburbs, and we have like an open backyard where the neighbors—everyone has their own backyard, but we cross over. And at that time we were the only ones with a swing set, so all the kids would come and play. So one day Sebastian was in one of his princess dresses and the neighbors came with two kids, a boy younger in age and a girl one year younger. And I could sense the parents feeling so uncomfortable and just saying, like, "*My* boy's all boy!" Like, they never talk to us like that. "'Oh, my boy's all boy! Look at him." And I'm like, okay, I don't like this.

Luciana noticed other parents restricting Sebastian's play as well. She said the initial encounter with Sebastian's femininity was often a surprise to other parents, and in the immediate aftermath they seemed to handle it well. But concerns often emerged later.

I will pick up Sebastian from a playdate, and so it will be something like the first time, "Hi, how was it?" And the mom, "The kids had a great time." I say, "What did they do?" "Well, they played different things. And they played dress-up." "Oh," I say, "Sebastian loves playing dress-up." "Yeah, but he was dressed up as the princess." And I say, "Oh, yeah, he loves it!" And she, "Oh, that was okay? I didn't know what to do." [...] And they are relieved, like whew! And then they have another playdate, and it happened with several families. So the next time I go to pick him up in the car I asked Sebastian, "How was it?" "Oh, it wasn't so cool." "What happened?" "We had to play outside all the time and we couldn't dress up." [...] So the parents were setting some limits where we're like, okay, you know, where do we stand here?

She recounted several stories of initial playdates, where Sebastian had his nails painted or was permitted to dress up in feminine costumes. It was rare, she said, for parents to restrict his behavior immediately. That generally came in later encounters, which made Luciana feel she couldn't rely on her initial impressions of other parents. She said she felt she couldn't be certain which parents would try to curtail Sebastian's gender behavior, or worse, who might shame or otherwise embarrass him for it. It made each new relationship a testing ground, each new interaction an occasion to be watchful.

Luciana found it difficult to withstand the critiques of other parents. She felt torn between two sets of impulses or reactions.

One is the rational one, to say, "So what? I love my son for who he is." But also there is shame and there is, again, trying to protect my son so he will understand that what the guy was saying had to do with him considering my son not-so-boyish. And what it meant to him.

Luciana and Raymond were tasked with assisting Sebastian in metabolizing the rejections he experienced and the residue of shame they left. It was a feeling she herself shared in some of the encounters she described, in the moments she imagined other parents prohibiting certain forms of play. These prohibitions represented symbolic rejections, messages to Sebastian—and by extension to her—that some parts of him were unacceptable. She began separating out which parents were safe hosts for Sebastian and which she felt might hurt him. This sort of risk-reduction strategy was familiar to many parents.

From the start, Yael was a very enthusiastic research participant. She and her husband were professors at one of the nation's most elite universities. Yael subscribed to the idea that knowledge can produce social change; she also had an inherent appreciation for rhetorically interesting ideas and arguments. She was a vocal participant in her community's play and parent group for families with gender nonconforming children. She was "out" about her child on campus and routinely participated in academic programs on LGBT issues. In her first email communication to me, she offered up an eloquent description of her son, Micah, and of the family context in which he lived:

Micah (age 7) is a biological boy who, since the age of 2 or 3, has always "liked girl things." He identifies as male, and tends to wear gender-neutral or gender-ambiguous clothes outside of the house; at home, he often wears dresses or skirts, and almost always sleeps in something feminine (a nightgown or dress). [...] He has been unconditionally supported in his gender expression by both of his parents and all of his teachers (he attends a progressive independent school), as well as by (most of) our extended family. He has an older brother (age 13) whom we call the "heteronormative enforcer" who is supportive of Micah's self-expression inside the home, but who often insists that, for instance, Micah take off his headband if he is coming to pick him up at the home of a new acquaintance.

The tension between her "unconditional support" of Micah and her own concern about his public presentation of self emerged in the afternoon we spent together at her home. At times, Micah and his older brother wandered into the room where we were speaking; Micah watched me quietly with what appeared to be both curiosity and trepidation.

Yael's descriptions of Micah confirmed my initial impression that he was exquisitely perceptive and attuned to the responses of others. She recounted stories of Micah hiding the small "Polly Pocket" dolls he favored under his body or in his pockets, when he worried someone would disapprove. He was particularly sensitive to the reactions of his thirteen-year-old brother, Ivan, who often cautioned Micah against being too feminine in social settings where he (Ivan) faced taunts or questions from his peers. Yael sensed that Micah was keenly aware of his brother's discomfort, and said she was waiting to see how Micah's presentation of self would change over the next school year, when the two children would be in different schools for the first time. Micah suggested to her that he might want to begin wearing skirts to school, once Ivan was no longer there.

Both Micah and his parents edited Micah's behavior around certain members of their extended family. Dimitri, Micah's father, was from Central Europe, and when the family traveled there each summer, Micah's clothing was always a concern. On their most recent trip, Yael dressed him "like a hippie": he wore loose pants, tie-dyed T-shirts, and bandanas to camouflage his headbands. And while Micah was excited to wear a beaded necklace, Yael was certain he understood the cause for the different attire. Yael's sister, a powerful, urban professional with three children of her own, came up frequently in our conversation. Yael told me that her sister had a son who also enjoyed feminine things, but he didn't identify as deeply with female characters and interests as Micah did. She felt her sister didn't seem to really "get" Micah. I asked if she thought her sister was uncomfortable around him.

> Yeah, she is uncomfortable. And on reflection, I do edit what Micah wears when we're up at my parents' with her. And had not, until you asked the question, noticed that I do it, and I do it in the easy way that parents control what their kids wear, which is by choosing what goes in the suitcase. And then there's no issues. And I know that Micah knows it because he wouldn't bring a nightgown with him when we went [there]; he brought his ambiguous pajamas.

Struck by her use of the word *edit* (a word I have since adopted), I asked Yael to describe what she meant. She told me that there were three completely safe spaces in Micah's life: his home and the homes of two friends he's known his entire life. Those were the places where he was free to be his most authentic self, and environments in which she gave little thought to his self-presentation. For time spent at other families' homes, at school, and out in public, she engaged Micah in a process of learning to assimilate the demands of others. This included limiting his choice of clothing and accessories, and talking with him at length about how to measure other people's affective states.

Even parents who facilitated gender nonconforming expression in their children did not do so unilaterly. There were many contexts, even in overwhelmingly supportive social environments, where parents "edited" clothing and toy choices, or the information about their child's identity or history they shared with others. Understanding these moments as merely coercive or rejecting, the typical frame of most theoretical work on social gender norm enforcement, misses the myriad ways conventional gender mediates social relationships. Parents knew their child must be gender literate enough to assimilate into their peer group and community, and these small, quotidian restrictions were a part of the intensive socialization process parents undertook with their children. It was a project, parents told me, that took constant, vigilant attention.

Whether parents or children chose to remain stealth, to leave their communities, or to urgently monitor social interactions, the insecurity parents felt drew them into ever more meticulous gendering processes. Facilitation was not merely the exercise of providing children with agency; it was a parenting project that extended into the most intimate registers of their child's life. Not merely clothing and toy choices, but identity disclosures, interaction styles, the architecture of sexual and romantic encounters—all of these things became topics of consideration, study, and discussion. While the underlying logic of facilitation makes these profoundly different from more repressive parenting practices of decades past, they do share a concern with social integration and with the high cost of transgression.

USING THE STATE

Gendering children—the monitoring, controlling, and enabling of certain forms of culturally coded identities, behaviors, and practices—is now one of the features of parenting at issue in negotiations with the state, with social institutions, and within individual communities and family systems. Securing a socially acceptable gender identity in children is among the many parenting practices the state monitors and mandates. For some families whose children transgressed social gender norms, the state was an intrusive and coercive presence; for others, the state became a vehicle through which they could advocate for the affirmation of a child's transgender identity, even against co-parents.

I first met Jerri, a grandparent caring for her son Scott's children, at a conference about two months into her middle grandchild's transition to living full time as Phoebe. Phoebe, then six, and her three siblings were living with Jerri and her husband while their parents ironed out the details of a divorce. Both military employees, Scott and Dina, the children's mother, had left the children with Jerri once before, when they went on a six-month deployment overseas. Phoebe was two and a half at the time of that first visit and was already confiding in Jerri that she was a girl. When the children resumed living with their parents, Jerri maintained an especially close relationship with Phoebe, who struggled to regulate her behavior in social settings. Jerri thought she often seemed anxious. Over the years, as Phoebe grew increasingly adamant about her need to express her female gender, Dina became more resistant and punishing in her refusal to accept Phoebe's femininity. Jerri recalled an incident when, having arrived early to meet the children and their mother, she decided to kill time in a local department store and realized Dina and the children were in there as well.

> They didn't know I was there, of course. And I could hear Phoebe begging her mom if she could please try on the pink sandals. Just begging: "You don't have to buy them for me, Mommy, I just want to try them on. How about the boots? Can I try on the pink—" And I almost cried, it was so sad. And Mom would say, "No, you're a boy! You're not wearing pink sandals!" And I wanted to cry. And I could hear them. So finally, I just went over to them and kind of winked at Phoebe. And Mom bought ... all boy clothes, everything boy, everything.

Scott, with significant prodding from Jerri, became more comfortable with Phoebe's gender identity with the aid of a family therapist. As his relationship with Dina dissolved, Jerri once again stepped in to care for the children, eventually assuming legal guardianship.

Initially, Dina's rejection caused mainly emotional distress to Phoebe. Once Phoebe began living in her affirmed gender and using a female name, Jerri realized that Dina's disapproval could cause far more wide-ranging problems. When I followed up with Jerri almost a year after our initial interview, Phoebe had successfully transitioned in school, though not without obstacles. Jerri was exhausted. "Dealing with these people ... it's like running a marathon. It's a full-time job just to make sure this kid is safe!" In March of the year Phoebe was to begin kindergarten, Jerri contacted her local school to prepare them for Phoebe's arrival that fall. She entered a long succession of meetings and consults with various school administrators—the principal, the assistant principal, an "adjustment counselor," the school psychologist— all of whom seemed confounded by the notion that they could accommodate Phoebe's gender in the classroom. While Jerri initially assumed Phoebe would be able to transition openly at school, it quickly became clear that privacy would be an important safeguard against harassment from school employees. Jerri offered to bring TYFA to train the teachers and staff, but the principal demurred. At that point, the school referred her to the district manager for "pupil services."

Jerri called a well-known LGBT rights attorney in her area, who coached her on local education law. Law, it turned out, wasn't itself a solution; law was only as helpful as the people enforcing it. "It was like everything I asked for, this woman said no." Jerri sighed. "I asked if they could change her name just on the roll call list. No. I asked, can we keep her medical and private information separate from her academic record? No." Jerri knew that, if nothing else, medical information was protected by federal law; but she didn't know how she was going to convince the school and the district to honor the law. One mention of Phoebe's gender history was all it would take to thwart her efforts at secrecy. "Once the cat's out of the bag, you can't really put it back in." At an administrator's suggestion, she met with the assistant superintendent, hoping he would be her ally. He seemed well prepared for her visit and fired questions at Jerri, one after the next. How did she know for certain that Phoebe had gender issues? What experts had confirmed this? How could she prove it? What did she really expect them to do about the bathrooms? "He was so obnoxious. Just his whole tone and demeanor. It was unsettling. And then, after that, even the administrators at the school wouldn't work with us anymore."

The school and the district repeatedly asserted that they needed to maintain consistency in Phoebe's written records, over all other considerations. The name on her medical files needed to match the one on the roll sheets, administrative documents, prescription medications, etc. Even when Jerri procured bottles of prescription pills marked "Phoebe," they refused to relent. It took repeated threats of a lawsuit and the retention of a lawyer from a national LGBT rights nonprofit to scare the school and the district into submitting to Jerri's demands for privacy. In the end, the school agreed to training for staff and teachers and to maintain Phoebe's privacy. When we spoke, only the senior school administrators, the school nurse, one teacher, and the secretary in charge of student records knew about Phoebe's history. Jerri told me that she walked away from the battle with the school having learned two things: one was the power of legal representation, and the other was the importance of a coherent legal identity. For that reason, she and Scott were then battling Dina for the right to legally change Phoebe's name.

While Jerri and Scott fought with the school and the state to harmonize Phoebe's legal identity, they also faced a constant battle with Dina to define the terms of Phoebe's care. Because Dina refused to recognize Phoebe's name and gender, each of the many small parenting decisions that relate to her gender received extensive review by the team of experts required by the state to adjudicate disagreements over parenting. Each adult party—Dina, Scott, and Jerri—had their own legal counsel. There was a pro bono attorney representing Phoebe. The local family court appointed a *guardian ad litem*[22] to represent Phoebe as well. Jerri and her attorney worked diligently to construct arguments to convince each of these people that every step they took to support Phoebe in making a social transition was the correct step.

Risk discourse featured prominently in these disputes. It was a powerful rhetorical tool for parents seeking to facilitate gender nonconformity over the objections of rejecting co-parents. Many of the arguments Scott and Jerri made concerned the negative consequences of family rejection on the emotional and physical health of trans children. Jerri went to her first meeting with the *guardian ad litem* fully prepared. She had compiled a dossier of information on transgender children that included studies documenting brain differences, information sheets on childhood gender diversity, news articles on families raising transgender children, studies linking family relationships to the health and well-being of transgender people, and a newsletter from an organization working with transgender youth in foster care. She included anything she thought might help this woman understand Phoebe's identity and her and Scott's efforts to support and empower her. Her attempts to educate the *guardian ad litem* about Phoebe's gender were less than successful:

> I went there with the purpose of introducing the topic and trying to edu-
> cate her, but she told me she was already educated on this stuff. But she had
> no idea [what] that looked like in day-to-day life. Because I can tell you,
> and I tried to tell her, that raising a trans kid and keeping that kid safe is a
> full-time job. You know, dealing with the school and the doctors, and we
> don't have a legal name change, so neighbors and activities ... and can the
> kid take swimming lessons or a tumbling class ... just like everything. It's a
> full-time job. [...] I just felt like I was the only one who truly understood,
> like, what it was taking to keep her safe and protected.

Scott and Dina continued to share joint legal custody of Phoebe, though Scott had full physical custody. Phoebe lived with him on the weekends; she spent the school week with Jerri, living apart from her siblings so that she could remain in the school they worked so hard to educate. Jerri continued to be her primary advocate in school and with the state. Phoebe attended school mostly stealth. Jerri filed a contested name change petition, over Dina's objections, with Scott's support and the help of their team of legal advocates.

Val found herself fighting a different sort of battle around her deci-
sion to allow Jesse to transition medically. When we met, she was in a protracted, private legal battle with her ex-husband, Dan, Jesse's stepfa-
ther, over the cost of his medical care. When Val and Dan married, Jesse was eight years old and living as a girl, though Val said he was always quite masculine. In the beginning, Dan and Jesse had a very strong relationship. Dan filled a void left by Jesse's biological father, who abandoned them shortly after Jesse's birth. Val relocated to a small Midwestern town to follow her then husband's career. When their relationship soured some years later, they came to a separation agreement that stipulated Dan's responsibility for Jesse's medical care.

Jesse, then seventeen and preparing to accept an attractive scholarship to a renowned fine arts college, had recently decided to transition. While Dan's medical insurance covered his routine medical needs, it did not cover his hormone therapy, and Val couldn't afford to provide it herself. Because Dan contested Val's decision to allow Jesse to transition, the issue of who would pay was left to the courts to resolve. When we spoke, Val worried that Jesse would postpone college if he was unable to transition.

Though I didn't encounter any such stories, there is evidence that, in extreme cases, parents may even use the state to intervene in their individual relationships with their children. In late 2016, news media reported that Anmarie Calgaro, a Minnesota mother of a seventeen-year-old transgirl, was suing her own child in federal court for transitioning without her consent.[23] (Also parties to the suit were the child's school district, a local health clinic at which she received clinical services, St. Louis County, and the state Department of Health.) The child, referred to by reports and in the original complaint only as J.D.K., had been living apart from her mother, in a different part of the state, for over a year before she used a state statute (Minnesota Statute 144.341)— that allowed minors living apart from their parents to provide their own consent for medical care—to seek transition-related services.[24] Calgaro, represented by a team of lawyers with ties to conservative political groups, attempted to use the court system to both halt her child's transition and access her school and medical files.[25] A federal judge eventually dismissed the suit, six months later, finding Calgaro's claims without merit.[26] Val and Jerri called upon state agencies to regulate issues related to their child's gender identity, actively using the agencies as tools to enforce support from otherwise rejecting parents. While Foucault's[27] suggestion that the modern era would be characterized by ever more complete state monitoring of its citizens rings true in these regulatory practices, sometimes individuals also find creative ways to summon regulatory power to enable and assist them in what we might otherwise consider private moral or emotional interpersonal disputes.[28]

SAFE FOLDER

"'Expect the best; prepare for the worst.' That's an important motto, if you've got a trans kid." Kim Pearson was speaking to a packed room at an East Coast conference for families. Close to sixty parents had assembled for a workshop on creating a "safe folder," a repository of documentation that TYFA suggested all parents of transgender children keep on hand, to insulate themselves from intrusions by state social services and confrontations with family members, and to scaffold demands for accommodations from schools. Kim warned, "Never wait until a situation arises. Always be prepared." A standard safe folder is a binder that includes a whole host of evidence that a child's identity is sui generis, consistent, and long-standing.[29] The file's contents—letters from experts and laypeople with no personal interest in the determination, along with evidence of immutability—were fashioned after the kinds of evidence that might be admissible in a family court.

TYFA suggested that all parents compile a letter from a physician (pediatrician or general practice doctor) confirming the child's gender identity and its persistence over time, confirming a GID diagnosis, and stating that the only effective treatment is allowing the child to live in their preferred gender.[30] They also suggested including corroboration from a therapist confirming the child's gender and family stability; letters from other healthcare professionals the child has seen; letters from multiple friends, family members, religious officials, and others testifying to the child's gender and good parenting within the family; and even drawings or writings the child has done that demonstrate their gender identity (specific examples include "natal males drawing themselves as princesses or natal females drawing themselves as soldiers").[31] Along with these testimonials, videos of the child, snapshots that demonstrate their gender in six-month intervals across their life, and legal documents such as birth certificates, social security cards, passports, and any name-change documents. Finally, parents were told to gather any home study information documenting family stability, if they have it, as well as State Department of Justice, Bureau of Criminal Information/ Analysis,[32] searches for all the child's parents and guardians.

Only a few families who had never been investigated had complete safe folders at the time we met, though most families with the means to have consistent medical care had trusted experts at the ready, should the need arise. Several parents, like Sean and Penny, had assembled them largely to stave off unexpected investigations. Others, like Val and Jerri, compiled expert research and their children's medical and social histories in an effort to buttress their own parenting decisions against challenges from co-parents. In all of these cases, parents became quasi-experts themselves, able to craft a factual record of their child's identity over time and to contextualize their decisions to facilitate their children's identities.

The inclusion of transgender children into the state's bureaucratic lexicon meant that its processes of optimization[33] now extended into gender. There were dossiers to be compiled, expert testimony to procure, and certifications of fitness to be acquired. Few individuals, even those with the most agentic relations to the state, assembled these prophylactically; most found themselves scrambling at the last minute to secure accreditation from recognized experts in gender and parenting. The reach of the state creeps ever more inward, concerning itself with smaller and smaller forms of parental decision-making and affect, moving most swiftly against those families it deems to be at highest risk or within easy reach. These are not value-neutral assessments; rather, they underscore existing biases and social hierarchies.

CONCLUSION

These stories paint a complex picture of the double life of the state. Its regulations exert their force in both positive and negative ways. On the one hand, the state confers recognition, in the form of legal name changes and gender changes, antidiscrimination protections, and disability rights paradigms (which can be particularly useful in schools). In this way, we can see gender as a resource distributed by the state. On the other hand, the state also both regulates and punishes deviance. This happens through the formal regulation of Departments of Children's Services, and reveals both the differential vulnerabilities of certain families to intrusion, and the role of the state in moderating parenting practices and family disputes.

Many of the families I met faced administrative inquiries initiated by the state into their parenting practices, because someone, sometimes a mandated reporter like a doctor or teacher, sometimes a nosy neighbor, disapproved of their choice to allow their child to transgress gender norms and alerted children's services. Formal state regulation was far more prevalent among families with black children, those with a gay or lesbian parent, and adoptive or foster families with preexisting relationships characterized by state surveillance.

When historian Margot Canaday argued that the advent of the idea of homosexuality developed in tandem with the consolidation of federal statehood, she noted that "the state defined the category, ... without ever fully capturing its subject."[34] Much as it did with homosexuality, the state constructs its gender categories and, through the mechanism of conferring recognition, invites individuals to pass, to hide the dissonance between their lived experience and their bureaucratic classifications. The rhetoric of the state imposes passing and covering demands on individuals, and denies that those demands exact their own forms of violence and coercion. It seems clear, however, that gender transgressions open up families to elevated forms of scrutiny, and also to more intricate involvement with the state and its administrative actors.

Penny's brush with state regulation infected her relationships in ways that endured far beyond the resolution of that inquiry. She was distrustful of me as a researcher, worried that I would reveal details of her parenting that would increase her exposure to harm by the state. She became a self-governing subject, one who retained a consistent consciousness of the potential vulnerability of her family, at a cost of silence. And Penny was one of the lucky ones. Parents targeted by the state for intervention often remained so frightened after those encounters that they felt unable to contest or, sometimes, even to disclose their experiences. The more violent the intervention, the more difficult speaking about it became.

Jerri interacted differently with the state. She learned that it was a tool she could mobilize to support her in her parenting. When Jerri's sensibilities conflicted with Dina's, she could enlist the assistance of state actors to facilitate negotiation of those disputes. The legal recognition of Phoebe's name and gender provided a form of institutional sanction she could import back into the context of her family, to create consensus where previously there had been discord. Its force could be harnessed and directed. Herein lies the double life of state regulation; it can be at once coercive and redemptive.

Families used a diverse array of strategies to avoid, confront, and make strategic use of the complexity of the administrative and regulatory state and its ever-intensifying engagement with the particulars of gendered parenting practices. This analysis demonstrates that institutions don't articulate their power in uniform ways. Institutional actors, like lawyers and caseworkers, work sometimes as advocates for and at other times adversaries of affirming parents. Power moves between and among government, social institutions, and community actors. Likewise, parents responded to these pressures in diverse ways, each developing their own thoughtful rationale for decisions to flee, to go stealth, or to monitor their child's behavior. Parents and children used these strategies in various combinations, actively negotiating boundaries between safety and danger, shame and defiance, public and private. While these families told classic tales of both external and internal gender regulation, parents were far from passive targets of bullying from social institutions. They were generating collective knowledge and gaining expertise in negotiating their children's gender with and through the state. Furthermore, coalitions of parents and families were consolidating information to assist in preparing for state interventions before they actually happened.

Parents of gender nonconforming children knew that they faced a variety of risks, both formal and within their particular social networks, as they worked to support their children and to facilitate their public expression. Far from merely advocating for their children to have equal access to opportunities, these parents were expert in mitigating emotional and material risk. From engaging in the gathering and tracking of evidentiary support for their parenting practices, to developing nuanced vocabularies for communicating with children and other adults, to the monitoring of their child's expressive conduct in public, assessing and responding to uncertainty became an automatic feature of how they parented.

Parents understood the relational nature of gender acquisition. They knew they needed to help their child assimilate socially with peers and extended family, in school and at home. Much work in the sociology of gender presumes that regulation is a dichotomous variable; either one regulates the behavior of children, or one doesn't. It appeared that even the families most affirming of gender diversity, who we might argue engage in some of the most liberatory parenting practices around gender and sexuality, engaged in the monitoring and restriction of their child's affect and behaviors. Yet these covering demands seemed to come not from an inherent aversion to gender nonconformity or any internal sense of role structure or value schema, but from a desire to minimize the risk of social sanction by the surrounding community, even by the state. It was a project they undertook with constant vigilance. These gender management projects required parents to develop a facility with communicating about complex gender histories with institutions, complex sexual dynamics with children, and myriad other more subtle negotiations with extended family and other parents.

CHAPTER SIX

Telling Gender Stories

At first glance, Sam's room looked much like you'd expect a seven-year-old's room to look. His mother opened the door for me, revealing a clutter of competing colors and shapes. As I stepped inside, I noted a kind of disharmony. Among the muddle of toys and books, a pouty baby doll lay dejected, slumped sideways against the silvery sheath of a weapon that resembled something from Star Trek. The bed was cheerfully dressed in royal blue sheets depicting train engines, a jarring contrast to the delicate pink, gauzy canopy speckled with tiny sequins that hung from the ceiling above. Sam's mother ushered me forward to the dresser and shelves that lined the far wall of the room. She pointed out the two shelves that held Sam's dresses, stopping at a small, folded piece of pink fabric. She held it with reverence and announced that it was Sam's "very favorite dress," the first one they allowed him to purchase, which he'd insisted on wearing to preschool over their admonishment and protest. She pulled open a dresser drawer to show me Sam's T-shirts, neat piles of pinks and blues topped by a neon orange shirt with a giraffe on its front. She took down a photo of Sam, smiling next to his favorite preschool teacher. He was wearing a pink T-shirt, his longish hair pulled upward into a rubber band.

Sam's mother, Sarah, lived in a liberal urban center with her husband and two children. She worked as a freelance journalist and writer, and as we sat together drinking coffee in the morning sunlight of her living room, she told me in thoughtful detail about her son's complicated gender. Sarah wrote about her experiences parenting Sam for local newspapers and websites and on her own personal blog. She thought carefully about how to explain Sam to people who don't know him, and over the course of the two hours we spent together she marshaled all of her best evidence of Sam's uniquely gendered self: his feminine clothing choices, female friend preferences, mixed interests and hobbies, acute physical sensitivities, and his emotional fortitude in the face of peer criticism. We even discussed the possible contributions of Sam's celiac disease—an autoimmune disorder that manifests in an intolerance for wheat products—to the ways he understands and expresses his gender. Several months before we met, National Public Radio profiled her family for a segment about gender nonconforming children. She received notes from grateful parents and a handful of rageful criticisms.

Sarah, at that point, was one of only a handful of parents who had gone public with stories about their kids and families. We met in 2009, just as the media firestorm on the issues surrounding transgender childhood ignited. Neither of us realized that in the ensuing few years, trans kids would become a mainstay of daily news cycles. When we met, Sarah was at work on a book for other parents of what she then termed "pink boys" and was thinking through her experience of raising a gender nonconforming son in contemporary culture and what she thought she learned about boyhood in general. She imagined a rapt mainstream audience listening for the stories of Sam and other children like him. (Little did she know just how right she was!) She and her husband, Ian, had already penned a children's book about a boy who likes dresses, and they traveled around the country doing readings. Sarah believed that the new media attention on trans kids was evidence that contemporary U.S. culture was poised for a sea change around gender, and that parents' voices about how gender and transgender happens would be key to inciting that change. Sarah and parents like her told articulate, well-honed gender stories, narratives about who their child was and where their gender came from. Contemporary culture gave them a wealth of material to work with.

Over the last century, there has been a proliferation of discourses within biomedicine, psychiatry, and popular culture discussing ways in which we can "know" our gender; as a result, individuals are called upon to understand and communicate gender in ever-increasing detail. The somatic indicia of gender, which social scientists have long argued underlie the cultural matter of gender, have become themselves a cultural product, a way of knowing and being known. And alongside transformations in biomedicine that allow the soma of gender to be manipulated, ever more emotional work is required to account for the "self" that inhabits the gendered body. Parents of transgender and gender nonconforming children did tremendous intellectual work to explain their child's gender, demonstrating that these identities are themselves a distinctly modern form of accounting. They produce a space in which a more explicit, outward, and nuanced examination of identity can take form—one heavily influenced by the popularization of biochemical and genetic explanations for human difference.

With this call to articulate the self comes an attendant proliferation of the ways in which gender can be regulated.[1] Because of the particular sets of cultural anxieties that attend adolescent identity, gender nonconforming youth are popular targets for normalizing projects within biomedicine, psychiatry, and religious contexts. And these regulatory projects become built into the ways in which their identities are conceptualized and understood within their families. While all rational systems confront exceptions to their rules,[2] there are rare circumstances where individuals must remake understandings in the absence of familiar tropes. We might expect parents to reject orthodox explanations for how gender happens, or to draw from new or invented constructs; instead, they redeployed familiar knowledge in unfamiliar and creative ways to make sense of their evolving realities.

Dominant narratives about transformations in medicine, psychiatry, and spirituality typically conclude that these knowledge projects function to secure formerly social phenomena as the exclusive province of established knowledge systems and, particularly for women and sexual minorities, produce increasingly restrictive gender regimes.[3] Yet such depictions miss important microprocesses of social transformation. Parents' gender stories demonstrate that medicine, psychiatry, and spirituality provide ready rhetorical tools for exploring, facilitating, and embracing the multiplicity and plasticity of contemporary gender identities. Parent accounts depict the ways our "selves" are both "organizationally embedded,"[4] produced by and through the publicly available institutionalized discourses, and at the same time subject to individual "interpretive discretion."[5]

ACCOUNTING FOR GENDER

Parents' accounts of their children's evolving and complex gender identities are inseparable from the lexicon with which they are equipped to speak and the audience who demands the explanation. In a sociological sense, accounts are "story-like constructions"[6] most typically solicited and produced to explain deviant behaviors.[7] We become uniquely *accountable* to others when social circumstances or individual decisions are complex or contested.[8] Accounts do specific social work, ameliorating moments of potential unrest; as such, they are also features of everyday life.[9] Judith Butler argues that accounts of identity often occur after some injury, or in the moments where explanation is demanded of us by another who occupies a higher position in the overarching system of justice. "I begin my story of myself only in the face of a 'you' who asks me to give an account."[10] Sometimes those demands are made plain; often, they are elicited indirectly by institutional contexts that require them for accommodation.

Accounts organize individual views of self, of others, and of the social world. How individuals make sense of themselves or others relies, in some part, on scientific knowledge, the things others consider "true" or "possible."[11] Parents occupy a unique position in accounts of children's gender; they are, at moments, the ones demanding explanations of their children, yet they are also the proxy voices permitted (and often required) to make declarative statements in the medical and social environments their children inhabit. They "give gender"[12] to their gender nonconforming children, and in so doing become the intermediaries between the entirely personal, emotional, and cognitive experiences of their children and the larger, surveilling glance of social institutions. The fact that they overwhelmingly mingle scientific and social knowledge in their accounts of their children's identities indicates larger shifts in public epistemologies of the self in modern times. Families are engaged in intellectual labor to reconstitute their understandings of gender and in emotional labor to carefully present the fruits of those new understandings to others. This labor was demanded from them by the social institutions with which they come into routine contact: schools, religious institutions, the state.

Biological Explanations

About two-fifths (39 percent) of the parents I spoke with at some point made reference to biological underpinnings of their child's gender. These explanations rooted gender in the physiological processes of the body, in its hormone receptors, in prenatal hormone washes. Some biological accounts invoked explanations from genetics, gene mutations, and in one case, the possible deleterious effects of environmental toxins.

For Sarah, understanding Sam's gender required understanding his somatic experience of the outside world. The many ways he chose to express his gender outwardly, his eclectic clothing and toy choices, were, in her mind, intrinsically connected to the ways he experienced touch, how he metabolized his food, the physiological nature of his mind. A few months before we sat down to talk, Sam spontaneously began shifting his clothing and toy preferences to more boyish things, and Sarah connected that directly to starting Sam on digestive enzymes for celiac disease. Within a week, she said, his behavior shifted. He began favoring pants over skirts, engaged in Star Trek fantasy games with classmates he would have previously avoided. She asked several doctors why his behavior might change on the medication and received conflicting accounts. Ultimately, she favored one explanation by a psychiatrist that connected internal swelling from his celiac to the suppression of testosterone.

> He said inflammation from any number of illnesses or problems in the body can blunt sex hormones. So while he may have had ample testosterone, his body was unable to read it. And this explanation made so much sense, in part because a number of people on the listserv have had their children have endocrine workups, but the thing that keeps shocking people is that their boys have ample testosterone. They don't lack it and yet they are very feminine. I've never seen a kid who does this 'cause they don't have enough sex hormone. So that made sense.

For Sarah, the shift in Sam's behavior toward more stereotypically masculine clothing and toys signaled a somatic shift in his body, even though some of his preferences and mannerisms remained markedly feminine. And yet, while she thought the recent change was produced within his body, she also believed some essential core part of him was distinctly feminine.

> I didn't realize ... how much of gender is ingrained. If [Sam's sister] was the way he was, I'd go wow, who's more feminine than me? She must be following my cues. I have makeup, she wants it on her. I have jewelry, she wants to wear it. She wants to go shopping. She wants me to wear a dress. She's like, "Mommy, could you stop wearing pants and wear something pretty?" You know? But you kind of think she's following gender cues. But then when a boy starts doing those things, well, they aren't following gender cues, and that taught me that gender is innate.

Central to many parents' rearticulations of their child's gender were detailed accountings of that child's subjectivity and the placing of that subjectivity in relationship to their body and to other bodies. In this way, contemporary transgender identities were not novel for their proof of gender's multiplicity. Transgender identities were themselves a distinctly modern form of accounting, a set of stories that drew from familiar knowledge systems in new and innovative ways.

Sarah's notion that an impairment in Sam's ability to "read" testosterone might lead to more feminine behaviors and preferences appeared to be a direct result of a specific transformation in modern medical thinking that locates gender directly in the physiological processes of the body. The popularization of discoveries within endocrinology, themselves products of deeply gendered social projects, was built into constructs of identity through which parents understand gender.

Sarah's focus on the physiology of gender was not unusual. Some parents offered a range of explanations for why gender was bound up in physiology, either in the function of hormone receptors or from prenatal "hormone washes." Others drew from popularized explanations of epigenetics and the common knowledge that there is a chromosomal element to gender to assert genetic explanations for gender difference. These narratives centered on rich descriptions of gene mutations, fears of the effects of environmental toxins, or creative ideas of ways in which conception might have gone awry.

For Christine, accepting Emmy's femininity was far less painful than coping with her community's reaction to it. She had easy access to support resources on the internet and through a national group for families. She read extensively about transgender in the beginning and said,

> From what I understand in the research I've done there's a hormonal wash in the third trimester and at that point a child either is given the hormones that matches their anatomy or not. Now, I don't believe that research is conclusive or something that someone can say, "This is it, we're done asking questions." But I do believe it points to a biological- or chemical-something answer to why a person is trans. I believe that our gender is not optional, and whether your body matches your gender or not, that that is who you are.

Ideas that biodiversity is multiple, informed by the media and their own education became resources that informed parents' understandings of gender. Christine continued:

I don't believe that there are just two genders. I do believe that there is an entire spectrum because from the research I've done it just seems to me if a hormonal wash can make you a girl or a boy, why couldn't it leave you somewhere in the middle, or a quarter of the way, or three-quarters of the way ... or something else entirely different, whatever that may be. Meaning that we have an unlimited number of genders, as of now nobody knows and I think they should teach that in school too.

This is far from scientific orthodoxy, but it makes practical sense. Rooting gender in the physiological processes of the body, and understanding that there are various moments in gender development where things could go awry, would seem to produce a kaleidoscope of possible gender outcomes.

Val told me multiple times during our conversation that she thought a lot about why her son Jesse was born female but felt like a boy, though she was quick to say she hadn't read too much medical research:

I really do believe that an egg that starts to split can be fertilized by two different sperm and it never splits. One can be different for the inside of the person, and one can be the imprint of the exterior of the person, and the very few percentage chances that that happens is because it's a sperm that just differentiates ... like you can actually have the inside of an X and an outside of a Y or vice versa.

Val, like many other parents, grasped for other examples of unexplainable childhood differences to help them not merely form explanations, but also make meaning out of the struggles they underwent. These material logics became emotional logics, as parents moved from ideas of difference to ideas of specialness. Val continued,

I don't know if it's ever medically provable, looking at that woman who ended up with twins, one was black and one was white, it almost proves it. It just happened that egg finished splitting. Okay? And they were identical twins, okay? You have a percentage of people that are going to have some kind of gender variance because that's the way genes and development are. You're gonna have the male and the female, which are at the opposite end of the spectrum. Irregardless to what society accepts, there are instances where people with gender variance fall in between, and [...] I believe the transgenders are the rare kind where physically they are one end of the spectrum and mentally they're on the other end of the spectrum.

Because Val struggled with her ex-husband to affirm Jesse's identity, because she faced disapproval from peers and some members of their community, she believed that these explanations, which rendered Jesse's gender nonconformity all but inevitable, were crucial to her advocacy efforts. And what acceptance they had found had been hard won. At the end of our interview, she wearily removed her glasses, rubbed her forehead, and said,

> I really do believe there is a different gene pool for how a person can be made up inside and how a person is made outside. Someday maybe people that are transgender will be accepted. It's just a matter of changing how the shell looks, because it's really what's in the inside that counts.

The notion that there is a genetic explanation for subjectivity empowered Val to argue for accommodations for Jesse in the conservative environment in which they lived. She felt that the connection between his mind and his body made his gender unimpeachable and grounded the moral imperative that others should treat him as the boy he felt himself to be.

Psychological Explanations

I met Sean Murphy, the single gay father whose child Michael incited a CPS investigation, for the first time the evening before our interview, when I attended an information session for parents at the middle school his youngest child attended. Sean immediately told me he always knew he wanted to be a parent. Thinking gay family life impossible, he didn't come out until his late twenties after moving to a large urban center from his suburban hometown. When by his mid-thirties Sean still hadn't settled down with a partner, he began thinking seriously about parenting on his own. After many discussions with an adoption placement agency, Sean says, he became very clear about his lifestyle and the sort of children he felt able to parent well.

> I'm a pretty on-the-go smart person out there in the world, kids with phys-
> ical disabilities wouldn't work for me. Kids with emotional difficulties and
> disabilities are the ones that I could really handle. [...] I think they knew
> that this is a pretty verbal environment, it's a pretty stimulating environ-
> ment in terms of conversation, travel, music, theater, et cetera. So I think
> that they probably had in mind that kids like that are gonna thrive. [...] I
> think that I just kind of knew to trust the folks at the agency and to sort of
> trust that the universe knows what it's doing. And I was right. And also, you
> know, I think that it's kind of like giving birth, you don't know what you're
> gonna get. You get what you get. And I wanted it to be that way for me.

Over the course of the following year, Sean adopted two little girls; first came eight-year-old Alessandra, who was part Italian and part Central American. Alessandra came to him saddled with a traumatic and violent past but immediately began to thrive in his care. And so, six months later, he received a call from the placement agency asking him if he'd be interested in adopting Jasmine, a five-year-old African Amer-ican girl. He asked how long he had to think about it. The agency replied, "Well, you've got about twenty minutes: she's on her way over to your house. So do you potentially want her for the rest of your life or not?" Sean said he thought for a second and replied, "Okay, sounds good."

When describing the family's early years together, Sean alternated between masculine and feminine pronouns for his younger child. Both Sean's children had significant histories of abuse in their natal and pre-vious foster families and myriad emotional struggles. He explained,

> My first impressions of Michael were, you know, here is this beautiful little
> girl who is outgoing and vociferous, and funny ... and just an amazing and
> charming individual. And yet scared. [...] I remember her first day here:
> "Oh, hi, are you gonna be my new daddy? Is that gonna be my room? Oh,
> this is great, this is fantastic." And then she was out in the yard and just
> standing there looking at all of us and started to pee in her pants.

Sean and his children all saw psychologists and psychiatrists. Sean practiced attachment therapy with his children, attending sessions with their therapists, holding them while they talked. He viewed their processes of healing as family processes, and was fiercely committed to building family bonds and helping them turn their gazes from the difficulties of their pasts to the prospects for their futures.

It didn't take long for Jasmine to come out of her shell. Sean imagined that Jasmine immediately felt safer than she ever had, that she'd never before been in a "kid-safe environment." He recalls a fairly rapid shift in her gender behavior as well. A month or two after her arrival, she favored a particular Hawaiian shirt, which she called her "boy shirt," and took to wearing it as often as she could. Sean didn't think much of it at the time. Over the next several years, she began asking for shorter and shorter haircuts. Sean and Alessandra called them her "Halle Berry" haircuts, and mostly thought of Michael as a tomboy.

By the end of third grade, Michael adamantly refused to wear anything feminine and began asking Sean to tell prospective camp counselors for that summer that his name was "Todd" and that he was a boy. School and summer camp administrators issued reports of Michael hanging out exclusively with boys and frequenting the boys' restroom. Eventually, Sean facilitated Michael's use of teacher restrooms. Some children at his summer camps would call him Jasmine, others called him Todd. Sean shrugged, "The other kids just seemed to get it." Soon thereafter, Sean took Michael to the emergency room to have a splinter removed. He went down the hall to get Michael a snack and returned to find the ER physician talking with him. She took Sean aside and said, "I just want you to know your daughter just asked me how old you have to be to have the operation to be changed into a boy." Sean assured her this was nothing new and shortly thereafter began to actively raise the issue of Michael's gender with Michael and his therapists. Michael told them all, in no uncertain terms, that he wanted to be a boy.

Sean told me that he considers gender identity and expression to be just another way in which individual people differ—along the same lines as sexuality and race. He questioned whether Michael's masculine gender represented a response to his history of abuse, but he eventually decided it was an unanswerable question. "We don't know, we may never know, and does it really matter if we know or not? If this is who he is or who he needs to be, then we gotta go with that." Sean was quick to point out that he also believed the reason Michael had been able to thrive in his male gender was that he and Sean had cultivated a relationship in which Michael could be authentic, while still feeling safe. For Sean, this kind of psychic safety was tied to the secure attachment he forged with Michael, as well as the conscious way he allowed Michael to explore his own sense of self. It seemed clear, listening to him speak, that his own identity as a gay man informed his parenting choices:

> I think that we live in a world where we use assumptions more than we discard them … and I think it's very hard for people just to be genuinely themselves … I think I started out by saying I wanted to grow up, get married, have kids. I probably wanted to have a nice big house, 'cause I didn't grow up in one. With a white picket fence, and a nice big station wagon, 'cause we didn't have one. And those were the assumptions that I grew up with for myself. And instead I've learned to live the life that's genuinely mine, not some picture I made up about myself … For me, Michael's just got to live his life as he wants to. I don't think parenting is having our kids grow up and making little us's. It's, how do we create the safe, comfortable, competent environment where they get to grow up and be themselves, whoever that is? And are there limits to that? Yes, but within a certain broad bandwidth they get to discover who they are.

Sean was acutely aware, however, that his family and his parenting choices are subject to scrutiny by the agencies through which they accessed the basic social services Michael needed. At one point, I told Sean I though it must be difficult at times to advocate for Michael within such complex bureaucracies. Sean bristled, becoming instantly defensive, and—taking the conversation in a slightly different direction than I had intended—replied:

I can't tell you how many people tell me how lucky my kids are to have gotten a dad like me. I just want to say, fuck you, you just don't get it, do you? You don't... like, no, they're not lucky, they deserve to have a parent that loves them for who they are, not for who he wants them to be. And I deserve to have children who are grateful and clean their room and do their homework. And scratch the grateful, right? I mean, just do your homework and clean your room. I'm the privileged one that I get to go through this with Michael—like, how many people get to do that? How many people get to do that in their lives? Parent a child who has had such a difficult life, who has the opportunity to fight a lot of the perceptions about who she used to be and be who he wants to be. That is a beautiful thing to help a kid find that, right? And not that many people get to do that.

While what I had meant with my comment was to signal empathy for the difficult bureaucracies he navigated, I suspect I hit upon the place in Sean where the weariness and sense of injustice lived. It took tremendous emotional labor for him to remain entitled and defiant in the face of "helping" systems that didn't always help. There was the labor he did to assist Michael in coming into an understanding of his identity. There was the work of advocacy in schools and social services organizations. There was the excruciating emotional work of parenting children with such complex histories and presents. Finally, there was the work it took to reframe the difficulties his family endured as a unilateral gift.

Sean believed that Michael's gender was reflective of the security of their relationship, a security forged through an active engagement with psychology. Sean spoke with confidence of the work he'd done as a parent to cement his relationship with his children, despite the myriad obstacles they've faced as a family. It was work, he said, that came with its own rewards. "I consider myself the privileged and lucky one. I'm the lucky one."

Patrick, a thirty-eight-year-old white landscape designer, seemed far more conflicted about the potential relationship between gender difference and psychic trauma, yet he was equally committed to psychotherapeutic projects with his child. He and his wife, Laura, formed their rambunctious family of five through a combination of biological and adoptive parenting. Pearl was their first addition. When I drove to their house on the outskirts of a major Pacific Northwestern city, she was eight, an African American transgirl who had come to them as an infant from a domestic adoption agency. They spoke with me at length about Pearl's early behavioral issues, their many trips to psychologists and trials with medication. It wasn't until she was about five years old that they realized that many of her defiant behaviors were around gendered moments, clothing choices in particular.

Patrick seemed reluctant to talk about the difficulties of parenting Pearl. He did, however, share his process of picking apart her gender identity and its relationship to her larger emotional struggles:

> I think there's definitely a more identifiable mental—that might be just particular to Pearl's situation, but there's definitely a more identifiable mental health component of a lot ... not a lot, but some ... gender issues. There's got to be some sort of mental health issues. What I'm saying by that is if people are making these choices, and not in a good environment because of split home or drug abuse, things like that where the kids are not supported in any way, it can manifest itself with some pretty significant mental health issues. Maybe those are things that are part of somebody's personality that gets to the point of manifesting that way or exhibited that way, or they can be tremendously more difficult if you're in an environment that is not supportive for you to make a choice like that. I don't know. Once again, that might be something that's particular to Pearl, because we deal with behavior issues a lot at the same time.

Patrick returned to this point several times. He wanted me to know that he didn't believe gender nonconformity to be itself evidence of psychopathology. He just couldn't understand how it all fit together.

Patrick struggled more actively with Pearl's gender than Sean did with Michael's, yet, both fathers believed strongly that engagement with psychotherapy was a path toward empowering a core aspect of their child's emergent self. Both families were also engaged in long-term psychotherapeutic projects with their children that covered a range of issues. While sociologists typically focus on the prescriptive rigidity of psychological theories about gender development, these families used psychology in a distinct way. For them, it offered a container in which to explore complex themes of human difference, and the ways they interact with social experiences like trauma, family, attachment, and love.

We can locate these accounts within larger shifts toward biological and psychiatric accounting in general,[13] yet the "regulatory power" of psychiatry is typically framed in social critique as a propensity toward sanction and social control whenever norm violations occur.[14] Psychiatric practice is opening up a space of possibility for benign gender variation and, in that sense, propelling the expansion of gender's possibilities. Parents are often acutely aware of and grateful for that transformation.

Spiritual Explanations

Some parents located their child's gender in their body, others in their psyche. A quarter (25 percent) of families invoked religious or spiritual tropes in their accounts. Some families described their child's unique and complex soul as one that could not contain a simple gender. Others viewed their child's gender atypicality as a spiritual project for the whole family. Still others appeared to reformulate Christian teachings to accommodate difference. Whatever the case, these explanations were often laden with intense affect.

Willow was twelve and a half when I first met her at a national conference for gender nonconforming children and their families. She was small of frame, with neatly composed dark, straight hair and serious brown eyes. Though she was dressed whimsically in a layered skirt with frills on its edges, in pink and purple pastels, she had a solemn comportment and a quiet demeanor. She seemed older than her years; when she spoke, it was often with a sort of wistful romanticism. She seemed to sit apart from some of the other youth, too young for the teenagers but older than her chronological peers. Her parents, Joseph and Michelle, described her as a creative genius who taught herself to knit and sew, who could mimic entire scenes in foreign language films with near perfect inflection, yet she struggled with the mundane tasks of classroom learning. They were also quick to tell me that the child I met at the conference scarcely resembled Oscar, the miserable, volatile, unpredictable boy they had raised for close to eleven years.

Joseph and Michelle described a distractible child who "lived in her own head" yet was capable of "profound thinking." They recalled routine encounters with strangers, who would seem mesmerized by Willow, telling them she was an "old soul" and that "there's just something about this kid." They faltered for words trying to explain their sense that she was somehow different from the start. Michelle described bringing four-year-old Willow along on a trip to take her grandmother to the eye doctor.

> I had Oscar in my lap and my grandma was sitting up on the table and the doctor was doing her thing. My grandma gets very nervous around doctors. After [the doctor] was done testing her, she had flipped on the light and my grandmother said, "Who was holding my arm?" Oscar, at the same time, had jumped down from my lap. My grandmother said, "Who was that who was touching my arm?" She said, "Oh, it was Oscar." I said, "No, Grandma, Oscar was in my lap. He just jumped down." She said, "Oh." Willow said something like, "It wasn't me, it was the angel." The doctor said, "Oh, what color is the angel?" She paused for a long time and said, "Purple." I was waiting for red, blue, a common color. Willow said, "Purple." The doctor said, "Yeah, that's right. There is a purple angel in this room. We've had reports of that."

Willow's unique sensitivity came packaged with a hypersensitive disposition and a stormy, unpredictable temperament. Her parents described her as a child reeling in pain, which she could contain through the school day but which would bubble up and spill over the moment she returned home. Her erratic behavior, even as a toddler, sent Joseph and Michelle from psychologist to psychologist, coming away each time with differing diagnoses: Asperger's, ADHD, anxiety. None of them could fully explain Willow's frequent tantrums and explosive temper.

Joseph lamented, "The terrible twos went to horrible threes and incredible, bad fours." Michelle chimed in, " ... explosive fives, want to sit her out in the middle of the freeway sixes. It was bad." "*It was bad*," Joseph concurred. They relayed the classic tales of emphatic rejection of "gender-appropriate clothing," tearful begging for feminine accessories, emotional distancing and withdrawal. Michelle became visibly shaken when she recounted a meeting in Willow's school, where administrators warned her that Willow's obvious depression was becoming dangerous. They said, "If you don't do something soon, she may not want to be on this Earth anymore." A few months later, Willow had a particularly frightening breakdown. "She'd been compromising for years," Michelle said. "She was totally at her wits' end."

> She had been playing with the kids, came in explosive, screaming, upset. She grabbed a knife out of the drawer and was doing this towards herself... [Michelle clasped her fists and made a motion like she was stabbing herself in the chest] ... because of whatever the hell happened outside, just screaming and pulling at her face. I just saw this knife coming like this. I just remember grabbing it and throwing it across the room. "What is wrong? What is going on?" She's just, "I hate the world! I hate the world!" and screaming and tearing at her face. "I want to die."

Willow was diagnosed with gender identity disorder (GID) a few months later. By then, Joseph and Michelle already suspected that Willow's struggles around gender might be the root of some of her emotional troubles. They researched gender identity on the internet, and actively searched for a clinician who could provide them with a GID diagnosis; after months of frustrating setbacks, it finally came. Shortly thereafter, they allowed Willow to attend a family vacation dressed as a girl. The change in her, they said, was immediate. I asked how she was different. They replied:

> MICHELLE: More relaxed, although she still had a little bit of anxiety, but it had come down about ten notches.
>
> JOSEPH: It went from volume 80 to volume 15. She was funny. She was interacting. She was participating in family stuff.

MICHELLE: She was always somebody on the outside looking in. I have a very huge family, six brothers and sisters, twenty-something nieces and nephews. We do get together a lot as a family. She'd always be on the outside looking in. She was totally participating, just happy, having a good time, playing on the beach with her older sister and holding hands and running from the waves, just laughing, feeling good.

JOSEPH: Skipping!

MICHELLE: Yeah, just feeling good, skipping and feeling good about being who she is. You could just tell a load had been lifted off her shoulder and she was just free.

Joseph and Michelle believed that Willow's behavior reflected the pain of containing and repressing her identity. Michelle said,

> For ten years of your life, if you've been living as the gender you're not and everybody around you who is supposed to love and protect you and take care of you is telling you you're wrong, you're wrong, and your whole innate sense of self is telling you something different, wouldn't you think you're a little crazy and you would live in your head?

Throughout the interview, Joseph and Michelle joked easily about the treachery of Willow's early years, yet their accounts were punctuated by long sighs, silences, moments of teary reflection and palpable pain. As they struggled to make sense of all of it, they tied the complexity of Willow's gender to their sense of her unique spirit. Joseph said,

> I think the souls who are given this status were not randomly selected. I don't think that Willow's sense of strength and courage is a result of her being transgender. I think the soul had courage, and it takes that to be transgender, if that makes sense. Why are some kids born transgender? I think the answer is because they have something about them that will enable them to survive that and to promote it, to advocate it, and to teach the rest of us. Not anybody can do that. It takes a very special soul and a very special set of characteristics to survive and to endure and to thrive in that status. [...] It isn't a medical condition, it isn't a deformity or a lack of an enzyme, it's not physiological—it's spiritual. It's a status that's entrusted to souls and not imposed on them.

Willow's soul provided a container both for her complex gender identity and for the challenging manner with which her internal conflicts were enacted within her family. For Joseph and Michelle, these parts of her were inextricable; they co-determined one another. The treachery of her rocky emotional makeup, which caused tremendous strain on Joseph and Michelle's marriage and their family life, was deeply connected to their sense of her uniqueness and beauty. Both lived within the deepest parts of her.

Tam and Elizabeth were a lesbian couple who had seven-year-old Finn with the help of a male friend. While they were both committed to some forms of gender-neutral parenting, like choosing a gender-neutral name for their child, and while Tam herself identified as a butch lesbian, they never imagined they would have a transgender child. By the time we met, Finn was going to school full-time as a boy. Tam believed Finn's gender was connected to his spirit, but that it also represented a spiritual project for the family itself:

> Since Finn was born, we always talked about how he seems to be an older spirit than either one of us. He's constantly telling us what we need to do to be better, sometimes just directly. I'm certainly learning a lot spiritually from this whole experience ... I need to keep stretching myself open more just to—I don't know ... to realize that my expectations and perceptions are not necessarily how it is. I constantly need to be listening more and opening up my imagination more for what could be. It's hard. For me, it's harder than I thought it would be, being a parent, period, then also being a parent of Finn and all his Finn-ness. I came from my Tam-ness, being not on a gender line myself.

Tom and Sandy, the family that left their unsupportive church community, were on a different kind of spiritual journey. They abdicated their church, but not their faith, which still informed their understandings of Alexander's gender:

> SANDY: What makes me so sad, though, is that I don't believe ... that Jesus Christ would ever come in and punish them. I just feel that, what did

he teach? He taught to follow him, but to love people. So my whole theory on my religion and that's totally changed.

TEY: Tom? You're smiling.

TOM: Yeah, no, I think the one primary thing is, you know, the testament that I see through Alexander's life, that this has been something that is innate and who he is, that was not encouraged by anything other than who he is. This is completely biological. This is something that can't be explained any other way. Therefore, if that's true, there are probably a lot of other things that are true about biological conditions of people and so on and so forth. So then, boy, that answers a lot of questions that I've always had . . .

TEY: What kinds of questions?

TOM: I guess, questions about why certain people are the way they are. You know, why—why is someone gay? Why does somebody believe that they're a man trapped in a woman's body? Why does that guy dress like that? All those types of things. I don't have to deal with that, so I'm gonna put it over here. Now, suddenly, it's like you know what, if you really think about it, this goes well beyond somebody just deciding one day, hey, I think I'll do this to myself . . . When there's gonna be consequences for it . . . And so my world has just been turned upside down, sideways.

SANDY [CUTTING TOM OFF]: We were not those—we were definitely not liberal people . . . but I laugh sometimes and I just look up and say, okay, Lord, you led me to this to rethink our thinking and, boy, have we done that, or at least I have on my part.

I asked Tom and Sandy to explain why they think some children are transgender.

SANDY: Okay. I don't know scientifically. I've heard, you know, the hormone wash and things like that. I believe it's, okay, I believe because of my religion that when Adam and Eve were here, that was that God had created a perfect world, once sin came into it, and I don't believe it's sin, but once then the world wasn't perfect, and that's when you started having sickness and birth defects and mental issues, you know, what have you. And I believe that we live in an imperfect world . . . Now, don't get me wrong, I'm not—see, this is the hard thing. I don't look at my child as imperfect, but I just look at my child as something that society says is not normal. I believe my child's normal. But more than anything, my child is a child of God. And it doesn't matter what that child is. That's how we all are related, that's how we all are in a family. Trans, not trans, gay, not gay, black, white, is we are children of God, period. And this is how I believe.

TOM: Yeah, I believe exactly the same. We live in a broken world. The world is broken. It can never be perfect ... If it was a perfect world, everyone would be born perfect, and that's not what we see.

A quarter of the families who accounted for their child's gender invoked notions of their unique souls or fashioned the challenges of having a gender nonconforming child into a spiritual project for the family as a whole. Some families, finding that their child's gender challenged long-standing engagements with (and faith in) more typical forms of organized religion, were able to modify or reformulate their belief system to accommodate their choices. If there was one thing that all the families agreed on, it was that their child's gender identity represented a core, often immutable, foundational piece of who they were. Michelle recounted a conversation she had with Willow shortly before our interview, in which Willow told her she'd known she was a girl since she was two. Michelle asked, "What is it that tells you that you're a girl? Is it your brain? Is it your heart? What is it that tells you?" Willow replied, "Mommy, it's my soul. My soul tells me I'm a girl, deep down where the music plays." "To me," Michelle said with a smile, "that was very profound."

CONCLUSION

The telling of life stories is always a social process; stories are mechanisms through which we create coherent narratives of our experience, yet they are also negotiations we undertake with others of what is true and possible.[15] They are calls for recognition, consideration, and integration. As Ken Plummer wrote, "Stories are social actions, embedded in social worlds."[16] Sociologists know that individuals create stories to order their experiences of self and others. Contemporary culture demands and rewards sexual storytelling in a whole host of contexts. But these families tell gender stories. And they are new stories, though they make use of familiar knowledge. The stories families offered of the gender identities of gender nonconforming and transgender children were deeply influenced not only by the context of the interview setting, but also by the sorts of explanations of gender we've made possible and what we might consider true. Families made routine use of logics imported from medicine, psychology, and spirituality to describe, explain, and occasionally provide justification for the increasing complexity of contemporary gender formations. These institutionalized discourses, often framed by sociology as separate sites through which gender is regulated, also functioned as personal resources for parents struggling to remake their conceptual frameworks for gender. With the same rigor and nuance with which we examine their regulatory potential, we might also consider the ways they function to expand the potential for gendered personhood, as regimes of truth, explanations for social life.

Likewise, with the same attention to detail with which sociologists describe transgender lives, we might also explain the ways understandings develop in response to those lives. For Sarah, Christine, and Val, biomedical discourse on gender diversity located it within a range of normal human variation. Contemporary psychiatry offered Sean and Patrick a concrete vehicle through which to engage the emotional work required to parent complicated children. It also provided them a kind of institutional sanction that can be, at times, very material. Looking concretely at what Courtney Bender calls "the spiritual," the circulating meanings, yearnings and imaginations that overlap and intersect with organized religions,[17] permits us to view the creative ways individuals like Willow and Alexander's parents made sense of struggles around difference. By engaging the issue of difference through the tropes families used to forge other understandings, we are better able to analyze their complex interactions with the institutions they inhabit.

In many ways, the families depicted here are atypical. They successfully sought and received the support of affirming professionals and advocacy organizations. Their children had all met other gender nonconforming youth. One might argue that their stories offer an unusual internal coherence. And yet the unresolved epistemological questions within medicine and psychology tend also to mirror the places where families' narratives falter. How is childhood gender nonconformity related to adult transsexualism and homosexuality? How does one determine the meaning behind a very young child's assertion that they are absolutely, positively not the gender the adults in their life believe them to be? When are gender choices merely choices, and when are they the stuff of a stable, core identity? Why are some children transgender?

There is no doubt that these children and families faced stigma in their daily lives. And yet, the typical techniques sociology suggests for managing "spoiled" identities[18]—deviance disavowal, passing, and denial[19]—didn't feature in these narratives as one might expect. These families instead forged a "shared construction of reality"[20] in which the very meanings of gender were expanded to include constellations of identity and behavior thought impossible by most conventional narratives. Their narratives were embedded in expert discourses, yet their meanings were reimagined through their own interpretive discretion. Families revised institutionalized tropes and reimported them back into the institutions they inhabited; in that way, they made social change.

These families afford the opportunity to witness the active working through of a new social identity category and the cultural lexicon with which they describe it. They offer a glimpse of processes of integration—how people reformulate their understandings of the world in response to queer lives. To paraphrase literary critic Michael Warner, they bring clarity to the process by which individuals make dissident identity articulate, how they challenge and reinterpret dominant frameworks.

These stories also suggest alternate ways of looking at the sex/gender distinction that vexes many gender theorists. Although the "queer" move of separating sex from gender provided feminists with analytic traction at a particular historical moment, conversations across disciplines urge bringing the material body back into gender theory. We see here the varied ways bodies are part of social accounts. We experience who we are with and through our bodies. These accounts demonstrate that there is no easy way to distinguish "what is materially true from what is culturally true about bodily gender."[21] Parent accounts give us some examples of ways to bring the body back in, to theorize fixity, without succumbing to notions of biological determinism. The body is a mechanism of meaning-making, irrespective of the veracity of the claims made upon it.

While these stories provide fascinating evidence of the creative and unique ways individuals account for deviance, they also demonstrate the role played by expert discourses in the formation of identities and social relationships. Parents speak institutionalized languages, yet experience them as deeply personal, meaningful, and individual resources.

They signal that in the contemporary moment, families are negotiating a novel social tension: with the increasing heterogeneity of social groups interacting in shared space and with associated calls for equality and recognition, metrics for delineating differences become ever more minute. Biomedicine, psychology, and spirituality offer tools for constructing a normative view of gender. Yet individuals can employ these restrictive knowledge systems in the service of expanding gender ideologies, not constricting them. They give us the concepts we use to make sense of who and what we are. Medicine and psychology locate gender within the structures of body and mind; in this way, they are at once natural and inevitable. Cultural, communicative dimensions of modern spirituality emerge ever more often outside of traditional organized religion. Those "evolving societal conversation[s] about transcendent meaning"[22] provide potent discursive resources families can employ to guide them in sense-making. This is religion in the creative and cultural sense. These explanations for difference issue a challenge to critical social theory, which seems at every turn to disavow reliance on expert discourse and hierarchies of knowledge-making, to ask itself: How can it assimilate the meaning-making processes of those who might be allies? Can it allow them to reconstruct their own meaning systems in response to new lives?

CHAPTER SEVEN

From Failure to Form

It had been close to five years since I'd last seen Rachel. I walked into the sprawling, suburban Italian restaurant where Rachel's boyfriend, Josh, worked as a waiter. It was a Saturday night, and the place was packed and noisy. It took me a few minutes to recognize her, but I finally spotted her seated in the back corner of the bar area, sipping a drink and tapping away on her phone. I approached and we greeted each other warmly but timidly. It had been a long time, and we both felt it.

She had grown her hair long. Her makeup was subtle but deliberate. She wore a flowing dress of brightly colored, dyed fabric that hung to the floor, with a sweater draped around her shoulders against the chill outside. Traces of Rafe's campy style were still visible. She wore sparkly black diamond-and-mesh earrings. Her cellphone case was bedazzled. She still held herself like a dancer. Her affect was softer now, though; she seemed more at ease in her body.

Rachel, then twenty-one years old, lived in an apartment with roommates in the most conservative suburb of a small Northeastern city. She worked as a hairstylist and makeup artist at a small salon, where everyone knew she was trans. On Sundays, Rachel performed as "Carlotta Trouble," a spicy drag queen at a local "drag brunch." Over plates of fried cheese and pasta, Rachel, now joined by her mother, Claudia, talked about her long process of coming to terms with her very complicated gender. As we talked, Josh came by to make sure we had everything we needed. He was warm and handsome and awkward; he smiled at Rachel often as we talked.

Rachel's parents and coworkers, including her drag friends, called her Rachel and used only female pronouns for her. Josh and other closest intimates called her Rafe and used male pronouns. Rachel could pass as female in most situations, and while she preferred that Josh called her Rafe, they had developed a signal for when she felt he should switch to Rachel and "she" for their safety. She stated adamantly that she had no preference for which name and pronoun I use, so I follow my commitment to honor parents' classifications here.

Claudia told me she had only recently begun using Rachel's female name and pronouns. When I asked what prompted Rachel to request the change, she replied, "She never did. I decided to make the switch." She recounted a conversation with a friend who also had a trans child, in which Claudia described the dissonance between Rachel's appearance and her seeming ease with male pronouns. The friend challenged her, "Well, have you ever tried using female pronouns for her? What would happen if you tried? Do you think she'd complain, or might she see it as affirming?" That night, Claudia discussed the conversation with Rick and they decided to begin calling their child Rachel and using female pronouns. Rachel, Claudia told me, never corrected her; she simply smiled.

Rachel does not have a stereotypical trans narrative. She elected to undergo certain medical treatments but not others. When we met, she was not on estrogen, and she had stopped and started blockers a handful of times, not liking the way her body felt when she was on them. She had gone abroad with her mother for breast augmentation surgery and a nose job. While she called herself "transgender," she lived her life in a kaleidoscope of genders often contingent on the relationship; she was male with her lover, female with her coworkers, somewhere in the middle with family and friends, and deeply invested in a camp culture that privileged the hyperbolic nature of femininity. Her sensibility was still campy, and her performances were raunchy and sexually saturated. She was, perhaps, somewhat of an anomaly, mixing the politics of sincerity with irreverence and play. It was a compelling combination.

To position Rachel as an example of gender's erosion would be to profoundly misunderstand the way she lived gender. Rachel's gender was very much at the center of her life, of her self-understanding, of the configuration of her relations to others. It was also something her family and intimates thought about, negotiated with her, grappled to understand, and explained routinely to others.

While Rachel's gender trajectory did not follow a linear path, it does illustrate many of the new questions faced by this generation of children and families. Rachel may never come to rest in a static, fully articulated, singular identity, though her family certainly spent years trying to discern what such an outcome might be. She will likely continue to make strategic use of medical interventions, as each iteration brings her either closer to or further from a self she can rest in. Her parents used a female name and pronouns for her in acknowledgment of the centrality of these processes in her life, and as an indication of their willingness to travel the sometimes difficult path along with her. Likewise, Rachel's brand of trans identity, while it could not be captured by a neat male/female dichotomy, did not eschew dyadic gender, either. She lived in intricate relation to the gender binary, approximating it, subverting it, even parodying it in her drag practice. Rachel was living a new version of social gender, one tied to many of the historical and contemporary social processes outlined in this book. Her story demonstrates that even in the moments when individuals contest the gender system, the categories and social processes into which they are interpellated, those categories are not evacuated of their meaning. Instead, they are drawn ever more deeply inward, as possibilities for a gendered life rearticulated on new terms.

GENDER CHANGES

Social change is produced not merely by social actions or organizations, but by bundles of emergent stories.[1] The new stories told about transgender and gender nonconforming children are changing the very terms by which gender categorization happens. Whereas once we understood gender to be the social expectations that adhere to biological sexual difference, we now understand it to be a fundamental, immutable part of the psychic self that needn't cohere, in any predictable way, with the materiality of the body. Perhaps paradoxically, the idea of a static "gender identity" as a core part of psychic structure opened up a cultural space for individuals to renegotiate gender's relationship to the body. If it is, as philosopher Gayle Salamon has argued, partly the "felt sense" of the body,[2] then individuals might assert feelings that conflict with their bodies. This seems different than even poststructuralist ideas of gender performativity.[3] The idea that there is no self behind the expressions that constitute it is in direct tension with people's deeply held ideas of the essence of who they are. While feminist theory has often wished to undo social ideas of the body in an effort to "free" the self, we find that the authentic, unbounded self must nonetheless contend with the body,[4] and must do so in interaction with institutions. This requires of us not only a new multivalent understanding of social gender, but also a move from a static understanding of the body to one that can account for the creative rearticulation of the body by the individual who possesses it.[5]

Whereas for over a century most considered gender atypicality in childhood a psychiatric ill warranting corrective intervention, parents, physicians, and even social institutions now understand it to be something else. These children are "transgender," "gender creative," "gender independent," "gender flexible," or a whole host of other terms that literally didn't exist ten years ago.[6] These are not just new words; they are new forms of subjectivity. That subjectivity "is constitutive of gender."[7] The idea of "gender identity" is the symbolic resource[8] that allows the social male/female boundary to become permeable. And not merely on the cultural level, but on the bureaucratic level as well, from biomedicine and psychiatry, to schools, to law.

These parents and children are part of a social process in which the transgender child is installed as a legitimate category of experience.[9]

It's not that gender-atypical children didn't exist before; of course they did, in different historical times, under different names, in interaction with different cultural forms. Yet, until recently we had no "functional understanding" of them as a type of person.[10] Atypical gender was considered psychopathology because it was a type of gender failure; the failure resided precisely in the fact that it was atypical. But now, atypical gender is understood *not as a failure of gender but as a form of gender.* One might say, it now marks the insufficiency of the gender category itself. Gender nonconformity used to be the debris that marked psychopathology; now it is the material that constitutes social identity. That shift from debris to identity was facilitated by changes in psychiatry and psychology, and mirrors precisely the recent move from the DSM-IV to the DSM-5. As medicine moves from the regulatory to the facilitative, parents learn to view atypical gender behaviors as the signposts of a different core identity.

Will Rachel and Avery grow up to be gay, straight, or transgender adults, or some combination of those things? The parents I interviewed have become ever more attuned to the vicissitudes of childhood gender, and asking those very questions is one part of that attunement. Likewise, new medical technologies that forestall puberty, either to buy parents time to allow their child's identity to mature or to avoid the physical manifestations of natal puberty, exerted their own normative pressures to taxonomize childhood gender nonconformity, to determine what forms correlate with adult transgender identities. Ashley's parents determined their child would continue to identify as a girl into adulthood. Bess understood that Benjamin identified as male and wondered where his sexuality would land. While Rachel's and Avery's parents understood their children had gender problems, neither one had yet completed the process of assuming a female identity.

Rachel's and Avery's parents noticed something atypical about what their child said or did. Since "sex category is omnirelevant,"[11] Rachel and Avery were held accountable for those behaviors, play styles, and identity declarations *as boys.* As West and Zimmerman note, "doing gender" did not always mean doing normative masculinity or femininity; rather, it was the "activity of managing situated conduct in light of normative conceptions ... for one's sex category," always "at the risk of assessment."[12] In previous generations, the negative assessments made of such boys would lead to psychiatric diagnoses and corrective treatment. This is the crux of the shift: the gender nonnormativity these boys exhibited was not merely assessed as an infraction; it now incited questions about the allocation of those children into gender categories themselves. While Jade's butterfly princess play was an atypical form of behavior, her parents did not understand it as "doing gender." Instead, David and Lyn understood Jade to "be" a gender that failed to conform to the expectation of others. They recognized their child's behavior as something deeper than social gender, emerging rather as a core aspect of her actively consolidating personal identity.

While these stories included struggles around the sorts of issues—clothing, toys, interactions—that prompt other parents to constrain gender, there was something different here, a fundamental self that parents understood as gendered in particular ways. They and their physicians interpreted ambiguity and uncertainty as intrinsic properties not of gender itself, but of the process through which gender comes to be understood by others. This happened differently for assigned male and female children, reflecting differences in the cultural value placed on masculinity and femininity. The idea of transgender, as a cultural resource, gave parents a context for interpreting gender behavior in ever more nuance. They looked at play styles, manner of dress, affect, imaginative play, even the length of hair as signposts of a core self. Some of those identities mapped neatly onto male and female; others required more nuanced articulations.

The parents I met were searching for ways to assist their children in articulating an authentic gender while also striving for social assimilation and connection. They searched one another, their own and others' children, adult transpeople, for evidence of what their child's trajectory might look like going forward. They thought about gender, asked questions, read books and articles, and talked about it constantly. As I watched them, they watched me back; we mirrored one another's processes of sense-making.

Some children moved from one social category to another. Their parents engaged in affective, interpersonal, and bureaucratic efforts to assist them in shifting their social classifications, and their labors illustrated what being a gender actually entails. There are multiple parts to this undertaking: there is the individual development of a self-understanding. There are also social, interactional, and institutional negotiations of that self to be made. Most of these processes are assumed or obscured for cisgender people, but they happen for everyone. To *be a gender*, in a social sense, is to incorporate a self-understanding, along with the recognition of that understanding, into the space of interaction, and then to appeal to the forms of institutional validation that scaffold and organize collective life. Even the state has a hand in the allocation of gender; some families found themselves acutely vulnerable to interventions into their parenting by social services, while others used the state as a tool in mediating intrafamily disputes. Forms of inequality we typically imagine as macrostructural, in fact, permeate the most intimate of all family relationships.

Psychologists were the first to identify gender identity, the intrapsychic consolidation of male or female identity, in the 1950s and 1960s.[13] Parents used this same construct to explain why individual children might understand themselves in a way that seems counter to the evidence their bodies present. As sociologist Rogers Brubaker wrote recently, "To make subjective identification the socially legitimate grounds for changing [classifications], it has been necessary to fortify and naturalize identity by casting it as a deep, stable, lifelong, unchosen, and probably biologically grounded disposition."[14] The concept of gender identity functions in precisely this way, to scaffold the efforts parents make to give gender to their children in interaction. But neither individual assertions of self nor even the collective agreement to validate that self by a community is sufficient to fully ensure an individual's transition from one social category to another. The varied and anxious interactions parents have with school officials, medical professionals, social services, and the administrative state demonstrate that gender classifications function in a host of bureaucratic contexts to structure access to resources and insulate those who conform to their mandates from intrusion and punishment.

The liberalization of psychiatry occurred in tandem with the production of a host of new medical technologies that assist individuals in their bodily expressions of gender. While for decades progress in adult transgender medicine was often accompanied by an intensified effort to constrain the gender behavior of children, now there is a vast medical complex that provides families with facilitative psychiatric and biomedical services. Because of the particular anxieties that attend medical decision-making for children, an intensified effort to identify the etiology of nonnormative gender and delineate predictable long-term outcomes accompanies these treatments. This activism both humanizes medical practice and stabilizes (some argue prematurely) the meaning of childhood transness, cementing protocols for its normalization.[15]

The expert landscape is also shifting dramatically. Formerly the world expert on gender nonconformity in children, Ken Zucker now works in partial isolation, contributing to research efforts and editing his journal, but seeing patients only on weekends and without the institutional support he enjoyed for decades. His clinic has been overtaken by university-based hospital clinics that offer a more consumer-based approach to treatment, some of which contain both psychiatric and medical services under a single awning. This is the future of trans medicine for children, and activists and parents hope it is a future that will feel more humanizing to its patients.

The very existence of transgender children and the emergence of a medical and social industry surrounding them is the direct result of a cultural shift in one of the most debated and fundamental of all social categories. When early critical social theorists outlined the historical evolution of homosexuality from a collection of discrete sexual acts to a form of individual personhood,[16] they never imagined the same would become true for gender. The transgender may represent just such a transformation. When adults quantify, label, and recognize transgender identities in children, they participate in the active construction of gender itself as an individual subjectivity, a feature of the self. It is a self intimately tied to both social relationships and institutions.

Gender identity, as a construct, came into being to explain why there might be a dissonance between individual identities, bodies, and social classifications. Gender identity separated gender both from the body and from our idea of sexual orientation. As transgender individuals (or their parents) assert dissident gender identities to medical and legal institutions, they become installed as legitimate categories of being, analysis, and study. If gender identity is an immutable feature of the self, there is a much stronger argument to be made that social classification systems ought to reflect that reality as well.

YOUR MOTHER'S TRANS

The Point looks like a cross between a Starbucks and a diner. During the week and in the evenings, it's a typical restaurant, but on Sundays until midafternoon it hosts a popular drag brunch. For $24, patrons can gorge on a huge breakfast of eggs, fried potatoes, and buffalo wings, mimosas and bloody marys, arranged buffet style along a long wall. Claudia and I seated ourselves at the very end of a large bar that ran the length of the room. She was clearly a regular, greeting the servers warmly and by name. While patrons ate breakfast, the loudspeakers blasted songs by Lady Gaga and Adele, show tunes and movie themes, and one of the half dozen or so drag queens would burst into the dining room, lip syncing and walking through the crowd rubbing against whomever was close by, dancing provocatively, soliciting tips, or posing for photographs. Midway through the performance, Lady Mother, the lead queen, would announce birthdays, bachelorette parties, and other special occasions, and the celebrants would be invited to the front of the room to receive her ridicule in exchange for her demands to tip, pointing to the crevice between her breasts and exclaiming, "Put it in the bank, honey!"

Claudia took Rachel there for the first time on her seventeenth birthday. When it came time for the birthday announcements, Rachel sauntered to the front, and when Lady Mother asked her what she wanted to be when she grew up, she replied, "A drag queen." They immediately ushered her backstage (Claudia quickly followed), did her makeup, and invited her to do a number with them. She was ecstatic. She quickly became a regular at The Point, at first just once a month, then a year or so later joining the weekly cast.

As we sat in the corner, Rachel sauntered into the room to Lady Gaga's "Bad Romance," wearing a long blonde wig and what looked almost like a black graduation gown, or a floor-length satiny version of the drape one wears at a hairstylist's. Poking out from the bottom were shiny silver platform high heels. She promenaded up the aisle, making a bee-line first for Claudia, kissing her cheek and accepting some cash. Claudia clapped along and followed to the edge of the bar to watch Rachel as she then disappeared around the corner. A moment later, she was pulling off her robe to reveal a diamond-studded string bikini. She twirled, climbed on the back of the booths, and at one point slid into full splits on the floor. Patrons cheered and slipped her money. She gleamed. She made her way over to us and her mom proudly snapped a photo of Rachel and me together. Rachel then slipped offstage, and we went back to our brunch.

After a few more performances, it was Rachel's turn again. This time, at her mother's request, she reprised a techno version of the Disney hit "Let It Go." This time, Rachel discarded a shiny blue smock to reveal tiny sequined shorts and pasties. As we watched, Claudia told me a friend had challenged her, after seeing Rachel perform, to explain how this was different from letting her daughter become a stripper. We sat in silence for a moment, hearing the reproach in the question and searching out minds for a way to articulate the difference. It was something, Claudia explained, about the difference between gender and sexuality. This was a performance of gender. Of course, we both acknowledged, it was often complicated, if not impossible, to fully separate the two. The performance was nothing if not sexually saturated. But perhaps its sexuality was less the point than its gender parody. Or, that in order to participate in the sexualization of the ritual, one had to inhabit their own desire for the kind of gender drag queens possess. That is, in itself, a politics.

One afternoon as she stood outside The Point, Claudia spotted a leader in the adult trans community, someone who ran a major lobbying group and who worked often on Capitol Hill. Let's call her Melanie. Melanie recognized Claudia and they chatted, but Melanie looked uncomfortable. She told Claudia that she didn't like hanging around The Point, that whenever she walked by she feared someone would mistake her for "one of them." (Claudia moved her body in a mock drag pose as she recounted this.) She asked Claudia what she was doing there, and Claudia explained that Rachel was "one of them." Melanie made an awkward joke about not being glamorous enough and scurried away. But the point was made: drag, overt sexuality, camp aesthetics, hyperbole—these are distinct from a politics of transgender that trades in notions of concrete identity and sincerity. This was, as Claudia said, "not your mother's trans."

Claudia, Rachel, and I carefully chose the image on the cover of this book. I hoped they would offer me something that captured both the complexity of Rachel's relationship to gender and the light touch with which she held some of gender's mandates. There were many options: Rafe in the context of his pink bedroom, Rachel face-forward in soft focus, Carlotta in full makeup. In the end, we returned again and again to an image taken not long before we first met, at a high school dance performance. Rafe in a "c jump," buoyant, fully himself.

Claudia and Rachel were different from many other families in this book. By and large, the parent movement was a cisgender movement. It was politically distinct from the transgender movements that came before. Rachel straddled these two worlds, the world of mainsteam trans rights and the more complicated world of drag, camp, and queer. Different articulations and investments in gender animate each. The parent movement has, over the last several years, effected tremendous change in institutional practices ranging from local schools to the federal government, around everything from identity recognition to access to medical care. It tapped into the activist energy that closed CAMH, and worked to help found the clinics that are replacing it with newer models of care. In many ways, trans kids are not merely an unprecedented social category; they are unusual in that their very existence depends on a vicarious social movement of supportive adults. Some wonder if this support comes with normative investments that will radically transform transness for this new generation. Some worry the politics of visibility will be lost, in favor of a more sanitized version of trans. Many transgender children growing up today will have the benefit of medical interventions that prevent them from going through their originary puberty. As such, they will have wider latitude to pass as adults and to disidentify with the label *transgender* and the movement it defined. Thus, both parents and children may be taking trans in a direction far different from where it began.

TYFA and Gender Spectrum have both undergone tremendous change in recent years. When the Mazzoni Center took over Philly TransHealth, TYFA found itself pushed out of its main family event. While some of the parents who worked with the organization still do limited trans advocacy, most now have grown children, and even Kim herself has largely stopped doing trans activism. We spoke as the book went to press and she told me that she had known for several years that TYFA was losing its relevance. The marketplace for expertise on trans had grown at a lightning pace, and with smaller local support groups for parents cropping up in many major cities, TYFA no longer had something unique to offer. While their website remains live, it is a hollow version of what it once was.

Gender Spectrum's day-to-day operations are now managed by Joel and a handful of other senior staff. The organization's mission has expanded from a focus on gender nonconforming kids to a broader focus on "gender inclusivity" for all children. Stephanie occasionally consults for the organization but is no longer its director. Parents with trans youth now have an array of options, from medical and psychiatric care, to specialized gender clinics, to summer camps and youth groups, that were unthinkable when Stephanie and Kim met in San Francisco a decade ago. While their models of advocacy have given way to a more professionalized trans advocacy, much of what now exists is a direct result of their efforts.

BEING A GENDER

In this moment of rapid social change, it might be tempting to think that the gender order is crumbling. But as queer theorist Jack Halberstam said, "Rumors of the demise of hegemonic sex/gender systems have been greatly exaggerated."[17] In fact, what is happening is that gender is at once proliferating and becoming more particular. While some feminist sociologists seem preoccupied with the "undoing" of gender, I would argue that these children and families provide potent, often heartbreaking evidence that gender is deeply valued cultural material, even by those whose practices seem most resistant to its mandates. Although the antiessentialist premises of early second-wave feminism extended into contemporary discourse, a funny thing happened on the way to that androgynous, gender-minimalist utopia. Instead of eroding, gender identities and gendered social forms have multiplied and gained importance, both socially and politically. Rather than further ossifying as contrasting explanatory frames, nature and culture have both been invested with an increase in significance. Gender desires and identities turn out to be quite profound, even more so than their presumed corporeal foundations. At the same time, many believe that the two are not, in fact, inextricable.

Finally, whereas some feminist theory appears, in the name of liberalizing gender restrictions, to denigrate both femininity and masculinity, newer work elaborates the intricate social pleasures that attend gendered life.[18] At conferences for transgender and gender nonconforming children, I saw parents and kids alike delight in their expressions of self and relationship. Whether enjoying the magical fantasy play common to all young children, wearing clothing their parents restricted in other contexts, or simply relaxing into the normlessness of a gender-inclusive space, children expanded into themselves with outward expressions of glee. And parents, offered a brief respite from the burden of being the radical translators of the gender order, could simply look on with relief and appreciation for the vast array of forms childhood gender can take. Gender did not evacuate the space; gender animated it.

Gender in its institutional forms gathers together various affects, interpersonal relations, medical and scientific apparatuses. All of this is the material that collects in gender categories. Ethnicity scholars Jan Blommert and Ben Rampton caution us not to make the intellectual mistake of talking "of multiple, fluid and ambiguous identities." Such "high octane dramatization of public discourse" ignores the fact that "people manage to bring a high degree of intelligible order to their circumstances."[19] Instead, they suggest we see how categories come to rest on humans, to constitute them and constrain them. Acceptance of mobility between categories does not necessarily destabilize the categories themselves, or even the boundaries between them. Indeed, it might fortify, or at least clarify, them. As some have argued, it may instead lead to the institutionalization (and, concomitantly, the acceptance) of categories beyond the binary pair.[20] This very proliferation is the contemporary gender moment.

Rather than abdicating identity discourse and focusing on fluidity, parents are now more inclined to contest the gender labeling practices of others, to engage in intricate relational work to assist children in identity development, and to push social institutions to recognize and reinforce those identities. The institutionalization of transgender identities in children indexes the ways processes of assessment are required to produce gender, even in its nonnormative forms. The future my subjects portend is in many ways the very inverse of widespread feminist ideals of gender neutrality. It is certainly true that securing a coherent and comprehensible gender in children has become part and parcel of what sociologist Sharon Hays calls "intensive parenting."[21] Gender has become an object of both knowledge and "concerted cultivation." But the classic analysis of "doing gender at the risk of assessment" doesn't work for these subjects. Some new forms of gender actually require the kinds of negative assessments that individuals previously sought to avoid.

As the clinical gaze penetrates new levels of bodily and psychic gender, the state is likewise solidifying its concern with the gendering of children. From interventions into family life, to the use of the state by individuals for mediating family disputes, to certification of expert discourse on gender diversity, the state and its administrative actors have joined other social institutions deepening their investments in the classification of and interaction with new forms of gender. Gender is not loosening its grip on institutional life; quite the opposite. A proliferation of cultural discourse on gender matches an intensified institutional push to incorporate gender into the business of the state.

It may look like gender is becoming more fluid, but in fact it is becoming more highly differentiated. Transgender children may well be the harbingers of a new gender order, but it will be one in which complex configurations of sexuality and gender get articulated in ever more nuanced ways. As the binary gender system shifts, we look to one another for clues about what comes next. We are all studying one another. We are all gendering one another. We all carry a gendered subjectivity, but we live that subjectivity intersubjectively. Gender is not merely something we do. It is something done to us, with us. It does and undoes us, constrains us and constitutes us.

It is some of the most basic material of social life.

A Note on the Language of Gender

I researched and wrote this book during a watershed moment for gender diversity. When I entered the field, parents referred to their children as "gender variant." Within two years, that terminology was no longer considered culturally sensitive; rather, dominant sentiment was that the term adopted a psychiatric lexicon long used to objectify and pathologize transgender people. Parents had begun using "gender nonconforming" instead, to signal a child's deviation from cultural expectations, rather than installing a normative gender taxonomy from which they might vary. In my first published work on this project, I used the former term. I shifted, along with the communities I studied, and now use the latter. I fully anticipate that the language will continue to evolve and that, sooner than I care to anticipate, the language in this book will seem archaic.

I have struggled mightily to figure out what names, pronouns, and descriptors to use for the children portrayed in this book. The solutions I have generated are imperfect. I elect to use the gendered names and pronouns for children their parents used at the time we spoke. I do this for two reasons: first, it allows me to keep the language parents use verbatim in moments when doing so seems crucial to preserving the temporality and complexity of their internal processes. Second, because I make claims to gender as fundamentally relational, and aim the analysis at parents as participants in the creation of gender, it is, in essence the parents' stories I am telling. Others, including many transgender children themselves, are now writing these stories from the other side.

The most daunting task has been determining how best to convey to you the particular gender configuration of individual children, in the contexts in which I describe them. You might notice a single child referred to as a "trans-girl" when I speak about her in the present, while also being lumped into the category of "feminine boys" for the purposes of analyzing when and how her parents came to understand that she was trans. I hope my readers, particularly those whose genders have been held roughly by others, will forgive the moments when I fail to reconcile the need for specificity of a parent's experience with the fullness of a child's internal sense of self. Rather than staking a claim as to how an individual child might identify, were I to ask that question today, descriptions of gender herein mirror the genders available to that child in the moment. Assigned male, feminine boy, gender nonconforming boy, and transgirl can all be stops along a single child's path to an enduring self, one that, sometimes after great struggle, merges their felt sense of self with their social world.

Methodology

This project began as pure serendipity, as is so often the case in ethnographic fieldwork.[1] I was miserable in graduate school, completing a dissertation prospectus for a project I thought was important but uninspiring. To distract myself, I decided to volunteer at the National Gay and Lesbian Task Force annual conference, Creating Change. They were running a day-long institute for activists on the current state of LGBT families that would feature social scientists, activists, and community organizers. I met Jordan Scott on that cold winter day. It was January 2009. Jordan was about five foot nine and small of frame. He had a neatly trimmed beard and kind eyes that crinkled slightly when he smiled, which was often. He sat down with a group of us during a break, and we went around and made introductions. Jordan described the work he was doing with an organization called Gender Spectrum. He explained that for the past three years he had been working as an ally and social support for the families of gender nonconforming and transgender children. The work took him into schools and communities in multiple states where children were transitioning from one gender category to another, or were being bullied for violating gender norms, and he conducted workshops on gender for youth, parents, teachers, and administrators. Someone in the group asked him how he had begun this work, and at that point he revealed to us that he himself is a transman. Several in attendance remarked on their surprise that, even in an LGBT context, the thought hadn't crossed their minds.

Like most people at the time, I hadn't given much thought to transgender children; I simply assumed that it was in late adolescence or early adulthood that the vast majority of transpeople fully realized, understood, and openly expressed their identities. Certainly, I had met dozens of transgender adults in my long history of activism in LGBT organizations in New York, but I'd never met a transgender child. And yet Jordan described doing dozens of workshops just in the city in which he lived. It was surprising to me that there was a trans-related social movement with which I was unfamiliar. As it turned out, the dominant organizations and public discussions about LGBT equality at the time were wholly separate from the movement of families with transgender children I was about to encounter. Mainstream transgender rights organizations often described the tremendous difficulties faced by gender nonconforming youth, but they were, at the time, oddly silent about the particular lives some openly trans youth with supportive families were living. As we see in the book, the generational tensions that kept the movement apart were felt from both sides. Much like the rapid development of PFLAG (Parents and Friends of Lesbians and Gays) in the mid-1970s,[2] the parent support movement functioned in isolation from (though on some rare occasions in shared spaces with) LGBT community-based interventions.

Whereas PFLAG was institutionalized in communities across the country and contributed to ongoing research on homosexuality and parenting,[3] the world of supportive families with gender nonconforming and transgender children was insular, nebulous, and well guarded by the parent advocates who formed organizations and held events. In meeting Jordan Scott, I had involuntarily stumbled into the epicenter of one of the two largest constellations of children and families in the United States networking around these issues. As we walked together after the conference, I asked him about how schools responded to these children and families, how he did the work of education, and about the mission and vision of his organization. With little idea of what it was I sought, I asked Jordan if I could observe Gender Spectrum doing its work. He generously agreed. Two months later, I boarded a plane, and this project began.

As with much research on emergent phenomena, I began by doing some "diagnostic participant observation."[4] Jordan put me in contact with Stephanie Brill and Joel Baum, and I spent a week watching them work in a variety of contexts. I met some of the families they supported and had some informal conversations about their lives and their children's transitions. I met several of the children as well, and spent time playing and interacting with them. These were not typical "pilot interviews";[5] they were largely informal and unstructured, and although I kept extensive field notes during that time, most of what occurred never made it into this text. What became apparent in those initial encounters was that I would need to engage a number of relevant actors in order to comprehend the rapid emergence of this new social form. After returning to New York and breaking the news to my mentors that I planned to discard my current project in favor of this new one, I began preparing for a multi-method, qualitative approach to studying the emergent phenomenon of the transgender child.

PARTICIPANT OBSERVATION

I located my larger fieldwork project within the social and institutional spaces where families gathered to seek support around their children's gender. This focus on a population of *social situations*[6]—my participant observation in these community spaces as well as individual in-depth interviews—produced the chance to observe social change in action. It also produced an unexpected opportunity to witness parents' individual processes of remaking their conceptual frameworks for gender. In keeping with a rich tradition in sociology of field-driven, emergent theory building,[7] I realized during the course of my research that these conferences, support groups, and, indeed, the interview setting itself, provided spaces wherein parents could consolidate their thought processes in dialogue with others.

This is certainly not ethnography in its most traditional sense. There is no singular, bounded "site" in which to witness and experience this emergent social group and its relations internally and to the outside world. My study is perhaps more closely aligned with the newer practice of "relational ethnography," which privileges "fields rather than places, boundaries rather than bounded groups, processes rather than processed people, and cultural conflict rather than group culture."[8] Taking my cue from another ethnographer of transgender phenomena, David Valentine, I constructed this study as an "ethnography of a category,"[9] and I endeavored at first merely to appear in sites where families with "transgender children" were also likely to appear. In doing so, I found myself "putting things together."[10] My field site is a kind of "assemblage,"[11] a collection of experiences and opportunities for participation that required flexibility, travel, and improvisation; it results from transient moments of "deep hanging out"[12] and from sustained, longer-term relationships.

In all, between 2009 and 2013 I attended twelve multiday conferences for families, children, and care providers in five different cities. I attended another eight professional conferences for mental health professionals working specifically with gender nonconforming and transgender youth, two of which also contained substantial parallel tracks for physicians providing medical care and hormonal therapies to youth. One of these, the World Professional Association for Transgender Health (WPATH) was a major international conference that brought together the top specialists working with transgender youth and adults from over twenty different countries. I shadowed TYFA and Gender Spectrum through a total of seventeen workshops in middle schools, high schools, parent association meetings, and churches. I attended countless talks, lectures, panel discussions, community networking events, parent group Christmas parties, ice skating and bowling events, and a multitude of other gatherings where there were critical discussions about trans youth issues or groups of families at work or play. I spent as much time "backstage" with these organizations as money and travel time permitted. I attended both telephone and in-person planning meetings for conferences, and talked informally with organizers about their aims and plans. I spent time, drank coffee, ate breakfast, and moved boxes with parent activists and movement leaders before, during, and after conferences. I sat in hotel lobbies, in cars, on trains, and in the homes of these people and their families. In short, I endeavored to make myself a fixture during moments when organizations were engaged in the business of their work, and when activist parents were engaged in the business of their lives. I took copious field notes after each event, and sometimes during events, carrying a small notepad with me wherever I went. Finally, I organized the teen programming for one major conference, wrote up a guide to families for dealing with researchers and media, and edited documents for both TYFA and Gender Spectrum, in an effort to repay in some small way the generosity both organizations showed me.[13]

IN-DEPTH INTERVIEWS

Between 2009 and 2013, I conducted a total of eighty interviews with sixty-two parents of fifty gender nonconforming and transgender children, some of whom I interviewed multiple times. There were two subsamples. Fifty parents of forty children were from "facilitative families," parents who worked with organizations of care professionals in the United States to facilitate their child's gender expression. All initial interviews with those families were conducted between 2009 and 2011, with some later follow-ups. The second subsample were "clinical families," those who utilized CAMH services. Those interviews were conducted in 2012 in Toronto, Canada. I only met the CAMH interviewees once. Interviews typically lasted between one and a half and three hours, though some lasted as long as five hours. They were recorded, transcribed, and hand-coded by me. After the first twelve interviews, I paused, coding and looking at transcripts for emergent themes, and then amended my interview protocol, largely removing questions I deemed unimportant and adding more open-ended prompts that allowed participants to generate more self-directed versions of their stories. I also noticed some clear trends I then knew to follow more closely. For example, I noticed that the question "When did you first reach out to someone else for support around your child's gender?," rather than prompting parents to reveal stories about the first confidence they shared with a friend or relative, generated stories of "aha!" moments, where comments from others or some significant emotional upset made them understand their child's gender as enough of problem that they needed professional support. I then became more attuned to what those moments looked like, resulting in the gendered analysis of fragile masculinity in chapter 2. My "grounded theory" approach to data analysis employed an emergent coding scheme that evolved as I went through the transcripts (and then went back to recode those that followed the introduction of a new code) and an inductive approach to theory building, beginning with significant observations and moving through connections between the observed and the theoretical architecture of the project.[14]

The sample of parents I interviewed is interesting in a few respects. It neglects four categories of parents that, for reasons related to relevance or accessibility, I chose to exclude. First, I excluded parents whose children were diagnosed intersex. Second, I excluded facilitative or supportive parents who did not seek support from organizations or mental health professionals. These families exist, but they live largely apart from the consolidated community of families with trans children. Third, I did not include families who are in "deep stealth"—those whose children have fully transitioned but who are never public about their children's gender history. These families are nearly impossible to find, for one thing, and in any case are unlikely to want to talk publicly about their experiences. And finally, I did not include families who deliberately engage in "gender-neutral"[15] child-rearing practices, those who attempt to resist labeling their child a gender at all, or who edit their child's surroundings in significant ways to minimize the extent to which they are labeled boys or girls by others or expected to confirm to gender stereotypes. I met several of these families during my fieldwork, but there are not many of them, and they tend to have distinct issues and belief systems. Because these parents deliberately injected a transgressive gender frame into their child's life and identity, their stories were qualitatively different from those profiled in this book.

Children had a range of different gender identities (see Appendix C: List of Interviewees). Of the forty children whose facilitative families participated, twenty-nine were identified by their parents as transgender. Sixteen were transboys (children born female who now identify as male), and thirteen were transgirls (children born male who now identify as female). The remaining eleven children were identified by their parents as gender nonconforming: ten were feminine boys and one was a masculine girl. Twenty-eight of the forty children were identified by their parents as white, three were Black, one was Latinx, one was Asian, and seven were multiracial (two white/Asian and five white/Latinx). Of the fifty-two facilitative parents interviewed, forty-five identified as white, four as Latinx, one as Black, and one as multiracial (white and Asian). Eight of the households were headed by a gay or lesbian parent (nine lesbian or gay parents total sat for interviews).[16] Twelve of the families were multiracial. At least six were formed through adoption or legal guardianship (not counting the lesbian- or gay-headed families who may have undertaken second-parent adoptions). Children were between four and a half and eighteen years of age at the time I interviewed their parents.

The clinical sample was much more homogenous. Of the ten families, nine had gender nonconforming children and one had a transgirl. Of the nine gender nonconforming children, eight were feminine boys and one was a masculine girl. Eight of the children were white, one was Italian and Filipino, and one was Egyptian and Trinidadian. All lived with at least one biological parent. One of the mothers was in a same-sex relationship; none of the others disclosed a nonheterosexual identification or history to me. Children were between seven and fifteen at the time of interview.

Almost everyone in this book is mentioned pseudonymously. While part of what I argue is that the complexities of gendered life are becoming ever more public, particularly when it comes to children, processes of exploration and change are often experienced as private. The exceptions to this include Dr. Ken Zucker, Joel Baum, Kim Pearson, and Stephanie Brill. Each occupied a uniquely conspicuous space in the marketplace for gender expertise, and attempts to conceal their identities felt, in some cases, impossible, and in others, unnecessary. Each of them allowed me to tell the stories of our encounters on my own terms. These were acts of trust in which I place great value.

Stories are constituted not just by what is told, but by the silences that surround the printed narrative. Three important interviews never made it to text. Those families contacted me between six months and two years after we met to withdraw consent. Two families were engaged in investigations by departments of children's services, both threatened with loss of custody for supporting their child's gender nonconforming behavior. The third was a supportive mother who was embroiled in a brutal custody dispute with a father who was unsupportive of her child's transgender identity. In all cases, parents worried that despite the use of pseudonyms, their stories, if printed, could be used against them in legal and administrative proceedings. Each agreed that I could tell you this much: they are and were too afraid to speak publicly about their children. The stakes felt too high.

WHY I STOPPED INTERVIEWING KIDS

Micah and I sat cross-legged on the floor of his bedroom, among a scattered array of "Polly Pockets" (tiny female figurines), crayons, and books. At his mother's suggestion, he was showing me some storybooks he had composed. His head was down, and he was flipping the pages, narrating his marker drawings of birds and dancing girls and flowers. Micah was a seven-year-old feminine boy whose mother enthusiastically proposed I spend time hanging out with him after our interview. She came in and out of the room several times during the forty-five minutes we sat playing together. Each time, she would look through the files of papers sitting atop his dresser, pulling out drawings he'd made at school, journals he'd kept of ideas for drawings and stories he'd composed. Each time, she'd ask him permission to show them to me. He granted it. And yet while we sat together, although Micah was warm and open and interactive, I felt a nagging discomfort. He answered my questions about school, about his interests, about his toys and dolls and drawings. He was compliant. I asked him a few questions about gender, masking them (or so I thought) by asking whether he and his older brother (whom I'd met earlier that morning on his way to karate class) liked to play the same games or different ones, if they liked the same stories, movies, clothing. I knew they didn't. And he knew I knew. He half answered me, eyes lowered, focused on his dolls.

When I emerged from Micah's room, I went back outside and sat with his mother on their porch. While we were talking, she remarked with a smile that she found it interesting that Micah discussed his Polly Pocket dolls with me.

Micah is fascinating about self-censorship. We were [away at the beach] two sum-
mers ago maybe, and there was a reporter there. And Micah was playing with his
Pollys, and he saw the reporter walk by ... and then lay down on top of them to hide
them from the reporter. And the reporter said, "Why can't I see your soldier?" And
Micah was totally ... he told me later, like he was totally relieved that the reporter
had thought they were soldiers, because he was afraid the reporter might have
known that they were Pollys. So he's very sensitive to who is and isn't a sort of safe
person.

I had passed the test; I was a safe enough person for discussions of dolls, a
slight nod at the precarious emotional territory of sibling relationships. I
should have felt satisfaction, but I didn't. Something felt familiar, but off center,
like a story I'd heard before. It took me a few hours to piece together what it
was, but then it hit me: it was a passage from a dissertation on childhood gender nonconformity I'd read in preparation for this project.

Karl Bryant, a sociologist at SUNY New Paltz, was a feminine boy. He was
among a handful of such boys whose parents enrolled him in a UCLA study in
the late 1960s that pioneered therapeutic cures for feminine behavior. As an
adult, Bryant discovered the book that resulted from the study and found
himself awash in complex feelings about his identity, his parents' rejection of
it, and the social scientific endeavor of which he was a part. While Bryant
described enjoying the opportunity to leave his small town and travel to the
excitement of the city, and while he admitted enjoying the attention and sense
of being "special," he also outlined far more pernicious effects of being the
object of scientific study, in an account of going back to visit Richard Green
years later, as an adult.

> I told Green I thought what he had done to me was harmful. I told him the study
> and the therapy I received made me feel that I was wrong, that something about me
> at my core was bad, and instilled in me a sense of shame that stayed with me for a
> long time. I don't remember everything that was said in our meeting. I remember
> Green asking me to discern between the effects of his actions and the effects of
> growing up in a culture that, with or without his help, would (and did) disapprove
> of me. One of my clearest recollections is of Green explaining why he conducted
> these studies in the first place—pure intellectual curiosity. He told me that he
> might as easily have studied why people decide to skydive out of airplanes, but he
> wanted to know about how people's sexual orientation and gender identity devel-
> oped. I had a vague uneasiness about his answer, and a great deal of frustration,
> since it struck me as evasive at best and disingenuous at worst.[17]

My discomfort, it turned out, was about my inability to predict and control
the emotional impact of my study on the children who would comprise its

subjects. I didn't want to be the vague memory that haunted some future adult, the researcher who showed up because there was something strange or different about their identity, their way of being in the world. I worried I might reproduce that same kind of othering psychiatric gaze that Bryant describes.

Although the present contains an intense focus on childhood and children, and on the ability of children to tell us things about our social world and its value systems,[18] I began to wonder just what, precisely, I wanted these children to tell me that they weren't already saying with their behavior. The pull toward "pediocularity," the idea of seeing through the eyes of the child, is, perhaps, not the best way to observe the tension between a child's agentic expression and the political, economic, and emotional will of the larger culture.[19] Children and adults, it seemed to me, had different languages. Children said things like "I'm a girl" or "I want to play with that." Parents did the work of translating those actions and statements into culture.

I decided in that moment that I would never formally interview another child. My discomfort wasn't shared by the university's institutional review board, which readily granted me permission to interview children with parental consent. It came, instead, from my own personal quest to understand and evaluate the possible impacts of the expansion of the social and clinical gazes at gender on the children coming up today. Since my initial interest was in social responses to childhood gender nonconformity, I thought, why not simply study that: social responses?

Thus, this book contains few direct quotations from the children and teens with whom I interacted during my fieldwork (unless relayed to me by their parents), and I ultimately decided against conducting a set of in-depth interviews with trans or gender nonconforming children or teens. During my fieldwork, I did spend a great deal of time around children. I drew pictures with them, read stories with them. I sat in on workshops and discussion groups. I went to ice skating parties and holiday parties. They took me on tours of their rooms, their doll collections, and in one case, a very elaborate ant farm. Early on in my fieldwork, however, it became clear to me that they would not be the subjects of my interviews or my analytic gaze.

ENACTIVE ETHNOGRAPHY?

The goal of ethnography is, as Erving Goffman and others have written, to subject ourselves to the same set of cultural contingencies that act upon our research subjects.[20] To paraphrase sociologist Kimberly Hoang, we put our bodies, positionalities, our own social situations in line with those we study, in the hope that our encounters with culture mirror theirs.[21] As I've noted throughout the book, this ethnographic project propelled my gender, my body, my comportment, my modes of interaction and imputed identity, to the forefront of many of the interactions I had. To relegate discussion of encounters with my gender in the field to an appendix, or to confine them to a discussion of "reflexivity" in fieldwork, would be to miss the fundamental way they are knitted to the phenomena I studied. Rather than merely understanding the perceptions others had of my gender/sexuality, and noticing when that either facilitated or restricted my access to people and conversations, or confining my analysis to the discourse of "reflexivity" by analyzing my presentation of self and political investments as disruptive to some objective scientificity, I think, as I argue elsewhere in this text, that these interactive processes are constitutive of the very social phenomenon I seek to explain. Gender is equal parts subjectivity, recognition, and evaluation. It can never be de-linked from the interactional. It is always, as Judith Butler has written, in the hands of others.[22]

It's useful here to think with the idea of "enactive ethnography," in Loic Wacquant's parlance, a "brand of immersive fieldwork based on 'performing the phenomenon'" one wishes to analyze.[23] Despite the fact that gender is "instituted through the stylization of the body," that the ways we do gender—the gestures, bodily acts, interactional choices—cohere to give the illusion of an "abiding gendered self," I did not do my gender differently in the course of this fieldwork. The idea of "enacting" appears counter to the idea of gender identity, in the sense that the latter presumes an independently occurring sense of self from which the outer manifestations of gender spring forth. I did not merely "do" gender in the field to gain competence in its doing. I entered the field already a "sensate, suffering, skilled, sedimented and situated corporeal creature."[24] But I did attune myself more carefully to the ways I was received by others, the meanings made of my corporeality, rather than to my own "felt sense"[25] of the materiality of my body. My emotional recall[26] became as essential a tool as my intellectual recall in some moments, and it provided me with crucial purchase on the lived, embodied experience of gender by those striving to live it.

Using the "skilled and sensate organism of the interviewer as an investigative tool,"[27] I became, in contexts like CAMH, both a researcher and indistinct from those I purported to research. The "embodied costs"[28] of doing this were often high. Self-consciousness, abjection, invasions of my privacy, the emotional sting of others' projections, the weight of their expectations, and hopes for what this project might accomplish in the way of making social change—all of these wore heavily on me in the field. I felt the tremendous weight of a very central tension between my desire to derive information from my subjects and their desire for the same from me. In that sense, in moments when my gender difference offered informants some comfort or paved the access road to research sites of individuals, I was even more keenly aware that the intimacy and apparent mutuality it afforded also brought an intensified risk of disappointment for my research subjects.[29]

This affective intensity followed me to one final site of ethnographic investigation that never made it into the main text: the academic departments I visited while writing up this project. The sets of anxieties, fascinations, and curiosities about gender diversity in the larger culture were echoed in the kinds of questions, critiques, and concerned warnings I received from colleagues who heard me describe the work. The emotional labor of doing what Kristen Schilt has termed "queer work in a straight discipline,"[30] the tremendous vulnerability[31] of self-revelation that accompanies work on sexual and gender minority populations, particularly in instances where one can be read as sharing significant characteristics with one's subjects. The trinity of "resistance, reduction, and ridicule"[32] that accompanied a handful of my talks reminded me that no matter how many ABC or Discovery Channel documentaries on transpeople air on network television, transpeople still appear to most as "pathologically anomalous or socially strange."[33] I fielded questions about children's genitals and about what potential social etiologies there might be for childhood gender nonconformity (with the implicit suggestion that they might then be eradicated), warnings about the unviability of this work in academia, and genuine concern for my future career trajectory. As I watched my colleagues—each of whom I believe to be both well intentioned and themselves enmeshed in the social processes at play around these issues—confront the vexing uncertainties of gender in the contemporary moment, I became ever more certain that the questions outlined in this book are urgent, emergent, and the stuff of complex and compelling social process.

When parents made associations to or assumptions about my gender, when colleagues or students ask me in the context of this work if I am transgender, I faced a complex choice. If I identified myself as transgender, I risked dismissal of the project as "me-search," inquiry motivated not by intellectual merit but by political and personal incentive. I risked alienating cisgender colleagues who felt uncomfortable around or even disgusted by transgender people, risked compromising my professional security. I risked being asked invasive questions about the configuration of my body, the structure of my genitals, my affective and sexual proclivities. Or, perhaps only slightly less pernicious, I risked becoming the symbolic repository for other people's emotional expansiveness, liberalism, or attempts at political correctness. Conversely, if I disidentified with transgender identity, if I told my cisgender audiences "I am like you," then I risked reinforcing the stigma associated with transgender identity. By deliberately disavowing that label, I might consolidate my authority as an "expert," yet I simultaneously position transgender children as *not me*, but *them*, objects of study, of political manipulation, the receptors of cultural ascription, outside myself. Because there was and continues to be no good or helpful reason to answer the question "Are you transgender?," because it delineates nothing about my affiliations or investments, because to answer would foreclose something in you, the reader, it is a question I do not answer.

I choose, instead, to underscore the social processes that produce the question in the first place.

List of Interviewees

Parents				Children			
Name	Age	Race	Location	Name	Age	Gender	Race
Alice	39	White	CAMH*	Addison	8	Masculine Girl	White
Sandy	44	White	Small West Coast town	Alexander	11	Transboy	White
Tom	47	White	Small West Coast town	Alexander	11	Transboy	White
Karen	37	White	Pacific Northwestern city	Andrew	4	Feminine Boy	White/Latinx
Sandra	42	White	Southeastern city	Ari	12	Feminine Boy	White/Asian
Charlotte	49	White	Small Midwestern town	Ashley	9	Transgirl	White/Latinx
Patti	48	White	Suburban Northeast	Avery	14	Feminine Boy	White
Bess	46	White	Small Northeastern town	Benjamin	18	Transboy	White
Joni	46	White	Midwestern suburb	Buddy	11	Transboy	Asian
Cole	44	White	CAMH	Charlie	15	Transgirl	White
Pam	49	White	Northeastern town	Colby	7	Feminine Boy	White/Latinx
Sophie	48	White	Canadian city	Collin	15	Transboy	White
Deirdre	49	White	Southern city	Colten	11	Transboy	White
Janine	37	White	CAMH	Connor	8	Feminine Boy	White
Penny	33	White	West Coast city	Delia	9	Transgirl	White
Natalie	50	White/Chinese	Large Canadian city	Devon	15	Transboy	White/Chinese
Jane	41	White	Pacific Northwestern city	Eli	7	Feminine Boy	White

Name	Age	Race	Location
Sylvia	42	White	Small East Coast town
Christine	36	White	Rural South
Shirley	47	White	Southern city
Elizabeth	41	White	Pacific Northwestern city
Tam	39	White	Pacific Northwestern city
George	45	White	Small Southeastern town
Roni	44	White	Small Southeastern town
Nan	37	White	Pacific Northwestern city
Susan	62	White	Pacific Northwestern city
Jose	42	Latinx	West Coast city
Lucia	42	Latinx	West Coast city
Carla	47	White	Small Great Lakes city
David	37	White	Small West Coast city
Val	40	White	Small Midwestern town
John	54	White	Large West Coast city
Nancy	51	White	Large West Coast city
Paula	49	White	West Coast city
Paula	52	White	Large West Coast city
Nora	22	Egyptian	CAMH

Name	Age	Identity	Race
Ella	10	Masculine Girl	White
Emmy	9	Transgirl	White
Ethan	17	Transboy	White
Finn	7	Transboy	White
Finn	7	Transboy	White
Haley	17	Transgirl	White
Haley	17	Transgirl	White
Hunter	6	Transboy	White
Hunter	6	Transboy	White
Isabelle	8	Transgirl	Latinx
Isabelle	8	Transgirl	Latinx
Jack	**	Transboy	White
Jade	8	Transgirl	White
Jesse	17	Transboy	White
Josephine	9	Transgirl	White
Josephine	9	Transgirl	White
Jovi	7	Transgirl	White
Jude	6	Feminine Boy	White
Kelso	8	Feminine Boy	Egyptian/Trinidadian

(continued)

Parents				Children			
Name	Age	Race	Location	Name	Age	Gender	Race
Grace	45	White	CAMH	Liam	15	Feminine Boy	White
Sabrina	35	White	CAMH	Lucien	10	Feminine Boy	White
Yael	44	White	Small Northeastern city	Micah	7	Feminine Boy	White
Sean	44	White	Large West Coast city	Michael	11	Transboy	Black
Giulia	40	Italian	CAMH	Nolan	12	Feminine Boy	Italian/Filipino
Mya	?	White	CAMH	Oliver	7	Feminine Boy	White
Victor	?	White	CAMH	Oliver	7	Feminine Boy	White
Ann	57	White	Southeastern city	Patrick	14	Transboy	White
Laura	39	White	Pacific Northwestern city	Pearl	8	Transgirl	Black
Patrick	39	White	Pacific Northwestern city	Pearl	8	Transgirl	Black
Jerri	49	White	Small Northeastern town	Phoebe	6	Transgirl	White
Claudia	51	White	Mid-Atlantic suburb	Rafe/Rachel	16	Feminine Boy	White
Rick	56	White	Mid-Atlantic suburb	Rafe/Rachel	16	Feminine Boy***	White
Yvonne	28	Black	Small Mid-Atlantic city	Raine	5	Transgirl	Black
Brenda	54	White	Suburban Northeast	Rory	17	Transboy	White
Sarah	38	White	Large West Coast city	Sam	7	Feminine Boy	White
Lucy	42	White	Southern city	Sawyer	13	Transboy	White
Arthur	37	White	CAMH	Scott	7	Feminine Boy	White

Paige	36	White	CAMH	Scott	7	Feminine Boy	White
Lucianna	48	Latinx	Small Northeastern town	Sebastian	9	Feminine Boy	White/Latinx
Casey	38	White	Canadian city	Skye	5	Feminine Boy	White
Jude	39	White	Canadian city	Skye	5	Feminine Boy	White
Linda	47	White	CAMH	Terence	11	Feminine Boy	White
Faye	49	White	Southern city	Van	19	Transboy	White
Joseph	50	Latinx	Pacific Northwestern city	Willow	12	Transgirl	Latinx/White
Michelle	47	White	Pacific Northwestern city	Willow	12	Transgirl	Latinx/White

*CAMH stands for the Centre for Addiction and Mental Health in Toronto.

**Jack pre-deceased the interview. (See chapter 4 for an explanation of the circumstances of his death.)

***This classification reflects Rafe's gender at the time I formally interviewed his parents, rather than the time, most recently, when we saw each other.

Notes

CHAPTER ONE. STUDYING EACH OTHER

1. Steinmetz 2014.
2. Meyerowitz 2002.
3. CBS News 2011; U.S. Department of State 2010.
4. Rule et al. 1983, 232.
5. Endocrine Society 2010.
6. Cha 2014.
7. Hembree et al. 2017.
8. California, Colorado, Connecticut, the District of Columbia, Illinois, Iowa, Maine, Massachusetts, New Jersey, Oregon, Vermont, and Washington State have such laws on the books. National Center for Transgender Equality 2017.
9. Human Rights Watch 2017.
10. Trotta 2017.
11. Ibid.
12. Beckford 2016; Blau 2017.
13. *National Geographic Explorer,* January 2017 issue.
14. See, e.g., New Day Films 2001, 2009, 2010a, 2010b, 2016a, 2016b; Still Point Pictures 2016; Zolten 2001.
15. Public Broadcasting Company 2015; British Broadcasting Company 2017.
16. Beam 2011; Keo-Meier 2017; Peters 2004.
17. Davids 2015; Herthel and Jennings 2014; Hoffman 2014; Kilodavis 2010; Zolotow 1985.

18. Angello and Bowman 2016; Brill 2008; Brill and Kenney 2016; Ehrensaft 2016; Tando 2016.

19. Brill 2008; Drescher and Byne 2014; Ehrensaft 2011.

20. Andrews 2015; Evans 2016; Kuklin 2015; Phillips 2014; Whittington 2016.

21. Alexis 2016; Testa and Coolhart 2015.

22. Henig 2017.

23. Clarke-Billings 2016.

24. O'Hara 2017.

25. Wilchins 2017a.

26. Brown 2011.

27. Ablow 2011.

28. Quoted in James 2011.

29. Schilt and Connell 2007, 596.

30. Kulick 1998, 9.

31. Ibid., 10.

32. West and Zimmerman 1987, 126.

33. See, e.g., Schilt and Connell 2007.

34. Butler 2011.

35. Blumer 1969.

36. E. Goffman 1959.

37. West and Zimmerman 1987, 127.

38. Butler 1990.

39. West and Zimmerman 1987; Pascoe 2007; Schilt 2010; Ward 2010.

40. West and Zimmerman 1987.

41. Pascoe 2007; Schilt 2010.

42. For an exception, see Pfeffer 2017, 41–42.

43. Althusser [1971] 2001.

44. Guralnik and Simeon 2010.

45. Althusser ([1971] 2001, 191) writes, "One of the practical effects of ideology is the practical *denigration* of the ideological character of ideology. Ideology never says 'I am ideological.' One has to be outside ideology, in other words, in scientific knowledge, to be able to say 'I am in ideology.'"

46. It is a central tenet of feminist ethnography that "knowing is itself determined by the relationship of knower to known" (Visweswaran 1994, 48). The products of the ethnographic endeavor are always "situated knowledges" (Haraway 1988, 1991) or "partial truths" (Clifford 1986). Everybody has gender, and gender always frames the perceptions of the researcher, the experience of the subject, and the knowledge produced by person-to-person encounters. An

ethnographer is "a positioned subject," who "occupies a structural location and observes with a particular angle of vision" (Rosaldo 1989, 19). Feminist standpoint theory long ago elaborated the effect not merely of the researcher's gender (Harding 1991), but also of her life experiences, and even her embodiment (Hartsock 1983; Reich 2003), on the products of ethnographic inquiry. What this means is that our informants are always looking to us and gauging how to interact. This is not a methodological obstacle; this is a social and empirical fact.

47. Stacey 1988, 23.

48. The process of "transition" from one gender category to another will be more fully explained in subsequent chapters, but transition is the social regendering process that distinguishes "transgender" children from those who simply transgress gender norms.

49. Wacquant 2004.

50. Rosario and Meyerowitz 2004.

51. Foucault 1978. The terms *gynephilia* and *gynophilia* have been used since the turn of the twentieth century to signal possession of a sexual orientation toward women or femininity. Contrary to models of homo- and heterosexuality, gynophilia (and its correlate androphilia) make no presumptions about the gender of the desiring subject, and thus more fluidly accommodate both trans and intersex people.

52. Mead, in *Sex and Temperament* (1935), argues that the variability across cultures in sex roles was occasioned by the "primary sex differences" conditioned by anatomy and the different roles in reproduction performed by men and women. In *Male and Female* ([1949] 1967, 37), for example, she described men's "natural springing potency" and women's "spontaneous slower-flowering responsiveness" as social outgrowths of their basic sexual anatomy.

53. Meyerowitz 2002.

54. Meyerowitz 2002; Germon 2009.

55. Meyerowitz 2002, 114.

56. Money, Hampson, and Hampson 1955, cited in Money 1973, 397.

57. Meyerowitz 2002, 114.

58. Ibid., 155.

59. Ibid.

60. Rubin 1975, 159.

61. West and Zimmerman 1987, 126.

62. Ibid.

63. Lorber 1994; Risman 2004; Valocci 2005.

64. See, e.g., E. Martin 1991.

65. Zucker et al. 2012.

66. Greenspan 2003.

67. Saketopoulou 2014.

68. Harris 2005.

69. Corbett 2009, 2011; Harris 2005; Saketopoulou 2014.

70. Saketopoulou 2014.

71. Deutsch 2007.

72. Risman, Lorber, and Sherwood 2012, 27.

CHAPTER TWO. GENDER TROUBLES

1. Merriam-Webster n.d.; Meadow n.d.

2. Butler 1988.

3. This is not "gender trouble" in the way Butler initially meant it, as a politically inflected, self-conscious performance of gender's incoherence or hyperbole. Though one might consider whether it may have a similar destabilizing effect on the gender system, by making plain the faulty assumptions that undergird it.

4. Parents of nontransgender children similarly tolerate a certain amount of gender-transgressive behavior. Emily Kane (2006, 2012) studied the gendered nature of child-rearing and found that parents abided a wide range of what they considered to be gender nonconformity in daughters, but their responses to sons were more complex. While they encouraged some stereotypical traits like empathy, they did so in the context of a more general hegemonic masculinity. This was especially true of fathers, whose own adherence to masculine norms drove their parenting practices, whereas mothers typically focused on accountability to others.

5. Kane 2006, 2012.

6. Sedgwick 1991.

7. Salamon contends that it is this "felt sense," what phenomenologists call "proprioception," that "delivers the body to consciousness" (2010, 3). As an experience, it is a product of and subject to cultural conventions, but it is also a structuring principle of psychic life, infinitely real to its possessor.

8. Arlie Hochschild (1983) described "emotional labor" in the context of the workplace as a process of managing the feelings and expressions of oneself and others, to fulfill the emotional requirements of a job. She differentiated this from "emotion work" (1979), which is specific to the self and undertaken in the

private sphere. My conceptualization of emotional labor here is a hybrid of the two: work done in the service of the concerted cultivation of children (which is, in many ways, like a job), and fundamentally relational, a process of managing one's own emotional experience as a parent and of creating possibilities for the emotional life of a child.

9. Ward 2010.

10. "When we recognize another, or when we ask for recognition for ourselves, we are not asking for an Other to see us as we are, as we already are, as we have always been, as we were constituted prior to the encounter itself. Instead, in the asking, in the petition, we have already become something new, since we are constituted by virtue of the address, a need and desire for the Other that takes place in language in the broadest sense, one without which we could not be" (Butler 2004a, 44). Schilt and Westbrook (2014, 32) have called this "determining gender" or the "social practices of placing others in gender categories."

11. Butler 2004b.

12. *Cisgender*, a word developed in the 1990s (and officially added to the *Oxford English Dictionary* in June 2015 [OED n.d.]), denotes someone whose personal sense of their gender (or "gender identity") corresponds to the gender category assigned to them at birth; or, as Kristen Schilt and Laurel Westbrook (2009, 461) have written, "individuals who have a match between the gender they were assigned at birth, their bodies, and their personal identity."

13. Cisnormativity is the correlate of heteronormativity. Where the latter references the taken-for-granted assumption that everyone is heterosexual, cisnormativity refers to the pervasive assumption that everyone has a gender identity that conforms to the category assigned to them at birth (E. Green 2006).

14. See, e.g., Connell 1995, 2012; Kane 2006, 2012; K. Martin 1998, 2005, 2009; Sedgwick 1991; Serano 2007.

15. Butler 2004b; Serano 2007.

16. This is certainly not to say that the race of research participants didn't matter; rather, it didn't determine levels of gender regulation or the proportion of difference between regulation of male femininity and female masculinity. Race mattered greatly in dealings with schools, social service agencies, and the state, as we will see in chapter 5.

17. Meadow n.d.

18. Corbett 2011; Pascoe 2007.

19. Garfinkel 1967; Kessler and McKenna 1978.

20. Butler 1990; Sedgwick 1991.

CHAPTER THREE. THE GENDER CLINIC

1. Ken Zucker, personal communication, September 22, 2016 (on file with author).

2. Centre for Addiction and Mental Health 2016.

3. Reparative or conversion therapies endorse treatment goals of eliminating gender nonconforming behavior.

4. Paul Preciado (2013) has called this the "pharmacopornographic era," a version of late capitalism in which the pharmaceutical industry becomes an agent in the social control of bodies.

5. Meyerowitz 2002, 99.

6. Ibid., 114.

7. Money, Hampson, and Hampson 1957, cited in Meyerowitz 2002.

8. Meyerowitz 2002, 116.

9. Ibid.

10. Stoller 1968, 102.

11. Ibid., 205.

12. Meyerowitz 2002, 254.

13. R. Green 1987.

14. G. Greenberg 1997, 256.

15. Zucker and Spitzer 2005.

16. Toscano and Maynard 2014.

17. Ault and Brzuzy 2009; Bem 1993; Kamens 2011; Langer and Martin 2004.

18. Zucker and Spitzer 2005.

19. Bem 1993, 106–107.

20. For a substantive overview of the history of sexual and gender identity diagnoses in the DSM, see Zucker 2010.

21. American Psychiatric Association n.d.

22. American Psychiatric Association 2013.

23. Zucker et al. 2013.

24. For varied commentary on the politics of the diagnosis, see Ault and Brzuzy 2009; Drescher 2002; Duschinsky and Zucker 2015; Kamens 2011; Langer and Martin 2004.

25. Duschinsky and Zucker 2015.

26. When children reach the onset of puberty (typically at eleven for males and ten for females), their bodies produce follicle stimulating hormone (FSH) and lutenizing hormone (LH). These hormones stimulate the sex glands (ovaries in girls, testes in boys) to begin producing the sex hormones that incite puberty. Blockers suppress the production of FSH and LH in the

pituitary gland, thus preventing the body from producing sex hormones and undergoing the associated masculinizing and feminizing effects of puberty. See Selva n.d.

27. Or, as Mary Douglas (1986, 124) wrote, "most profound decisions … are not made by individuals as such, but by individuals thinking within or on behalf of institutions."

28. Others included clinical protocols, review articles, studies of intersex individuals, co-incidence of homosexuality and gender nonconformity, and comorbidities with conditions like autism.

29. See, e.g., Bailey and Pillard 1991; Hamer et al. 1993; LeVay 1991.

30. Halley 1994.

31. LeVay 1997.

32. The analysis of published literature involved a rigorous review of peer-reviewed studies in the following databases: *Psych Abstracts*, *Psycho Info*, *Academic Search Premier (EBSCOhost)*, *Annual Review*, *PubMed*, *Google Scholar*, and *Web of Science*. Reference lists were hand-checked for additional sources missed in the original search. Search terms included "gender identity disorder," "gender variant," "gender deviant," "GID," "feminine boys," "masculine girls," "cross gender," "gender dysphoria," and "transgender." Children were defined as those under the age of eighteen (United Nations General Assembly 1989). We limited our search to articles published in English, but did not limit by country of origin.

The initial search generated 676 peer-reviewed articles. Among them, top cited articles included "Endocrine Treatment of Transsexual Persons: An Endocrine Society Clinical Practice Guideline" (Hembree et al. 2009) and longitudinal psychological outcome studies like "Consequences of Moderate Cross-Gender Behavior in Preschool Children" (Fagot 1977). Of those, 73 were deemed irrelevant to the topic. Of the 603 that remained, the breakdown of article topics was as follows: etiology (N = 128 or 21.2%); treatment protocols (N = 99 or 16.4%); gender socialization (N = 93 or 15.4%); literature reviews or demographics (N = 70 or 11.6%); intersex and disorders of sex development (N = 59 or 9.8%); comorbidities with other psychiatric conditions (N = 42 or 7%); homosexuality (N = 40 or 6.6%); longitudinal outcome studies (N = 36 or 6%); and psychometric measures for gender (N = 36 or 6%).

33. The TransYouth Project at the University of Washington is a new addition to this slate (https://depts.washington.edu/transyp/), after securing a grant from the National Science Foundation for its own longitudinal study of children (Ernst 2017).

34. Bakwin 1968; Davenport 1986; Drummund et al. 2008; R. Green 1987; Kosky 1987; Lebovitz 1972; Money and Russo 1979; Wallen and Cohen-Kettenis 2008; Zucker and Bradley 1995; Zuger 1984.

35. Ehrensaft 2012; Olson 2016; Steensma et al. 2013.

36. Anonymous 2017; Herzog 2017; Serano 2017; Wilchins 2017c.

37. Herzog 2017.

38. Corbett 2011.

39. Cretella 2017.

40. Olsson and Möller 2006, 501. It seems significant that suicide is mobilized as the danger on both sides of the transition argument. Proponents of transition access argue that transgender people will commit suicide without it. Opponents argue that transitioning and regretting it will lead to suicide.

41. Despite steady consideration of potential regret among theoretical and popular writing, no actual empirical studies of detransition exist. (Medical and psychiatric literature searched for keywords detransition*, de-transition, and retransition produced no results.)

42. Dhejne et al. 2014.

43. Lawrence 2003.

44. Some sex-change regret studies report rates as high as 10 percent (Blanchard, Steiner, and Clemmenson 1989) or 30 percent (Lindemalm, Körlin, and Uddenberg 1986). These were based on early surgical outcomes and unclear criteria. The latter study had a sample size of thirteen, and their 30 percent regretter statistic meant that one patient had officially requested reversal of sex change and another three were judged as repenting surgery in more indirect ways.

45. Lindemalm, Körlin, and Uddenberg 1986.

46. Bouman 1988.

47. Olsson and Möller 2006, 502.

48. Anonymous 2017.

49. Kenneth Zucker, personal communication, September 22, 2017 (on file with author). This is not to say that some children don't experiment with transgender identity and then decide that it isn't right. But that configuration seems more like desistence than regret. See Steensma et al. 2013.

50. Saketopoulou 2014, 773.

51. Saketopoulou 2011.

52. Gozlan 2015, xi.

53. This concept is often attributed to Foucault, though the precise phrase appears to have been developed by Butler (1993, 1). Donna Haraway also called them "regulatory fictions" (1991, 135).

54. Gozlan 2015.

55. Bradley and Zucker 1997.

56. Hospital for Sick Children n.d.

57. Conway 2009.

58. Awad 1999.

59. Bradley 2010.

60. Awad 1999.

61. Centre for Addiction and Mental Health n.d.

62. Singh 2012.

63. Butler discusses this idea in relation to sexuality (2004b, 14), attempting to free it from the duality of being theorized as either a total product of regulatory power or a wild and untamed locus of freedom. I'm extrapolating its usefulness to gender here.

64. Trans Road Map 2015a.

65. Conway 2009.

66. Ibid.

67. Singal 2016.

68. Trans Road Map 2015b.

69. Singal 2016.

CHAPTER FOUR. BUILDING A PARENT MOVEMENT

1. When C.J. Pascoe described her research methods for her ethnography of adolescent masculinity, *Dude, You're a Fag!*, she described deliberately cultivating a "least gendered self," an attempt to deflect sexualization by her research subjects and to distance herself from conventional femininity by adopting a soft-butch self-presentation and "camped-up" sexuality (Pascoe 2007, 180–183). My notion of a "best gendered self" is a play on this notion that cultivating a strategic gender that invites particular forms of attention and connectedness and deflects others.

2. Hart 2014, 284.

3. Hochschild 1983.

4. W. Gamson 1988; Polletta 1996; McAdam, McCarthy, and Zald 1996.

5. W. Gamson 1992; Klandermans 1997.

6. White 1984, cited in Polletta 1996, 422.

7. Polletta 1996, 422.

8. Broad et al. 2004, 2008; Naples 1992.

9. Lareau 2003.

10. Ruddick 1989.

11. Fields 2001.

12. J. Gamson 1995.

13. For histories of lesbian family planning in the United States, see Agigian 2004; Sullivan 2004.

14. Thomas Beatie, the self-proclaimed "first pregnant man," gained media notoriety in 2007 and 2008 when he published an autobiographical account of his pregnancy (Beatie 2008; Trebay 2008). A female-to-male transgender adult, Beatie had not altered his reproductive organs and so was able, with the help of assisted reproductive technology, to become pregnant. His story sparked a media firestorm, as well as debates among medical practitioners on the ethics of assisting transgender patients with fertility treatments (Murphy 2010). Although Beatie's story was the first to receive such widespread attention, he was by no means the world's first pregnant man. In her midwifery practice, Stephanie Brill estimated she'd seen dozens over the years. What differed was the public attention, the cultural sense that such a thing was possible.

15. *Stealth* is a term used commonly in transgender communities for individuals whose previous gender assignments are not known to one or more communities in which they participate. Stealth is distinct from "being in the closet," in that there is no "secret life" as the other gender (Schilt 2006); it is viewed, instead, as an instance of maintaining privacy about one's history (Brill 2008).

16. See, e.g., J. Green 2003; Spade 2004; Stone 1991.

17. National studies estimate a prevalence rate for attempted suicide among transgender-identified adults of between 41 and 46 percent (Grant et al. 2011; Haas et al. 2014), and between 32 and 50 percent internationally (Virupaksha et al. 2016). Other studies have found even higher levels of suicidal ideation in transgender youth (see, e.g., Grossman and D'Augelli 2007). To put these numbers in perspective, one study of youth found that 4.2 percent of heterosexual males and 28.1 percent of gay and bisexual males in grades 7–12 had attempted suicide at some point in their lives (Remafedi et al. 1998). Other studies estimate that the prevalence of suicide is three to four times higher for lesbian and gay youth than it is for heterosexual youth, and likely higher for transgender youth (Suicide Prevention Resource Center 2008).

18. Waidzunas 2012.

19. Gander 2014; Margolin 2015; Mohney 2014.

20. Alcorn 2014.

21. Johnston 2014.
22. Buncombe 2015.
23. Kellaway 2015; Nichols 2015.
24. Vultaggio 2014.
25. McCormick 2015.

CHAPTER FIVE. ANXIETY AND GENDER REGULATION

1. George Herbert Mead (1925) wrote that social control functions not solely through overt, external coercion, but also through the voluntaristic participation of individuals upholding the social order through self-regulation. In this case, parents internalized the gender expectations others carried for both their own behavior and that of their children, in an effort to avoid negative social consequences.

2. This is consistent with much of the sociological literature on the ambivalent relationship contemporary parents often have with gender norms. For example, Emily Kane (2012) found that many parents, particularly mothers but often fathers as well, are reluctant to cultivate traditional masculinity and femininity in their children; yet they often do just that in their efforts to promote socially desirable behaviors.

3. Marianne Hirsch writes about the concept of postmemory, which she describes as "the relationship of the second generation to powerful, often traumatic, experiences that preceded their births but that were nevertheless transmitted to them so deeply as to seem to constitute memories in their own right" (2008, 103). Dilara Caliskan (2015) uses this idea to fashion a concept of "queer postmemory," or the affective residue of traumatic injury to one's predecessors, which in the context of queer life operates through fictive kinship structures and with a more flexible temporality. Indeed, as parents become immersed in trans communities, these trauma narratives are part of their induction and, eventually, part of their emotional heritage.

4. Cott 2000; Luibheid 2002.

5. Most families I met during the ethnographic portion of my work who reported interactions with CPS did not want to go "on record" with their stories. Thus, any estimate I could make about the prevalence of these interventions would be completely unreliable. I will therefore confine my analysis to anecdotes, rather than estimates.

6. It seems noteworthy that two of three parents who spoke at length and allowed me to use stories about interventions they faced by children's services

were gay or lesbian. Heterosexual parents were, on the whole, much more reluctant to discuss these experiences with me, though I met several who had had them. Perhaps part of the traumatic legacy that adheres to gay identities includes an expectation of confrontation with government systems and a more vocal resistance to those forms of state violence.

7. While over 25 percent of the 486,000 married same-sex couples living in the United States are raising children (Gates and Brown 2015), there is no automatic mechanism within contemporary family law to protect the parental rights of nonbiological parents in same-sex couples. As a result, many same-sex couples who live in states that permit it will conduct "second-parent adoptions" to secure their parental rights (Richman 2008). In 2017, fourteen states had appellate jurisprudence expressly allowing second-parent adoptions by same-sex parents, and at least fourteen others had some jurisdictions where these adoptions are expressly permitted; in contrast, seven states (Alabama, Kansas, Kentucky, North Carolina, Nebraska, Ohio, and Wisconsin) have adoption restrictions that effectively ban such adoptions, though some married same-sex couples have adopted under stepparent statutes (National Center for Lesbian Rights 2017).

8. A home study is required in many states for any adoption process, even if a child is currently living with the prospective adoptive parent. These in-home visits typically consist of efforts to educate prospective parents on the realities of adoption and parenting and to evaluate the fitness of the prospective parent and home environment (Child Welfare Information Gateway 2010).

9. Salamon 2018.

10. Becker 1963.

11. For one notable exception, see Kane 2006.

12. Jones, Scott, and Marcus (1984) augmented Goffman's (1963) identification of stigma and its relationship to social identity by enumerating six dimensions of stigma management. Disruptiveness related to the extent to which the stigmatized trait and the reactions of others to it impedes social relationships. One might consider this a measure of the robustness of the stigma itself.

13. Psychologist Mark Snyder (1974) describes "self-monitoring" as the imposition of "expressive controls" on one's own behavior to tailor it to actual or perceived social expectations in a given context. In this case, parents are not self-monitoring; instead, they are limiting the kinds of expressive resources their children have in select social contexts.

14. Erving Goffman wrote, "It is a fact that persons who are ready to admit possession of a stigma (in many cases because it is known about or immediately apparent) may nonetheless make a great effort to keep the stigma from looming

large" (1963, 125). He calls this response to stigma "covering," which is distinct from "passing" or the attempt to gain regard as a member of a group to which others indicate one does not belong.

15. Larson [1929] 1986; E. Goffman 1963.

16. E. Goffman 1963, 42.

17. Ibid., 87.

18. Brill 2008; Ehrensaft 2011.

19. Snyder 1974.

20. Kenji Yoshino (2007) built on Goffman to describe the ways law imposes "covering demands" on individuals, distributing rights on the basis of adherence to mainstream expression. He describes "sex-based covering" as the downplaying of gender-atypical behavior and the performance of masculinity or femininity in compliance with social demands. This concept has tremendous utility outside the legal context as well, as a way of understanding the imposition of norms on one person by another.

21. E. Goffman 1963, 103.

22. A *guardian ad litem* (GAL) is a court-appointed adult who has the authority (and a corresponding legal duty) to care for and protect the personal and property interests of another person who is deemed by the court to be incapable of undertaking that responsibility on their own. Children who have not reached the age of majority are often appointed GALs when there are disputes among their legal caregivers over decision-making or custody (National Guardianship Association n.d.).

23. Greenfield 2016.

24. The statute reads, "Any minor who is living separate and apart from parents or legal guardian, whether with or without the consent of a parent or guardian and regardless of the duration of such separate residence, and who is managing personal financial affairs, regardless of the source or extent of the minor's income, may give effective consent to personal medical, dental, mental and other health services, and the consent of no other person is required."

25. The anti-abortion group the Thomas More Society provided legal counsel in the case *Calgaro v. St. Louis County et al.* and posted the original complaint on its website, at www.thomasmoresociety.org/wp-content/uploads/2016/11/Verified-Complaint-11–16–16-w-exhibits.pdf.

26. Cordell-Whitney 2017.

27. Foucault 1975.

28. A. Goffman 2009.

29. Trans Youth Family Allies n.d.(a).

30. Trans Youth Family Allies n.d.(b).

31. Ibid.

32. This is a centralized database of child abuse reports.

33. Douglas 1986.

34. Canaday 2009, 256.

CHAPTER SIX. TELLING GENDER STORIES

1. Foucault 1978, 1988.

2. Weber 1958.

3. See, e.g., Foucault 1978, 1980; Halpern 1990; Pawluch 1983 on knowledge systems; and, on medicine, Zola 1983. For critiques of the hetero-centricity and implicit race bias of these discourses, see Bayer 1981; Foucault [1973] 2004; D. Greenberg 1988; Lunbeck, 1994; Stevens and Hall 1991.

4. Gubrium and Holstein 1997; Gubrium and Holstein 1990, 165.

5. Gubrium and Holstein 1990, 167.

6. Harvey, Orbuch, and Weber 1992, 3.

7. E. Goffman 1959; Scott and Lyman 1968.

8. Garfinkel 1967.

9. Ibid.; Goffman 1959.

10. Butler 2005, 11.

11. Bourdieu and Waquant 1992; Butler 2005; Foucault 1988.

12. Ward 2010, 237.

13. Laqueur 1990; Hausman 1995.

14. Blum 2007; Conrad 1992, 2005; Horwitz 2002.

15. Butler 1993, 2004b.

16. Plummer 1995, 17.

17. Bender 2010.

18. Goffman 1963.

19. Edgerton 1993.

20. Gubrium and Holstein 1990; Taylor 2000.

21. Butler 2004b, 87.

22. Besecke 2005, 179.

CHAPTER SEVEN. FROM FAILURE TO FORM

1. Fine 2002.

2. Salamon 2010.

3. Butler 1990.
4. Saketopoulou 2014.
5. Salamon 2010.
6. Ehrensaft 2011, 2016.
7. Brubaker 2016, 432.
8. Lamont and Molnar 2002.
9. Ian Hacking (2002) described this process as "making up people," the recursive interaction between individuals and institutions that, at times, allows for new forms of personhood to emerge and to be installed in social and interpersonal practices.
10. Ibid.
11. West and Zimmerman 1987, 136.
12. Ibid., 127, 136.
13. Germon 2009; Meyerowitz 2002.
14. Brubaker 2016, 436.
15. Halberstam 2017.
16. Foucault 1978; McIntosh 1968; Plummer 1995.
17. Halberstam 2017.
18. Meadow and Schilt n.d.
19. Blommert and Rampton 2011, 36.
20. Brubaker 2016.
21. Hays 1996, 10.

APPENDIX B. METHODOLOGY

1. Geertz 1973; Mears 2011.
2. Owens 2005; Parents and Friends of Lesbians and Gays n.d.
3. See, e.g., Broad et al. 2008.
4. Schilt 2010, drawing from Duneier 1999 and Luker 1984.
5. Weiss 1995.
6. Stinchcombe 1980, cited in Burawoy 1998.
7. Becker 1992.
8. Desmond 2014, 547.
9. Valentine 2007.
10. This is not precisely how George Marcus (1986) would have phrased it, but largely how he has been taken up by anthropologists. See, e.g., Borneman and Hammoudi 2009, 4.
11. Borneman and Hammoudi 2009, 11.

12. Geertz 1998.

13. For discussions on the importance of "giving back" to studied communities, see Small 2004; Schilt 2010.

14. Glasser and Strauss 1967.

15. K. Martin 2005.

16. The sample contains an unusually high number of lesbian and gay parents. The cofounder of one of the two organizations through which I recruited participants has personal and professional ties to LGBT activist communities, which was reflected in the pool of prospective interviewees. Gay and lesbian parents also may be more familiar with the benefits of accessing supportive community around a stigmatized identity; they may be more likely to agree to participate in research, particularly anonymously, out of a belief in its relevance to larger rights struggles.

17. Bryant 2007, 10.

18. Pugh 2009; Schor 2005.

19. Cook 2004.

20. E. Goffman 1989.

21. Hoang 2015, 192–195.

22. Butler 2004b.

23. Wacquant 2015, 2.

24. Ibid.

25. Salamon 2010, 2.

26. Ellis 1999; Orne 2017.

27. Wacquant 2015, 4.

28. Hoang 2015, 181.

29. Stacey 1988.

30. Schilt 2018.

31. Ellis 1999, 672.

32. Schilt 2018.

33. Meyerowitz 2002, 4.

Glossary of Gender Terminology

AFFIRMED FEMALE Typically refers to a child assigned male at birth, who currently identifies as female and is recognized as such by the outside world. (See also *affirmed gender.*)

AFFIRMED GENDER Many transgender people view the process of transition to be an affirmation of a core gender identity they has always held, rather than a movement from one gender category to another. As a result, the language of "affirmed gender" references the recognition by others of the psychological gender identity held by the individual (Fenway 2010). The word "affirm" is used to signal that it is not the gender of the individual that is changing; rather, it is the perception of the outside world. Some parents of transgender children prefer this terminology for these reasons.

AFFIRMED MALE Typically refers to a child assigned female at birth, who currently identifies as male and is recognized as such by the outside world. (See also *affirmed gender.*)

ASSIGNED FEMALE An individual whose gender, as assigned at birth, is female. They may identify as female, male, or something else entirely. This term does not denote either a transgender or cisgender identity; it merely references social assignation. (See also *assigned gender.*)

ASSIGNED GENDER The declaration at birth of an individual's gender, generally based on the outward appearance of their body (Gender Equity Resource Center 2008). These determinations are usually made by a physician, based on standardized medical metrics for outward genital anatomy, though in some small percentage of cases, genital configurations fail to match either standard (Fausto-Sterling 2000).

ASSIGNED MALE An individual whose gender, as assigned at birth, is male. They may identify as female, male, or something else entirely. This term does not denote either a transgender or cisgender identity; it merely references social assignation. (See also *assigned gender.*)

BIOLOGICAL SEX/BIOLOGICAL GENDER Typically refers to the anatomy and physiology of an individual's body. Bodies are classified by physicians as male, female, or intersex. Some theorists argue that this term is misleading, since biological categories themselves are forged through complex social processes (Fausto-Sterling 2000; Laqueur 1990).

CISGENDER Cisgender is a new colloquial term for an individual whose assigned gender at birth, bodily characteristics, and social gender identity correspond (Serano 2007). The term makes use of the cis/trans dichotomy, wherein the Latin-derived *cis* means "on the side of" (Oxford English Dictionary, 2nd ed.). The term is meant to complement the use of "transgender" (Schilt and Westbrook 2009) and to mark non-transgender folks as "gender normative" (Aragon 2006).

CISNORMATIVE The cultural assumption that all people are cisgender, or that they have an internal gender identity that conforms to the sex they were assigned at birth.

CROSS-GENDER This is a qualifying term, usually used in conjunction with forms of behavior or identity to denote movement across gender categories. For example, cross-dressing means dressing in clothing typical of the gender different from that which was assigned.

GENDER EXPRESSION The "external manifestation of a person's gender identity" (Fenway Health 2010), as expressed in clothing choices, hairstyles, mannerisms, and ways of speaking and moving.

GENDER IDENTITY A person's deeply felt, internal, psychological identification as a man, a woman, or something else, which may or may not correspond to their external body, assigned sex at birth, or the identity afforded to them by law or the state (Fenway Health 2010). "Gender identity is who you are, not who you like" (TYFA 2008).

GENDER NONCONFORMING A descriptive terms for people whose gender is (1) neither masculine nor feminine), or (2) different from traditional or stereotypic expectations for how males and females behave (Fenway Health 2010).

GENDER VARIANT This term refers to individuals whose behaviors and/or gender-coded interests fall outside what is considered typical for their assigned gender at birth. While some researchers still use this term, it has been largely abandoned in advocacy contexts.

GENDERQUEER This term is generally used in two different ways: (1) as an umbrella term for anyone whose gender departs from the norm, akin to the way "queer" is used to describe nonnormative, and occasionally oppositional, sexual identities and politics; (2) to describe individuals who were born with anatomically typical male or female bodies but whose subjective identities are *neither* male nor female (Fenway Health 2010). (Other terms associated with genderqueer include gender bender, bi-gender, gender fluid, gender outlaw, gender nonconforming, and the list is always expanding.)

MEDICAL TRANSITION Generally refers to the process of undergoing medical interventions to alter the physical/sexual characteristics of one's body in order to affirm gender identity. This can include puberty suppression in adolescents, and cross-hormone or hormone-replacement therapy and/or surgery in adults.

PUBERTY BLOCKERS Medications prescribed by an endocrinologist to delay the onset of puberty. The effects of these medications are reversible. These drugs prevent the unwanted secondary sexual characteristics that occur during adolescence for children whose gender identity conflicts with their birth sex (TYFA 2008). (Also referred to as puberty inhibitors, GnRh inhibitors, puberty suppressors, hormone suppressors.)

SEXUAL ORIENTATION An individual's "romantic, spiritual, or emotional attraction to another" (TYFA 2008), typically referencing the gender category of persons to whom an individual is attracted.

SOCIAL GENDER The gender category one makes use of in the social world. This may or may not correspond to biological gender or internal gender identity.

SOCIAL TRANSITION The process of changing the gender category an individual inhabits in public. This term signifies the desire to take on a social role different from the one assigned. It can also signify the outward change in appearance or presentation that one may undergo in order to express gender identity. This may include dress, hairstyle, name change, and pronoun usage.

STEALTH "Stealth" is a term used commonly in transgender communities for individuals whose previous gender assignments are not known to one or more communities in which they participate. Stealth is distinct from being "in the closet," in that there is no "secret life" as the other gender

(Schilt 2006); it is viewed, instead, as an instance of maintaining privacy about one's history (Brill 2008), to avoid either negative social sanctions or risk of nonrecognition.

TRANS An abbreviated form of the word "transgender," sometimes used as a prefix meaning *to cross.*

TRANSBOY Child assigned female at birth, but living as a boy.

TRANSGENDER This term has historically been used as an umbrella term for "anyone whose gender identity or expression differs from conventional expectations of masculinity and femininity" (Currah and Minter 2000). This included transsexual people (those whose psychological gender is in direct opposition with their chromosomal or biological sex), be they preoperative, postoperative, or nonoperative; cross-dressers; intersex people; masculine women and feminine men. When used to label a child, however, it most often references a change in social gender categories from one gender to the other (Brill 2008).

TRANSGIRL Child assigned male at birth, but living as a girl.

TRANSITION The process through which transgender people change their social gender category; some also change their outward gender expression and/or physical appearance to conform with their internal, psychological gender (Fenway Health 2010). For some people, this involves only changes in dress and bodily adornment. For others, it can include hormone therapies and surgical alternations to their bodies. (See also *social transition; medical transition.*)

TRANSSEXUAL A person whose gender identity differs from the sex they were assigned at birth. Generally speaking, this term refers to individuals who identify within the binary gender structure of male/female (Fenway Health 2010). Some transsexual people will choose to make social and medical transitions and to live full time in their gender identity; others may not.

References

Ablow, Keith. 2011. "J. Crew Plants the Seeds for Gender Identity." *Fox News,* April 11. www.foxnews.com/health/2011/04/11/j-crew-plants-seeds-gender-identity.

Agigian, Amy. 2004. *Baby Steps: How Lesbian Alternative Insemination Is Changing the World.* Middletown, CT: Wesleyan University Press.

Alcorn, Leelah. 2014. "Suicide Note." Originally on Tumblr; archived at https://web.archive.org/web/20150101052635/http://lazerprincess.tumblr.com/post/106447705738/suicide-note.

Alexis, Hugh. 2016. *Psychotherapy Workbook for Gender Nonconforming Children and Adolescents: A Therapeutic Tool for Working with Gay, Lesbian, Bi, Pansexual, and Transgender Youths.* CreateSpace Independent Publishing.

Althusser, Louis. [1971] 2001. "Ideology and Ideological State Apparatuses." In *Lenin and Philosophy and Other Essays,* 121–176. New York: Monthly Review Press.

American Psychiatric Association. N.d. "What Is Gender Dysphoria?" www.psychiatry.org/patients-families/gender-dysphoria/what-is-gender-dysphoria.

———. 2013. *Diagnostic and Statistical Manual of Mental Disorders,* 5th ed. *(DSM-5).* Arlington, VA: American Psychiatric Association.

Andrews, Arin. 2015. *Some Assembly Required: The Not-So-Secret Life of a Transgender Teen.* New York: Simon & Schuster.

Angello, Michelle, and Alisa Bowman. 2016. *Raising the Transgender Child: A Complete Guide for Parents, Families, and Caregivers.* Berkeley: Seal Press.

Anonymous. 2017. "Experience: I Regret Transitioning." *Guardian*, February 3. www.theguardian.com/lifeandstyle/2017/feb/03/experience-i-regret-transitioning.

Aragon, Angela P. 2006. *Challenging Lesbian Norms: Intersex, Transgender, Intersectional, and Queer Perspectives.* New York: Harrington Park Press.

Ault, Amber, and Stephanie Brzuzy. 2009. "Removing Gender Identity Disorder from the Diagnostic and Statistical Manual of Mental Disorders: A Call for Action." *Social Work* 54 (2): 187–189.

Awad, George. 1999. "Review: Gender Identity Disorder and the Psychosexual Problems in Children and Adolescents." *American Journal of Psychotherapy* 53 (2): 265.

Bailey, J. Michael, and Richard C. Pillard. 1991. "A Genetic Study of Male Sexual Orientation." *Archives of General Psychiatry* 48 (12): 1089–1096.

Bakwin, H. 1968. "Deviant Gender-Role Behavior in Children: Relation to Homosexuality." *Pediatrics* 41 (3): 620–629.

Bayer, Ronald. 1981. *Homosexuality and American Psychiatry: The Politics of Diagnosis.* New York: Basic Books.

Beam, Cris. 2011. *I Am J.* New York: Little, Brown.

Beatie, Thomas. 2008. *Labor of Love: The Story of One Man's Extraordinary Pregnancy.* Berkeley: Seal Press.

Becker, Howard. 1963. *Outsiders: Studies in the Sociology of Deviance.* New York: Simon & Schuster.

———. 1992. *What Is a Case? Exploring the Foundations of Social Inquiry.* New York: Cambridge University Press.

Beckford, Checkey. 2016. "New Jersey School Board Votes to Adopt Transgender Bathroom Policy." *NBC News,* April 12. www.nbcnewyork.com/news/local/NJ-School-Board-Set-to-Vote-for-2nd-Time-on-Transgender-Policy-375224591.html.

Bem, Sandra L. 1993. *The Lenses of Gender: Transforming the Debate on Sexual Inequality.* New Haven, CT: Yale University Press

Bender, Courtney. 2010. *The New Metaphysicals: Spirituality and the American Religious Imagination.* Chicago: University of Chicago Press.

Besecke, Kelly. 2005. "Seeing Invisible Religion: Religion as a Societal Conversation about Transcendent Meaning." *Sociological Theory* 23 (2): 179–196.

Blanchard, Ray, Betty W. Steiner, and Leonard H. Clemmenson. 1989. "Prediction of Regret in Postoperative Transsexuals." *Canadian Journal of Psychiatry* 24 (1): 43–45.

Blau, Reuven. 2017. "Every NYC School Must Provide a Single-Stall Bathroom for Students with Gender Identity Concerns." *New York Daily News*, May 2. www.nydailynews.com/new-york/nyc-schools-single-stall-bathroom-trans-students-article-1.3131006.

Blommert, Jan, and Ben Rampton. 2011. "Language and Superdiversity." *Diversities* 13 (2): 1–21.

Blum, Linda. 2007. "Mother-Blame in the Prozac Nation: Raising Kids with Invisible Disabilities." *Gender & Society* 21 (2): 202–226.

Blumer, Herbert. 1969. *Symbolic Interactionism: Perspective and Method*. Berkeley: University of California Press.

Borneman, John, and Abdellah Hammoudi. 2009. *Being There: The Fieldwork Encounter and the Making of Truth*. Berkeley: University of California Press.

Bouman, F.G. 1988. Sex Reassignment Surgery in Male to Female Transsexuals. *Annals of Plastic Surgery* 21 (6): 526–531.

Bourdieu, Pierre, and Loic J.D. Waquant. 1992. *An Invitation to Reflexive Sociology*. Chicago: University of Chicago Press.

Bradley, Susan. 2010. "Interview with Susan Bradley." *Journal of the Canadian Academy of Child and Adolescent Psychiatry* 19 (1): 51–52.

Bradley, Susan J., and Kenneth J. Zucker. 1997. "Gender Identity Disorder: A Review of the Past 10 Years." *Journal of the American Academy of Child and Adolescent Psychiatry* 36 (7): 872.

Brill, Stephanie A. 2008. *The Transgender Child*. San Francisco: Cleis Press.

Brill, Stephanie A., and Lisa Kenney. 2016. *The Transgender Teen: A Handbook for Parents and Professionals Supporting Transgender and Non-binary Teens*. San Francisco: Cleis Press.

British Broadcasting Company. 2017. *Transgender Kids: Who Knows Best?* Film. United Kingdom: BBC.

Broad, K.L., Helena Alden, Dana Berkowitz, and Maura Ryan. 2008. "Activist Parenting and GLBTQ Families." *Journal of GLBT Family Studies* 4 (4): 499–520.

Broad, K.L., Sara L. Crawley, and Lara Foley. 2004. "Doing 'Real Family Values': The Interpretive Practice of Families in the GLBT Movement." *Sociological Quarterly* 45 (3): 509–537.

Brown, Erin R. 2011. "J. Crew Pushes Transgendered Child Propaganda: Women's Clothing Company Highlights Pink Nail-Polish Wearing Boy in Promotional Email." *Culture and Media Institute*, April 8. Retrieved May 25, 2011; no longer available online.

Brubaker, Rogers. 2016. *The Dolezal Affair: Race, Gender, and the Micropolitics of Identity*. Princeton, NJ: Princeton University Press.

Bryant, Karl. 2007. "The Politics of Pathology and the Making of Gender Identity Disorder." PhD diss., University of California, Santa Barbara.

Buncombe, Andrew. 2015. "Leelah Alcorn Suicide: Petition Calls for Transgender Teenager's Chosen Name to be Used on Tombstone." *Independent*, January 1. www.independent.co.uk/news/world/americas/leelah-alcorn-suicide-petition-calls-for-transgender-teenagers-chosen-name-to-be-used-on-her-9953239.html.

Burawoy, Michael. 1998. "The Extended Case Method." *Sociological Theory* 16 (1): 1–33.

Butler, Judith. 1988. "Performative Acts and Gender Constitution: An Essay in Phenomenology and Feminist Theory." *Theatre Journal* 40 (4): 519–531.

———. 1990. *Gender Trouble: Feminism and the Subversion of Identity*. New York: Routledge.

———. 1993. *Bodies That Matter: On the Discursive Limits of "Sex."* New York: Routledge.

———. 2004a. *Precarious Life: The Powers of Mourning and Violence*. London: Verso.

———. 2004b. *Undoing Gender*. New York: Routledge.

———. 2005. *Giving an Account of Oneself*. New York: Fordham University Press.

———. 2011. "Interview: Your Behavior Creates Your Gender." Big Think. http://bigthink.com/videos/your-behavior-creates-your-gender.

Caliskan, Dilara. 2015. "We Don't Use the Word 'Generation' in the Way Heteros Do: Can We Speak of Queer Postmemory?" Draft; on file with author.

Canaday, Margot. 2009. *The Straight State: Sexuality and Citizenship in Twentieth-Century America*. Princeton, NJ: Princeton University Press.

CBS News. 2011. "U.S. Changes Transgender Passport Policy." *CBS News*, June 10. www.cbsnews.com/stories/2010/06/10/national/main6567935.shtml.

Centre for Addiction and Mental Health. N.d. "Milestones and History." www.camh.ca/en/research/about_research_at_CAMH/milestones_and_history/Pages/Milestones-and-History.aspx.

———. 2016. "Summary of the External Review of the CAMH Gender Identity Clinic of the Child, Youth, and Family Services." www.camh.ca/en/hospital/about_camh/newsroom/news_releases_media_advisories_and_backgrounders/current_year/Documents/GIC-Review-26Nov2015.pdf.

Cha, Ariana E. 2014. "Ban Lifted on Medicare Coverage for Sex Change Surgery." *Washington Post*, May 30. www.washingtonpost.com/national/health-

science/ban-lifted-on-medicare-coverage-for-sex-change-surgery/2014/05/30
/28bcd122-e818–11e3-a86b-362fd5443d19_story.html.

Child Welfare Information Gateway. 2010. "The Adoption Home Study Process."
Washington, DC: Administration for Children's Services. www.childwelfare
.gov/pubs/f_homstu.cfm.

Clarke-Billings, Lucy. 2016. "What Do Tinder's 37 New Gender Identity
Options Mean?" *Newsweek*, November 18. www.newsweek.com/what-do-
tinders-37-new-gender-identity-options-mean-522679.

Clifford, James. 1986. "Introduction: Partial Truths." In *Writing Culture: The
Poetics and Politics of Ethnography*, edited by J. Clifford and G. E. Marcus, 1–26.
Berkeley: University of California Press.

Connell, R. W. 1995. *Masculinities*. Berkeley: University of California Press.

———. 2012. "Transsexual Women and Feminist Thought. *Signs* 37 (4):
857–881.

Conrad, Peter. 1992. "Medicalization and Social Control." *Annual Review of
Sociology* 18 (1): 209–232.

———. 2005. "The Shifting Engines of Medicalization." *Journal of Health and
Social Behavior* 46 (1): 3–14.

Conway, Lynn. 2009. "The War Within: CAMH Battles Notorious Reparation
of Zucker's and Blanchard's Gender Clinics with Scathing Report." April
30. http://ai.eecs.umich.edu/people/conway/TS/News/US/Zucker/The
_War_Within_CAMH.html.

Cook, Daniel T. 2004. *The Commodification of Childhood: The Children's Clothing
Industry and the Rise of the Child Consumer.* Durham, NC: Duke University Press.

Corbett, Ken. 2009. *Boyhoods: Rethinking Masculinities.* New Haven, CT: Yale
University Press.

———. 2011. "Boyhood Femininity, Gender Identity Disorder, and the Anxiety of Regulation." *Psychoanalytic Dialogues* 19: 353–370.

Cordell-Whitney, Dionne. 2017. "Minnesota Mom Loses Fight against Teen's
Sex Change." *CourtHouseNews.com*, May 24. Anmarie Calgaro.

Cott, Nancy. 2000. *Public Vows: A History of Marriage and the Nation.* Cambridge,
MA: Harvard University Press.

Couric, Katie, and World of Wonder, producers. 2017. *The Gender Revolution:
A Journey with Katie Couric.* Film. Washington, DC: National Geographic.

Cretella, Michelle. 2017. "I'm a Pediatrician: How Transgender Ideology Has
Infiltrated My Field and Produced Large-Scale Child Abuse." *Daily Signal*,
July 3. http://dailysignal.com/2017/07/03/im-pediatrician-transgender-
ideology-infiltrated-field-produced-large-scale-child-abuse.

Currah, Paisley, and Shannon Minter. 2000. "Unprincipled Exclusions: The Struggle to Achieve Judicial and Legislative Equality for Transgender People." *William and Mary Journal of Women and the Law* 7 (1): 37–66.

Davenport, C. W. 1986. "A Follow-Up Study of 10 Feminine Boys." *Archives of Sexual Behavior* 15 (6): 511–517.

Davids, Stacy B. 2015. *Annie's Plaid Shirt*. North Miami Beach, FL: Upswing Press.

Desmond, Matthew. 2014. "Relational Ethnography." *Theory and Society* 43 (5): 547–579.

Deutsch, Francine M. 2007. "Undoing Gender." *Gender & Society* 21 (1): 106–127.

Dhejne, C., K. Öberg, S. Arver, and M. Landén. 2014. "An Analysis of All Applications for Sex Reassignment Surgery in Sweden, 1960–2010: Prevalence, Incidence, and Regrets." *Archives of Sexual Behavior* 43 (8): 1535–1545.

Douglas, Mary. 1986. *How Institutions Think*. New York: Syracuse University Press.

Drescher, Jack. 2002. "Causes and Becauses: On Etiological Theories of Homosexuality." *Annual of Psychoanalysis* 30: 57–68.

Drescher, Jack, and William Byne. 2014. *Treating Transgender Children and Adolescents: An Interdisciplinary Discussion*. New York: Routledge.

Drummund, Kelly D., Susan J. Bradley, Michele Peterson-Badali, and Kenneth J. Zucker. 2008. "A Follow-Up Study of Girls with Gender Identity Disorder." *Developmental Psychology* 44 (1): 34–45.

Duneier, Mitchell. 1999. *Sidewalk*. New York: Farrar, Strauss & Giroux.

Duschinsky, Robbie, and Kenneth J. Zucker. 2015. "Interview," University of Cambridge. www.repository.cam.ac.uk/bitstream/handle/1810/254436/Zucker & Duschinsky 2015 Psychology & Sexuality.pdf.

Edgerton, Robert B. 1993. *The Cloak of Competence: Stigma in the Lives of the Mentally Retarded*. Berkeley: University of California Press.

Ehrensaft, Diane. 2011. *Gender Born, Gender Made: Raising Healthy Gender Nonconforming Children*. New York: The Experiment Publishing.

———. 2012. "From Gender Identity Disorder to Gender Identity Creativity: True Gender Self Child Therapy." *Journal of Homosexuality* 59 (3): 337–356.

———. 2016. *The Gender Creative Child: Pathways for Nurturing and Supporting Children Who Live Outside Gender Boxes*. New York: The Experiment Publishing.

Ellis, Carolyn. 1999. "Heartful Autoethnography." *Qualitative Health Research* 9 (5): 669–683.

Ernst, Douglas. 2017. "University Awarded Federal Grant to Study 'Internal Gender Identity' of Four-Year-Olds." *Washington Times*, September 8. www .washingtontimes.com/news/2017/sep/8/university-of-washington-awarded-federal-grant-to-/

Evans, Cheryl. 2016. *I Promised Not to Tell: Raising a Transgender Child.* Self-published.

Fagot, Beverly I. 1977. "Consequences of Moderate Cross-Gender Behavior in Preschool Children." *Child Development* 48 (3): 902–907.

Fausto-Sterling, Anne. 2000. *Sexing the Body: Gender Politics and the Construction of Sexuality.* New York: Basic Books.

Fenstermaker, Sarah, and Candace West, eds. 2002. *Doing Gender, Doing Difference: Inequality, Power, and Institutional Change.* New York: Routledge.

Fenway Health. 2010. Glossary of Gender and Transgender Terms. http://fenwayhealth.org/documents/the-fenway-institute/handouts/Handout_7-C_Glossary_of_Gender_and_Transgender_Terms__fi.pdf.

Fields, Jessica. 2001. "Normal Queers: Straight Parents Respond to their Children's 'Coming Out.'" *Symbolic Interaction,* 24 (2): 165–187.

Fine, Gary Alan. 2002. "The Storied Group: Social Movements as Bundles of Narratives." In *Stories of Change: Narrative and Social Movements,* ed. Joseph E. Davis, 239–246. Albany: SUNY Press.

Foucault, Michel. 1975. *Discipline and Punish: The Birth of the Prison.* New York: Random House.

———. 1978. *The History of Sexuality,* vol. 1: *An Introduction.* New York: Random House.

———. 1980. *Power/Knowledge: Selected Interviews and Other Writings, 1972–1977.* New York: Pantheon Books.

———. 1988. "Technologies of the Self." In *Technologies of the Self: A Seminar with Michel Foucault,* ed. L. Martin, H. Gutman, and P.H. Hutton, 16–49. Amherst: University of Massachusetts Press.

———. [1973] 2004. *The Birth of the Clinic: An Archaeology of Medical Perception.* New York: Vintage Books.

Gamson, Joshua. 1995. "Must Identity Movements Self Destruct? A Queer Dilemma." *Social Problems* 42 (3): 390–407.

Gamson, William A. 1988. "Political Discourse and Collective Action." *International Social Movement Research* 1: 219–244.

———. 1992. *Talking Politics.* New York: Cambridge University Press.

Gander, Kashmira. 2014. "Transgender Teenager Leelah Alcorn Took Her Life Because Parents Would Not Allow Her to Transition." *Independent,* December 30.

Garfinkel, Harold. 1967. "Passing and the Managed Achievement of Sex Status in an Intersexed Person, Part 1." In *Studies in Ethnomethodology,* 116–185. Englewood Cliffs, NJ: Prentice-Hall.

Gates, Gary T., and Taylor N. T. Brown. 2015. "Marriage and Same-Sex Couples after *Obergefell.*" Williams Institute, November. http://williamsinstitute .law.ucla.edu/wp-content/uploads/Marriage-and-Same-sex-Couples-after-Obergefell-November-2015.pdf.

Geertz, Clifford. 1973. *The Interpretation of Cultures.* New York: Basic Books.

————. 1998. "Deep Hanging Out." *New York Review of Books* 45 (16): 69–72.

Gender Equity Resource Center. 2008. "Gender/Sex: What Is the Difference between Gender and Sex?" Unpublished flyer; on file with author.

Germon, Jennifer E. 2009. *Gender: A Genealogy of an Idea.* New York: Palgrave Macmillan.

Glasser, Barney G., and Anselm L. Strauss. 1967. *The Discovery of Grounded Theory: Strategies for Qualitative Research.* Chicago: Aldine.

Goffman, Alice. 2009. "On the Run: Wanted Men in a Philadelphia Ghetto." *American Sociological Review* 74 (3): 339–57.

Goffman, Erving. 1959. *The Presentation of Self in Everyday Life.* New York: Anchor Books.

————. 1963. *Stigma: Notes on the Management of Spoiled Identity.* Edgewood Cliffs, NJ: Prentice-Hall.

————. 1989. "On Fieldwork." Translated by Lyn H. Lofland. *Contemporary Ethnography* 18 (2): 123–132.

Gozlan, Oren. 2015. *Transsexuality and the Art of Transitioning: A Lacanian Approach.* New York: Routledge.

Grant, Jaime M., Lisa A. Mottet, Justin Tanis, Jack Harrison, Jody L. Herman, and Mara Keisling. 2011. *Injustice at Every Turn: A Report of the National Transgender Discrimination Survey.* Washington, DC: National Center for Transgender Equality and the National Gay and Lesbian Task Force.

Green, Eli R. 2006. "Debating Trans Inclusion in the Feminist Movement: A Trans-Positive Analysis." *Journal of Lesbian Studies* 10 (1/2): 231–248.

Green, James. 2003. *Becoming a Visible Man.* Nashville, TN: Vanderbilt University Press.

Green, Richard. 1987. *The "Sissy Boy Syndrome" and the Development of Homosexuality.* New Haven, CT: Yale University Press.

Greenberg, David. 1988. *The Construction of Homosexuality.* Chicago: University of Chicago Press.

Greenberg, Gary. 1997. "Right Answers, Wrong Reasons: Revisiting the Deletion of Homosexuality from the DSM." *Review of General Psychology* 1 (3): 256–270.

Greenfield, Beth. 2016. "A Mom Is Suing Her Transgender Daughter for Transitioning from Male to Female." Yahoo News, November 18. http://

sports.yahoo.com/news/a-mom-is-suing-her-transgender-daughter-for-transitioning-from-male-to-female-220252766.html.

Greenspan, Stanley I. 2003. *The Clinical Interview of the Child.* Washington, DC: American Psychiatric Publishing.

Grossman, Arnold H., and Anthony R. D'Augelli. 2007. "Transgender Youth and Life Threatening Behaviors." *Suicide and Life-Threatening Behavior* 37 (5): 529–537.

Gubrium, Jaber F., and James A. Holstein. 1990. *What Is a Family?* Mountain View, CA: Mayfield.

———. 1997. *The New Language of Qualitative Method.* New York: Oxford University Press.

Guralnik, Orna, and D. Simeon. 2010. "Depersonalization: Standing in the Spaces between Recognition and Interpellation." *Psychoanalytic Dialogues* 20: 400–416.

Haas, Ann P., Phillip L. Rudgers, and Jody L. Herman. 2014. "Suicide Attempts among Transgender and Gender Non-Conforming Adults: Findings of the National Transgender Discrimination Survey." The Williams Institute. https://williamsinstitute.law.ucla.edu/wp-content/uploads/AFSP-Williams-Suicide-Report-Final.pdf.

Hacking, Ian. 2002. "Making Up People." In *Historical Ontology*, 99–114. Cambridge, MA: Harvard University Press.

Halberstam, Jack. 2017. *Trans*: A Quick and Quirky Account of Gender Variability.* Berkeley: University of California Press.

Halley, Janet E. 1994. "Sexual Orientation and the Politics of Biology: A Critique of the Argument from Immutability." *Stanford Law Review* 46 (3): 503–568.

Halpern, Sydney. 1990. "Medicalization as a Professional Process: Postwar Trends in Pediatrics." *Journal of Health and Social Behavior* 31 (2): 28–42.

Hamer, Dean H., Stella Hu, Victoria L. Magnuson, Nan Hu, and Angela M. L. Pattatucci. 1993. "A Linkage between DNA Markers on the X Chromosome and Sexual Orientation." *Science* 261 (5119): 321–327.

Haraway, Donna. 1988. "Situated Knowledges: The Science Question in Feminism and the Privilege of Partial Perspective." *Feminist Studies* 14 (3): 575–599.

———. 1991. *Simians, Cyborgs, and Women: The Reinvention of Nature.* New York: Routledge.

Harding, Sandra. 1991. *Whose Science? Whose Knowledge? Thinking from Women's Lives.* Ithaca, NY: Cornell University Press.

Harris, Adrienne. 2005. *Gender as Soft Assembly.* Hillsdale, NJ: Analytic Press.

Hart, Brendan. 2014. "Autism Parents and Neurodiversity: Radical Translation, Joint Embodiment, and the Prosthetic Environment." *BioSocieties* 9 (3): 284–303.

Hartsock, Nancy C. M. 1983. "The Feminist Standpoint: Developing the Ground for a Specifically Feminist Historical Materialism." In *Discovering Reality: Feminist Perspectives on Epistemology, Metaphysics, Methodology, and Philosophy of Science,* ed. Sandra Harding and Merrill B. Hintikka, 283–310. Dordrecht, Neth.: D. Reidel.

Harvey, John H., Terri L. Orbuch, and Ann Weber, eds. 1992. *Attributions, Accounts, and Close Relationships.* New York: Springer-Verlag.

Hausman, Bernice. 1995. *Changing Sex: Transsexualism, Technology, and the Idea of Gender.* Durham, NC: Duke University Press.

Hays, Sharon. 1996. *The Cultural Contradictions of Motherhood.* New Haven, CT: Yale University Press.

Hembree, Wylie, Peggy Cohen-Kettenis, Henriette A. Delamarre-Van-de-Waal, Louis J. Gooren, Walter J. Meyer III, Norman P. Spack, Vin Tangpricha, and Victor M. Montori. 2009. "Endocrine Treatment of Transsexual Persons: An Endocrine Society Clinical Practice Guideline." *Journal of Clinical Endocrinology and Metabolism* 94 (9): 3132–3154.

Hembree, Wylie, Peggy Cohen-Kettenis, Lousi Gooren, Sabine E. Hannema, Walter J. Meyer, M. Hassan Murad, Stephen M. Rosenthal, Joshua D. Safer, Vin Tangpricha, and Guy G. T'Sjoen. 2017. "Endocrine Treatment of Gender Dysphoric/Gender Incongruent Persons: An Endocrine Society Practice Guideline." *Journal of Clinical Endocrinology and Metabolism* 102 (11): 1–35.

Henig, Robin Marantz. 2017. "How Science Is Helping Us Understand Gender." *National Geographic,* January. www.nationalgeographic.com/magazine/2017/01/how-science-helps-us-understand-gender-identity.

Herthel, Jessica, and Jazz Jennings. 2014. *I Am Jazz.* New York: Penguin.

Herzog, Katie. 2017. "The Detransitioners: They Were Transgender, Until They Weren't." *The Stranger,* June 28. www.thestranger.com/features/2017/06/28/25252342/the-detransitioners-they-were-transgender-until-they-werent.

Hirsch, Marianne. 2008. "The Generation of Postmemory." *Poetics* 29 (1): 103–128.

Hoang, Kimberly. 2015. *Dealing in Desire: Asian Ascendency, Western Decline, and the Hidden Currencies of Global Sex Work.* Berkeley: University of California Press.

Hochschild, Arlie Russell. 1979. "Emotion Work, Feeling Rules, and Social Structure." *American Journal of Sociology* 85 (3): 551–573.

———. 1983. *The Managed Heart: Commercialization of Human Feeling.* Berkeley: University of California Press.

Hoffman, Sarah. 2014. *Jacob's New Dress.* Chicago: Albert Whitman.

Horwitz, Allan. 2002. *Creating Mental Illness.* Chicago: University of Chicago Press.

Hospital for Sick Children. N.d. "Susan Bradley Staff Profile." www.sickkids.ca/AboutSickKids/Directory/People/B/Susan-Bradley-Staff-Profile.html.

Human Rights Watch. 2017. "World Report 2017—United States: Events of 2016." www.hrw.org/world-report/2017/country-chapters/united-states.

James, Susan Donaldson. 2011. "J. Crew Ad with Boy's Pink Toenails Creates Stir." *ABC News,* April 13. http://abcnews.go.com/Health/crew-ad-boy-painting-toenails-pink-stirs-transgender/story?id=13358903.

Johnston, Maura. 2014. "Transgender Teen Leelah Alcorn: 'My Death Needs to Mean Something.'" *Boston Globe,* December 31. www.bostonglobe.com/lifestyle/2014/12/31/transgender-teen-leelah-alcorn-death-needs-mean-something/4hw6uPd8NtjIbn8kAdyAbM/story.html.

Jones, Edward E., Robert A. Scott, and Hazel Marcus. 1984. *Social Stigma: The Psychology of Marked Relationships.* W. H. Freeman.

Kamens, Sarah R. 2011. "On the Proposed Sexual and Gender Diagnoses for DSM-5: Histories and Controversies." *Humanistic Psychologist* 39 (1): 37–59.

Kane, Emily. 2006. "'No Way My Boys Are Going to be Like That!': Parents' Responses to Children's Gender Nonconformity." *Gender & Society* 20 (2): 149–176.

———. 2012. *The Gender Trap: Parents and the Pitfalls of Raising Boys and Girls.* New York: NYU Press.

Kellaway, Mitch. 2015. "New Details Emerge as Officials Rule Leelah Alcorn's Death a Suicide." *Advocate,* May 1. www.advocate.com/politics/transgender/2015/05/01/new-details-emerge-officials-rule-leelah-alcorns-death-suicide.

Keo-Meier, Colt. 2017. *Stacey's Not a Girl.* Self-published.

Kessler, Suzanne, and Wendy McKenna. 1978. *Gender: An Ethnomethodological Approach.* New York: Wiley.

Kilodavis, Cheryl. 2010. *My Princess Boy.* New York: Aladdin Press.

Klandermans, Bert. 1997. *The Social Psychology of Protest.* Oxford: Blackwell.

Kosky, R.J. 1987. "Gender Disordered Children: Does Inpatient Treatment Help?" *Medical Journal of Australia* 146 (11): 565–569.

Kuklin, Susan. 2015. *Beyond Magenta: Transgender Teens Speak Out.* Somerville, MA: Candlewick Press.

Kulick, Don. 1998. *Travesti: Gender and Culture among Brazilian Transgendered Prostitutes.* Chicago: University of Chicago Press.

Lamont, Michele, and Virag Molnar. 2002. "The Study of Boundaries in the Social Sciences." *Annual Review of Sociology* 28: 167–195.

Langer, Susan J., and James I. Martin. 2004. "How Dresses Can Make You Mentally Ill: Examining Gender Identity Disorder in Children." *Child and Adolescent Social Work Journal* 23 (1): 5–23.

Laqueur, Thomas. 1990. *Making Sex: Body and Gender from the Greeks to Freud.* Cambridge, MA: Harvard University Press.

Lareau, Annette. 2003. *Unequal Childhoods: Class, Race, and Family Life.* Berkeley: University of California Press.

Larson, Nella. [1929] 1986. *Quicksand and Passing.* New Brunswick, NJ: Rutgers University Press.

Lawrence, Anne A. 2003. "Factors Associated with Satisfaction or Regret Following Male-to-Female Sex Reassignment Surgery." *Archives of Sexual Behavior* 32 (4): 299–315.

Lebovitz, P.S. 1972. "Feminine Behavior in Boys: Aspects of Its Outcome." *American Journal of Psychiatry* 128 (10): 1283–1289.

LeVay, Simon. 1991. "A Difference in Hypothalmic Structure between Heterosexual and Homosexual Men." *Science* 253 (5029): 1034–1037.

———. 1997. *Queer Science: The Use and Abuse of Research into Homosexuality.* Boston: MIT Press.

Linde, Charlotte. 1993. *Life Stories: The Creation of Coherence.* New York: Oxford University Press.

Lindemalm, G., D. Körlin, and N. Uddenberg. 1986. "Long-Term Follow-Up of 'Sex Change' in 13 Male-to-Female Transsexuals." *Archives of Sexual Behavior* 15 (3): 187–210.

Lorber, Judith. 1994. *Paradoxes of Gender.* New Haven, CT: Yale University Press.

Luibheid, Eithe. 2002. *Entry Denied: Controlling Sexuality at the Border.* Minneapolis: University of Minnesota Press.

Luker, Kristen. 1984. *Abortion and the Politics of Motherhood.* Berkeley: University of California Press.

Lunbeck, Elizabeth. 1994. *The Psychiatric Persuasion: Knowledge, Gender, and Power in Modern America.* Princeton, NJ: Princeton University Press.

Marcus, George E. 1986. "Contemporary Problems of Ethnography in the Modern World System." In *Writing Culture: The Poetics and Politics of Ethnography,* ed. J. Clifford and G.E. Marcus, 165–193. Berkeley: University of California Press.

Margolin, Emma. 2015. "Leelah Alcorn's Suicide Note Pointed Out Societal Problems." *MSNBC,* April 10. www.msnbc.com/msnbc/leelah-alcorns-suicide-note-pointed-out-societal-problems.

Martin, Emily. 1991. "The Egg and the Sperm: How Science has Constructed a Romance Based on Stereotypical Male-Female Roles." *Signs* 16 (3): 485–501.

Martin, Karen. 1998. "Becoming a Gendered Body: Practices of Preschools." *American Sociological Review* 63 (4): 494–511.

———. 2005. "William Wants a Doll. Can He Have One? Feminists, Child Care Advisors, and Gender-Neutral Child-Rearing." *Gender & Society* 19 (4): 456–479.

———. 2009. "Normalizing Heterosexuality: Mothers' Assumptions, Talk, and Strategies with Young Children." *American Sociological Review* 74 (2): 190–207.

McAdam, Doug, John D. McCarthy, and Mayer N. Zald. 1996. *Comparative Perspectives on Social Movements: Political Opportunities, Mobilizing Structures, and Cultural Framings.* New York: Cambridge University Press.

McCormick, Joseph Patrick. 2015. "Amazon's 'Transparent' Writer Dedicates Golden Globe to Leelah Alcorn." *PinkNews,* January 12. www.pinknews.co.uk/2015/01/12/amazons-transparent-writer-dedicates-golden-globe-to-leelah-alcorn.

McIntosh, Mary. 1968. "The Homosexual Role." *Social Problems* 16 (2): 182–192.

Mead, George Herbert. 1925. "The Genesis of the Self and Social Control." *International Journal of Ethics* 35 (3): 251–277.

Mead, Margaret. 1935. *Sex and Temperament in Three Primitive Societies.* New York: HarperCollins.

———. [1949] 1967. *Male and Female.* New York: HarperCollins.

Meadow, Tey. N.d. "From Failure to Form: The Transgender Child and the Evolution of Gender Nonconformity." Draft; on file with author.

Meadow, Tey, and Kristen Schilt. N.d. "The Pleasures of Gender." Draft; on file with author.

Mears, Ashley. 2011. *Pricing Beauty: The Making of a Fashion Model.* Berkeley: University of California Press.

Merriam-Webster. N.d. "Problem" (definition). www.merriam-webster.com/dictionary/problem.

Meyerowitz, Joanne. 2002. *How Sex Changed: A History of Transsexuality in the United States.* Cambridge, MA: Harvard University Press.

Mohney, Gillian. 2014. "Leelah Alcorn: Transgender Teen's Reported Suicide Note Makes Dramatic Appeal." *ABC News,* December 31. http://abcnews.go.com/US/leelah-alcorn-transgender-teens-reported-suicide-note-makes/story?id=27912326.

Money, John. 1973. "Gender Role, Gender Identity, Core Gender Identity: Usage and Definition of Terms." *Journal of the American Academy of Psychoanalysis and Dynamic Psychaitry* 1 (4): 397–402.

Money, John, Joan G. Hampson, and John L. Hampson. 1955. "An Examination of Some Basic Sexual Concepts: The Evidence of Human Hermaphroditism." *Bulletin of Johns Hopkins Hospital* 97 (4): 301–319.

———. 1957. "Imprinting and the Establishment of Gender Role." *American Medical Association Archive of Neurology and Psychiatry* 77: 333–336.

Money, John, and A. J. Russo. 1979. "Homosexual Outcome of Discordant Gender Identity/Role: Longitudinal Follow-up. *Journal of Pediatric Psychology* 4 (1): 29–41.

Murphy, Timothy F. 2010. "The Ethics of Helping Transgender Men and Women Have Children." *Perspectives on Biology and Medicine* 53 (1): 46–60.

Naples, Nancy. 1992. "Activist Mothering: Cross-Generational Continuity in the Community Work of Women from Low-Income Urban Neighborhoods." *Gender & Society* 6 (3): 441–463.

National Center for Lesbian Rights. 2017. "Legal Recognition of LGBT Families." www.nclrights.org/wp-content/uploads/2013/07/Legal_Recognition_of _LGBT_Families.pdf.

National Center for Transgender Equality. 2017. "What Are My Rights at School?" www.transequality.org/know-your-rights/schools.

National Geographic. 2009. "National Geographic Explorer: Sex, Lies, and Gender." Available at www.youtube.com/playlist?list=PLDA4E37E7D90 C5E32.

National Guardianship Association. N.d. "What Is Guardianship?" www .guardianship.org/what-is-guardianship.

New Day Films. 2001. *No Dumb Questions.* Film. Directed by Melissa Regan. Epiphany Productions.

———. 2009. *Straight-Laced: How Gender's Got Us All Tied Up.* Film. Directed by Debra Chasnoff. GroundSpark Films.

———. 2010a. *I'm Just Anneke.* Film. Directed by Jonathan Skurnik. Youth and Gender Media Project.

———. 2010b. *The Family Journey.* Film. Directed by Jonathan Skurnik. Youth and Gender Media Project.

———. 2016a. *Creating Gender Inclusive Schools.* Film. Directed by Jonathan Skurnik. Youth and Gender Media Project.

———. 2016b. *Becoming Johanna.* Film. Directed by Jonathan Skurnik. Youth and Gender Media Project.

Nichols, James. 2015. "Leelah Alcorn's Death Inspires Fastest Growing Change. org Petition of 2014." *Huffington Post,* January 8. www.huffingtonpost.com /2015/01/08/leelah-alcorn-death-petition_n_6438918.html.

O'Hara, Mary Emily. 2017. "Oregon Becomes First State to Add Third Gender to Driver's Licenses." *NBC News*, July 15. www.nbcnews.com/feature/nbc-out/oregon-becomes-first-state-add-third-gender-driver-s-licenses-n772891.

Olson, Kristina R. 2016. "Prepubescent Transgender Children: What We Do and Do Not Know." *Journal of the American Academy of Child and Adolescent Psychiatry* 55 (3): 155–156.

Olsson, Stig-Eric, and Anders Möller. 2006. "Regret after Sex Reassignment Surgery in a Male-to-Female Transsexual: A Long-Term Follow-Up." *Archives of Sexual Behavior* 35 (4): 501–506.

Orne, Jason. 2017. *Boystown*. Chicago: University of Chicago Press.

Owens, Tom. 2005. "One Mother's Voice: PFLAG Cofounder Recalls Group's Beginnings." www.pflag.org/jeannemanford.

Oxford English Dictionary. N.d. "Cisgender" (definition). www.oxforddictionaries.com/us/definition/american_english/cisgender.

Parents and Friends of Lesbians and Gays (PFLAG). N.d. "PFLAG's Rich Past Provides a Solid Foundation for the Future." Retrieved March 25, 2011; no longer available online.

Pascoe, C.J. 2007. *Dude, You're a Fag! Masculinity and Sexuality in High School.* Berkeley: University of California Press.

Pawluch, Dorothy. 1983. "Transitions in Pediatrics: A Segmental Analysis." *Social Problems* 30: 449–65.

Peters, Julie Anne. 2004. *Luna*. New York: Little, Brown.

Pfeffer, Carla. 2017. *Queering Families: The Postmodern Partnerships of Cisgender Women and Transgender Men.* New York: Oxford University Press.

Phillips, Marilyn. 2014. *The Daughter We Didn't Know We Had: The Tears, Fears, and Joys of a Mother of a Transgender Child.* Bloomington, IN: Author House.

Plummer, Ken. 1995. *Telling Sexual Stories: Power, Change, and Social Worlds.* New York: Routledge.

Polletta, Francesca. 1996. "Contending Stories: Narrative in Social Movements." *Qualitative Sociology* 21 (4): 419–446.

Public Broadcasting Company. 2015. *Growing Up Trans. Frontline* episode. www.pbs.org/video/frontline-growing-up-trans.

Pugh, Allison. 2009. *Longing and Belonging: Parents, Children, and Consumer Culture.* Berkeley: University of California Press.

Reich, Jennifer A. 2003. "Pregnant with Possibility: Reflections on Embodiment, Access, and Inclusion in Field Research," *Qualitative Sociology* 26 (3): 351–367

Remafedi, Gary, Simone French, Mary Story, Michael D. Resnick, and Robert Blum. 1998. "The Relationship between Suicide Risk and Sexual

Orientation: A Population-Based Study." *American Journal of Public Health* 88 (1): 57–60.

Richman, Kimberly D. 2008. *Courting Change: Queer Parents, Judges, and the Future of American Family Law.* New York: NYU Press.

Risman, Barbara J. 2004. "Gender as a Social Structure: Theory Wrestling with Activism." *Gender & Society* 18: 429–450.

Risman, Barbara J., Judith Lorber, and Jessica Sherwood. 2012. "Toward a World beyond Gender: A Utopian Vision." Paper prepared for the 2012 American Sociological Association Annual Meetings. Available at www.ssc.wisc .edu/~wright/ASA/Risman-Lorber-Sherwood Real Utopia Proposal— Beyond Gender.pdf.

Rosaldo, Renata. 1989. "Introduction: Grief and the Headhunter's Rage." In *Culture and Truth: The Remaking of Social Analysis,* 1–21. London: Taylor & Francis.

Rosario, Vernon A., and Joanne Meyerowitz. 2004. "Transforming Sex: An Interview with Joanne Meyerowitz, Ph.D., Author of *How Sex Changed: A History of Transsexuality in the United States.*" *Studies in Gender and Sexuality* 5 (4): 473–483.

Rubin, Gayle. 1975. "The Traffic in Women: Notes on the 'Political Economy' of Sex." In *Toward an Anthropology of Women,* ed. Rayna R. Reiter, 157–210. New York: Monthly Review Press.

Ruddick, Sara. 1989. *Maternal Thinking: Towards a Politics of Peace.* New York: Ballantine.

Rule, James B., Douglas McAdam, Linda Sterns, and David Uglow. 1983. "Documentary Identification and Mass Surveillance in the United States." *Social Problems* 31 (2): 222–234.

Saketopoulou, Avgi. 2011. "Minding the Gap: Intersections between Gender, Race, and Class in Work with Gender Variant Children." *Psychoanalytic Dialogues* 21 (2): 192–209.

———. 2014. "Mourning the Body as Bedrock: Developmental Considerations in Treating Transsexual Patients Analytically." *Journal of the Psychoanalytic Association* 62 (5): 773–806.

Salamon, Gayle. 2010. *Assuming a Body: Transgender and Rhetorics of Materiality.* New York: Columbia University Press.

———. 2018. *The Life and Death of Latisha King: A Critical Phenomenology of Transphobia.* New York: New York University Press.

Schilt, Kristen. 2006. "Just One of the Guys? How Transmen Make Gender Visible at Work." *Gender & Society* 20 (4): 465–490.

―――. 2010. *Just One of the Guys? Transmen and the Persistence of Gender Inequality.* Chicago: University of Chicago Press.

―――. 2018. "The 'Not Sociology' Problem: Identifying the Strategies That Keep Queer Work at the Disciplinary Margins." In *Other, Please Specify: Queer Methods in Sociology*, ed. D'Lane Compton, Tey Meadow, and Kristen Schilt. Berkeley: University of California Press.

Schilt, Kristen, and Catherine Connell. 2007. "Do Workplace Gender Transitions Make Gender Trouble?" *Gender, Work, and Organization* 14 (6): 596–618.

Schilt, Kristen, and Laurel Westbrook. 2009. "Doing Gender, Doing Heteronormativity: 'Gender Normals,' Transgender People, and the Social Maintenance of Heterosexuality." *Gender & Society* 23 (4): 440–464.

Schor, Juliet B. 2005. *Born to Buy: The Commercialized Child and the New Consumer Culture.* New York: Scribner.

Scott, Marvin B., and Stanford M. Lyman. 1968. "Accounts." *American Sociological Review* 33 (1): 46–62.

Sedgwick, Eve K. 1991. "How to Bring Your Kids Up Gay." *Social Text* 29: 18–27.

Selva, Karin. N.d. "Puberty Blockers and Puberty Inhibitors." TransActive Gender Center. www.transactiveonline.org/resources/youth/puberty-blockers.php.

Serano, Julia. 2007. *Whipping Girl: A Transsexual Woman on Sexism and the Scapegoating of Femininity.* Emeryville, CA: Seal Press.

―――. 2017. "Stop Pitting Detransitioners against Happily Transitioned People." *Whipping Girl Blog*, June 30. http://juliaserano.blogspot.com/2017/06/stop-pitting-detransitoners-against.html.

Singal, Jesse. 2016. "How the Fight over Transgender Kids Got a Leading Sex Researcher Fired." *New York Magazine*, February 7. www.thecut.com/2016/02/fight-over-trans-kids-got-a-researcher-fired.html.

Singh, Devita. 2012. "A Follow-Up Study of Boys with Gender Identity Disorder." PhD diss., Department of Human Development and Applied Psychology, University of Toronto.

Small, Mario. 2004. *Villa Victoria: The Transformation of Social Capital in a Boston Barrio.* Chicago: University of Chicago Press.

Snyder, Mark. 1974. "Self-Monitoring of Expressive Behavior." *Journal of Personality and Social Psychology* 30 (4): 526–537.

Spade, Dean. 2004. "Resisting Medicine/Remodeling Gender." *Berkeley Women's Law Journal* 18: 15–37.

Stacey, Judith. 1988. "Can There Be a Feminist Ethnography?" *Women's Studies International Forum* 11 (1): 21–27.

Steensma, Thomas D., Jennifer K. McGuire, Baudewijntje P.C. Kreukels, Anneke J. Beekman, and Peggy T. Cohen-Kettenis. 2013. "Factors Associated with the Desistence and Persistence of Childhood Gender Dysphoria: A Quantitative Follow-Up Study." *Journal of the American Academy of Child and Adolescent Psychiatry* 52 (6): 582–590.

Steinmetz, Katy. 2014. "The Transgender Tipping Point." *Time*, June 9. http://time.com/135480/transgender-tipping-point.

Stevens, Patricia, and Joanne Hall. 1991. "A Critical Historical Analysis of the Medical Construction of Lesbianism." *International Journal of Health Services* 21 (2): 291–308.

Still Point Pictures. 2016. *Growing Up Coy*. Film. Directed by Eric Juhola. New York: Outcast Films.

Stinchcombe, Arthur. 1980. "Erving Goffman as a Scientist." Unpublished lecture, Northwestern University, Evanston, IL.

Stoller, Robert. 1968. *Sex and Gender: The Development of Masculinity and Femininity*. New York: Science House.

Stone, Sandy. 1991. "The Empire Strikes Back: A Posttransexual Manifesto." In *Body Guards: The Cultural Politics of Gender Ambiguity*, ed. K. Straub and J. Epstein, 280–311. New York: Routledge.

Suicide Prevention Resource Center. 2008. "Suicide Risk and Protection for Lesbian, Gay, Bisexual, and Transgender Youth." Newton, MA: Education Development Center, Inc. www.samaritanbehavioralhealth.com/files/SPRC_LGBT_Youth.pdf.

Sullivan, Maureen. 2004. *The Family of Woman: Lesbian Mothers, Their Children, and the Undoing of Gender*. Berkeley: University of California Press.

Tando, Darlene. 2016. *The Conscious Parent's Guide to Gender Identity: A Mindful Approach to Embracing Your Child's Authentic Self*. Avon, MA: Adams Media.

Testa, Rylan J., and Deborah Coolhart. 2015. *The Gender Quest Workbook: A Guide for Teens and Young Adults Exploring Gender Identity*. Oakland, CA: New Harbinger Publications.

Toscano, Marion E., and Elizabeth Maynard. 2014. "Understanding the Link: 'Homosexuality,' Gender Identity, and the DSM." *Journal of LGBT Issues in Counseling* 8 (3): 248–263.

Trans Road Map. 2015a. "Background: The Clarke Institute." May 31. www.tsroadmap.com/info/clarke-institute.html.

———. 2015b. "$325,000+ in Salaries for Zucker & Blanchard to Pathologize Trans People." www.tsroadmap.com/info/zucker-blanchard-salary.html.

Trans Youth Family Allies. N.d.(a). "Assembling a Safe Folder." Unpublished flyer; on file with author.

―――. N.d.(b). "Guidelines for Confirming a GID Diagnosis: Letter from Pediatrician/Family Practice Doctor." Unpublished flyer; on file with author.

―――. 2008. "Learning the Lingo." www.imatyfa.org/assets/learning-the-lingo-06–08(1).pdf.

Trebay, Guy. 2008. "He's Pregnant. You're Speechless." *New York Times,* June 22. www.nytimes.com/2008/06/22/fashion/22pregnant.html.

Trotta, Daniel. 2017. "Trump Revokes Obama Guidelines on Transgender Bathrooms." *Reuters,* February 22. www.reuters.com/article/us-usa-trump-lgbt-idUSKBN1612 43.

United Nations General Assembly. 1989. "Convention on the Rights of the Child." United Nations, *Treaty Series,* vol. 1577, page 3.

U.S. Department of State. 2010. "Gender Change." *U.S. Department of State Foreign Affairs Manual,* vol. 7: *Consular Affairs,* 7 FAM 1300, Appendix M. https://fam.state.gov/fam/07fam/07fam1300apM.html.

Valentine, David. 2007. *Imagining Transgender: An Ethnography of a Category.* Durham, NC: Duke University Press.

Valocci, Stephen. 2005. "Not Yet Queer Enough: The Lessons of Queer Theory for the Sociology of Gender and Sexuality." *Gender & Society* 19 (6): 750–770.

Virupaksha, H.G., Daliboyina Muralidhar, and Jayashree Ramakrishna. 2016. "Suicide and Suicidal Behavior among Transgender Persons." *Indian Journal of Psychological Medicine* 38 (6): 505–509.

Visweswaran, Kamala. 1994. *Fictions of Feminist Ethnography.* Minneapolis: University of Minnesota Press.

Vultaggio, Maria. 2014. "Leelah Alcorn's Transgender Suicide Prompts Response from Laverne Cox, Andreja Pejic, Janet Mock." *International Business Times,* December 30. www.ibtimes.com/leelah-alcorns-transgender-suicide-prompts-response-laverne-cox-andreja-pejic-janet-1770446.

Wacquant, Loic. 2004. *Body and Soul: Notebooks of an Apprentice Boxer.* New York: Oxford University Press.

―――. 2015. "For a Sociology of Flesh and Blood." *Qualitative Sociology* 38 (1): 1–11.

Waidzunas, Tom. 2012. "Young, Gay, and Suicidal: Dynamic Nominalism and the Process of Defining a Social Problem with Statistics." *Science, Technology, and Human Values* 37 (2): 199–225.

Wallen, M.S.C., and Peggy T. Cohen-Kettenis. 2008. "Psychosexual Outcome of Gender-Dysphoric Children." *Journal of the American Academy of Child and Adolescent Psychiatry* 47 (12): 1413–1423.

Ward, Jane. 2010. "Gender Labor: Transmen, Femmes, and the Collective Work of Transgression." *Sexualities* 13 (2): 236–254.

Weber, Max. 1958. *The Protestant Ethic and the Spirit of Capitalism*. New York: Scribner.

Weiss, Robert S. 1995. *Learning from Strangers: The Art and Method of Qualitative Interview Studies*. New York: Free Press.

West, Candace, and Sarah Fenstermaker. 1995. "Doing Difference." *Gender & Society* 9 (1): 8–37.

West, Candace, and Don Zimmerman. 1987. "Doing Gender." *Gender & Society* 1 (2): 125–151.

Westbrook, Laurel, and Kristen R. Schilt. 2014. "Doing Gender, Determining Gender: Transgender People, Gender Panics and the Maintenance of the Sex/Gender/Sexuality System." *Gender & Society*, 28 (1): 32–57.

White, James B. 1984. *When Words Lose Their Meaning: Constitutions and Reconstitutions of Language, Character, and Community*. Chicago: University of Chicago Press.

Whittington, Hillary. 2016. *Raising Ryland: Our Story of Parenting a Transgender Child*. New York: HarperCollins.

Wilchins, Riki. 2017a. "Is Trans Over?" *Advocate*, June 13. www.advocate.com /transgender/2017/6/13/trans-over.

———. 2017b. *Trans/gressive: How Transgender Activists Took on Gay Rights, Feminism, the Media, and Congress . . . and Won*. New York: Riverdale Avenue Books.

———. 2017c. "No, De-transitioning Is Not a Thing." *Advocate*, July 7. www .advocate.com/commentary/2017/7/07/no-de-transitioning-not-thing.

Yoshino, Kenji. 2007. *Covering: The Hidden Assault on Our Civil Rights*. New York: Random House.

Zola, Irving. 1983. *Socio-Medical Inquiries*. Philadelphia: Temple University Press.

Zolotow, Charlotte. 1985. *William's Doll*. New York: Perfection Learning.

Zolten, Sam. 2001. *Just Call Me Kade*. Film. San Francisco: Frameline Films. Available at www.youtube.com/watch?v=4pRt9pxmP0s.

Zucker, Kenneth J. 2010. "The DSM Diagnostic Criteria for Gender Identity Disorder in Children." *Archives of Sexual Behavior* 39 (2): 477–498.

Zucker, Kenneth, and Susan J. Bradley. 1995. *Gender Identity Disorder and Psychosexual Problems in Children and Adolescents*. New York: Guilford Press.

Zucker, Kenneth J., Peggy T. Cohen-Kettenis, Jack Drescher, Heino F. L. Meyer-Bahlburg, Friedemann Pfafflin, and William T. Womack. 2013. "Memo Outlining Evidence for Change for Gender Identity Disorder in the DSM-5." *Archives of Sexual Behavior* 42 (5): 901–914.

Zucker, Kenneth J., and Robert L. Spitzer. 2005. "Was the Gender Identity Disorder of Childhood Diagnosis Introduced into DSM-III as a Backdoor Maneuver to Replace Homosexuality? A Historical Note." *Journal of Sex and Marital Therapy* 31 (1): 31–42.

Zucker, Kenneth J., Hayler Wood, Devita Singh, and Susan J. Bradley. 2012. "A Developmental Biopsychosocial Model for the Treatment of Children with Gender Identity Disorder." *Journal of Homosexuality* 59 (3): 369–397.

Zuger, B. 1984. "Early Effeminate Behavior in Boys: Outcome and Significance for Homosexuality." *Journal of Nervous and Mental Illness* 172 (2): 90–97.

Index